A LINGUISTIC ANALYSIS OF THE ṚGVEDA-PADAPĀṬHA

SRI GARIB DASS ORIENTAL SERIES No. 142

Pre-Pāṇinian Grammatical Traditions
(Part - I)

A LINGUISTIC ANALYSIS OF THE ṚGVEDA-PADAPĀṬHA

By
Vashishtha Narayan Jha
Director,
Centre of Advanced Study in Sanskrit,
University of Poona

Sri Satguru Publications
A Division of
Indian Books Centre
Delhi-India

Published by:
Sri Satguru Publications
Indological and Oriental Publishers
A division of
Indian Books Centre
40/5, Shakti Nagar,
Delhi - 110 007
(INDIA)

First Edition : Delhi, 1992
ISBN 81-7030-320-6

Printed at :
D.K. Fine Art Press,
Delhi

PRINTED IN INDIA

Preface

The Present work is the revised verson of my Thesis submitted to the University of Poona for Ph.D. Degree in 1974. About sixteen years have passed. I still find that the results arrived at are valid. Not only that the results are confirmed by further studies in the same line conducted by my students. It was discovered that the entire analysis of Śākalya centres around the concept of *pada*. The study of the *Taittirīya Padapāṭha* by my student has confirmed it. The development of the concept of *pada* is quite clear now. Śākalya's as well as Ātreya's concepts of *pada* are Pre-Pāṇinian concepts. While Śākalya's concept is little remote, that of Ātreya is closer to Pāṇini. There seems to be two lines of development (1) Śākalya to Kātyāyana, the Vārttikakāra and (2) Ātreya to Pāṇini.

I am indebted to Dr. S.D.Joshi, the then Professor and Head of the Department of Sanskrit and Prakrit languages, University of Poona, my revered *guru* under whose guidance I could give the work its present shape.

I am also grateful to Prof. Dr. R.N.Dandekar, the first Director, Centre of Advanced Study in Sanskrit (CASS), University of Poona, for giving me the opportunity to work with Prof.Joshi.

Dr Kashinath Hota, Dr Subas Dash, Dr Sanjay Deodikar, Smt. Suvarna Shete have seen the proofs through the press. I bless them.

My sincere thanks are due to the staff of the CASS library and the library of the Deccan College.

I also thank Indian Books Centre for taking up the publication of this work.

V.N. Jha.

Vijayādaśamī
1991.

Preface

[illegible] the present version of my thesis [illegible] to the University [illegible] for the Ph.D. Degree [illegible] years [illegible] I still find that the [illegible] [illegible] valid [illegible] the same [illegible] [illegible] [illegible] [illegible] [illegible] [illegible] [illegible] [illegible] Tamil [illegible] [illegible] [illegible] [illegible] and [illegible]

[illegible] to Dr. [illegible], the then Professor and Head of the Department of [illegible] and [illegible] Languages, University [illegible] for his [illegible] and guidance [illegible] [illegible]

[illegible] [illegible] [illegible] [illegible] University of [illegible] for [illegible] me the [illegible] to work [illegible]

[illegible] [illegible] have seen the book through the press [illegible]

My sincere thanks are due to [illegible] and the library of the [illegible]

I also thank [illegible] for [illegible] the publication of this work.

[illegible]

[illegible]
199[illegible]

Contents

Abbreviations* and Symbols

ABORI	Annels of the Bhandarkar Oriental Research Institute
AiĀr	*Aitareya Āraṇyaka*
AIG	Altindische Grammatik
aor.	aorist
APr	*Atharvavedaprātiśākhya*
ASS	Anandashrama Sanskrit Series
Aṣṭā.	*Aṣṭādhyāyī* of Pāṇini
AV	*Atharvaveda*
BDCRI	Bulletin of the Deccan College Research Institute
BSS	Bombay Sanskrit Series
cp	compound
fn.	foot-note
GK	Greek
Gr.	Grammar
HOS	Harvard Oriental Series
IC	Immediate Constituent
ICA	Immediate Constituent Analysis
IE	Indo-European
IHQ	Indian Historical Quarterly
IL	Indian Linguistics
JAOS	Journal of the American Oriental Society

* For the full references to the works and articles mentioned here see 'WORKS OF REFERENCE'.

JGJKV	Journal of the Ganganatha Jha Kendriya Sanskrit Vidyapeeth
JOIB	Journal of the Oriental Institute, Baroda.
JUPHS	Journal of the University of Poona, Humanities Section
KWA	*KurzgefaBtes etymologisches Wörterbuch des Altindischen* of MAYRHOFER
KZ	Zeitschrift für Vergleichende Sprachforschung auf dem Gebiete der Indogermanischen Sprachen
Lat.	Latin
MBhā	*Mahābhāṣya* of Patañjali
MW	Monior-Williams *Sankrit-English Dictionary*
NIA	New Indian Antiquary, Bombay
Nir	*Nirukta* of Yāska
P	Pāṇini
PAIOC	Proceedings of the All-India Oriental Conference
Pdk	*Padakāra*
pl	plural
Pp	*Padapāṭha*
Pr	*Prātiśākhya*
PW	St. Petersburg *Sanskrit-Wörterbuch* of BÖHTLINGK and ROTH
ṚPr	*Ṛkprātiśākhya*
RV	Ṛgveda
Śāk	Śākalya
ŚatBr	*Śatapatha Brāhmaṇa*
ŚāṁkhĀr	*Śāṁkhāyana Āraṇyaka*
Sāy.	Sāyaṇa
sg	singular
Sp	*Saṁhitā-pāṭha*

SV	*Sāmaveda-saṁhitā*
tr.	translation
TS	*Taittirīya-Saṁhitā*
VPr	*Vājasaneyī Prātiśākhya*
VS	*Vājasaneyī Saṁhitā*
VSM	*Vaidika Saṁśodhana Maṇḍala*
Wb	*Wörterbuch zum Ṛgveda* of GRASSMANN

✔	root
>	becomes
<	comes from or, is derived from
⇒	rewrite as

PART I
INTRODUCTION

1. Introduction

I.1.0 The General background of Pp

The continuous recitation of a Vedic *mantra* with applied *sandhis* is known as the Sp, and the recitation without such *sandhis*, i.e., the recitation by dissolving the *Sandhis*, is known as the Pp.

All the four Vedas have a Pp along with the Sp. Since the danger of text-corruption is inherent in oral transmission it became necessary to ensure the correct Vedic text. This gave rise to the composition of the Pp.[1]

The process of explaining the Vedic *mantras* had already started in the Brāhmaṇa-period which shows some traces of grammatical analysis. Yet, this incidental analysis is mainly ritually motivated. The main aim of the Brāhmaṇas is to connect the Vedic *mantras* with the sacrifices. However, the Pp represents the earliest record known to us of purely grammatical analysis quite different from the Brāhmaṇas.

The Pp served two purposes. First, it established the base for preserving the Vedas, and, secondly, and consequently, it served to clarify the meaning of the Vedic *mantras*.

Now, the question became how to ensure the transmission of the Sp? For that purpose several mnemonic techniques were developed. They go by the name of *vikṛti*. Traditionally eight *vikṛtis* are known to us, namely, *jaṭā mālā, śikhā, rekhā, dhvaja, daṇḍa, ratha, and ghana.*[2]

Before these vikṛtis had been devised, a *pāṭha* known as *kramapāṭha* was in use. The *vikṛtis* are, in fact, a further elaboration of the *kramapāṭha* which is directly based on the Pp. The *kramapāṭha* was merely a recitation of the Pp in which words were repeated as AB, BC, CD, DE, and so on. The pattern in which words are repeated is still very simple. But, from the *jaṭāpāṭha* onwards the pattern of word- repetition became more and more complicated. Just to give an example, in the *jaṭāpāṭha* the words repeated six times, for instance, ABB, AAB, BCC, BBC, and so on. In the *ghanapāṭha*, the very intricate pattern of word-repetition was adopted in which words were repeated thirteen times.

The term *vikṛti* does not apply to the Pp and the *kramapāṭha* because neither of these *pāṭhas* changes the order of the words in a *mantra*. But, in the eight *vikṛtis* mentioned above, the order of the words is reversed also. This might be the reason for calling them as *vikṛtis*.

The invention of all these *vikṛtis* shows how much trouble people took in memorising the orally transmitted text, so as to keep the *Saṁhitā* text free from corruption. However, the display of mnemonic techniques has less value for preserving the text than showing the achievements of human memory. We are not sure when these *vikṛtis* were introduced. Their origin may be relatively late.

I.1.1 The Pp of the RV

The Pp of the *RV* is the oldest Pp that we have. It is generally believed that this Pp was composed around 600 B.C. We will discuss this point later.

The author of this Pp is Śākalya.[2a] The authors of the Pps of the *TS* and the *SV* are Ātreya and Gārgya respectively. The authors of the Pp on the *VS* and the *AV* are not known. The Pps of the *RV*, the *AV* and the *VS* follow common principles, whereas the Pp of the TS shows much improvement over the other Pps. One thing these Pps having common is that they show only one cut in a compound word. But the Pp of the *SV* goes one step ahead and shows more than one cut in a compound-word following the morphemic division of the word. Therefore, it can be said that the Pps of the *RV*, the *AV* and the *VS* are earlier than the Pp of the *TS*. The Pp of the *SV* is the latest. On the other hand, out of the Pps of the *RV*, the *AV*, the *VS* and the *TS*, the Pp of the *RV* is the oldest, because the mention of Śākalya's name is found in the AiĀr.[3]

I.1.2. Nature and Scope of the thesis

For the present study, the Pp of the *RV* alone is taken. An attempt is made to get a complete picture of the principles on which the *Pada*-text is based. To reach this goal the method of descriptive analysis is adopted. Each suffix is individually studied in order to discover the principles why some suffixes are separated from the stems and others not. Likewise, the analysis of compounds is also studied. Further, the separation of individual words by way of *daṇḍa* is studied. After the completion of study of data an attempt is made to formulate the principles which guided the Pdk in separating linguistic elements. It is further attempted to assess the Pdk's knowledge of grammar. *Sandhi* - rules known to him are reconstructed. His ideas on notions like *pragṛhya, pada, non-pada,* and *avasānasandhi* are also reconstructed as far as possible.

The entire study of the Pp has been divided into two parts. Part I contains the results and conclusions based on the analysis of the actual data given in Part II. This latter part describes how the Pdk treats individual types of forms.

I.1.2.1

The Pp of the *RV* being the oldest Pp occupies a unique position in the history of grammatical thought in India. It presupposes a considerable knowledge of the grammar of the Vedic language on the part of Pdk. The first available text on grammar of the Sanskrit language is P's *Aṣṭā*. But before P there must have been a long tradition of grammarians. P himself mentions not less than ten predecessors. One of these is Śākalya, the author of the Pp of the *RV*. Probably P's reference to Śākalya is based on the Pp and not on a grammatical treatise by Śākalya. There is no work available today under the name of Śākalya except the *Pada*-text of the *RV*. From his procedure adopted for word-analysis it is clear that Śākalya was a trained grammarian. Therefore, if we study the *Pada*-text from this grammatical angle, we are certain to derive much information about the state of the science of grammar in the time of Śāk.

But no serious attempt has been made so far to ascertain Śāk's contribution to grammar. The *ṚPr* which is based on the *Pada*-text of the *RV* does not go beyond listing data collected from the Pp. It does not attempt to phrase the rules on which the Pdk's analysis was based. It mainly tells us how to reconstruct the Sp from the Pp. Only from the *Apr* and the *Vpr* onwards we see that attempts have been made to account for the way in which the Pp is derived. But these *Prātśākhyas* too do not study the *Pada-text* systematically.

No modern scholar either has attempted to find out the principles behind the Pdk's treatment of the Sp. However, some attempts have been made to point out inconsistencies in the Pp.[4] Obviously, these studies were not undertaken with the aim to discover the basic principles underlying the composition of the *Pada*-text. These scholars did not base their studies on the *Pada*-text as a whole and they could not, therefore, explain a number of points which they take to be 'error' on the part of the Pdk. In fact, many of them are not errors but simply exceptions to the general rules made to achieve a certain purpose.[5]

Recently, K.V. ABHYANKAR has published an article on the Pp.[6] In broad terms he discusses certain aspects of the Pp. He tried to formulate the rules of the Pp on the basis of the rules laid down in the *APr* Chapter IV and *VPr* Chapter V. Therefore, this study does not tell us anything more than what the *APr* and the *VPr* tell.

That is why there is still a need to have comprehensive survey of the Pp of the *RV*.

Another reason for undertaking the study of the Pp is to assess in how far the Pp is helpful for our understanding of the *Vedas*.

The third reason for undertaking the present study has to do with the question why Śāk chose the method of *pada-* analysis?

I.1.3. Śākalya, the Pdk

The tradition ascribes the authorship of the Pp to Śāk. But, since we have more than three Śāk.s. a problem arises regarding the identification of Śāk the author of the Pp the *RV*. We find reference to Sthavira Śākalya in the *AiĀr* which states:"....if we repeat the verses according to the *saṁhitā*, if we say the teaching of Maṇḍukeya, then the letters ṇ and ṣ are obtained for us"[7]. This is the view of Sthavira Śākalya. Obviously, the word *sthavira* refers to the senior Śāk. But, awkwardly enough, the same statement is ascribed to the junior Māṇḍukeya in the *AiĀr* 3.2.6.[8] Both these statements obviously refer to the conversion of the Pp into the Sp. In the Pp, both *ṇ-sandhi* and *ṣ-sandhi* have been dissolved and *n* and *s* are restored.

We have one more reference to the Sp and the Pp in the *AiĀr* which states : "Ṇ is the strength *(bala)* and ṣ is the life *(prāṇa)* in the Sp and one who knows this conversion of *n* and *s* into ṇ and ṣ is said to have known the *Saṁhitā* with strength and life".[9]

In the Śāṁkhyāyana Āraṇyaka 7.16 and 8.1, 11 also both these names (Sthavira Śākalaya and Hrasva Māṇḍukeya) appear in a similar context.[10]

The ŚatBr[11] refers to Vidagdha Śākalya who gets himself involved in a dispute with Yājñavalkya at the court of king Janaka and finally dies. We cannot say definitely that this Vidagdha Śākalya is the author of the Pp of the *RV*, because his discussion with Yājñavalkya does not involve anything relating to the Pp.

The ṚPr mentions Śāk to quote Śāk's authoritative opinion regarding the following technical points:

i) *ṚPr* III. 13 states that according to Śāk the result of a *sandhi, udātta plus anudātta* will be *svarita.*[12]

ii) *ṚPr* III. 22 states that according to Śāk the *pracaya*-accent has distinctive features which we do not find in the *jātya-svarita.*[13]

iii) *ṚPr* IV. 13 states that the sequence *c / ñ* plus *ś* does not became[14] *c / ñ* plus *ch* according to Śāk.[15]

iv) *ṚPr* XIII. 31 states that the restoration of ṣ and ṇ in the *Pada*-text is termed as *samāpādya* by Vyāḷi, Śāk and Gārgya.[16] ṚPr II. 81 refers to one Sthavira Śākalya according to whom 'the hiatuses in the Prācya and Pāñcāla *(padavṛttis)* have their following vowels resembling their preceding ones'.[17]

One interesting fact noted by the ṚPr IV. 5 is that according to the father of Śāk, the sequence *c / ñ* plus *Ś* becomes *c / ñ* plus *ch;* whereas according to Śāk the sequence remains as it is in *sandhi*[18]. Similarly, in ṚPr II. 81 it is stated that in the *sandhi*-sequence *-e / o* plus *a-*, *a* is pronounced more or less like the preceding e or o. This is the opinion of Sathavira *Śāk*. But, the settled practice is otherwise *(itarā sthitiḥ ṚPr II. 82).* The commentators explain *itarā Sthitiḥ as itarā anyavidhā Śākalānāṁ sthitiḥ prākṛtodayatvaṁ nāma*. Thus, according to śākala-school *a* in the above mentioned situation is not influenced by the preceding *e* or *o* in pronuciation. This clearly shows that *Śākalyapitā* or Sthavira Śākalya and Śākalya are two different personalities. It seems that *Śākalapitā* (ṚPr IV. 5) may be identical with Sthavira Śākalya (ṚPr II. 81 and AiĀr 3.2.6).

Yāska[19] and P [20] name Śāk as the Pdk.

The question before us is that who among Sthavira Śāk, Vidagith Śāk, Śākalyapitā, and Sākalya is the author of the *Pada*-text. It has been already pointed out that in connection with grammatical discussion the opinion of Sthavira Śāk or Śākalyapitā or Śāk is mentioned. The name of Vidaghda śāk finds no place in connection with grammatical discussion. That is to say, he is never refered to as a grammarian or a *padakāra* in any grammatical text. This may be the reason why OLDENBERG rejects Vidagdha Śāk for being the Pdk of the *RV*[21]

If we take into account Purāṇas we find that the problem of authorship is further complicated. The Brahmāṇḍapurāṇa [22] and the Vāyupurāṇa [23] describe Vidagdha Śāk as the Pdk of the *RV*. On the basis of the Purāṇa-descriptions GELDNER [24] and KASHIKAR[25] think that Vidagdha Śāk may be the Pdk of the *RV*.

It is not seldom that Purāṇas give different account, names etc. in their own way, than what we have in earlier texts. For instance, Vedamitra of *ṚPr* 1.51 is found as Devamitra in the Purāṇas.

Although it has been admitted that Śāk is the Pdk of the *RV*, it is not easy to fix with certainty that this Śāk among many mentioned above, composed the *Pada*-text.

I.1.4 Date of Composition of the Pada-text

The earliest occurrence of the name of Śāk is found in the *śatBr*[26]. The Purāṇas [27] identify him as the Pdk and the *śākhāpravartaka* of the *RV*. Against the view of OLDENBERG [28] and KEITH,[29] GELDNER[30] and KASHIKAR[31] support the identification of śāk of the *śatBr* with the Pdk of the *RV*. OLDENBERG and KEITH, however, think of no connection between śāk of the *śatBr* and the Pdk śāk of the *RV*. According to these scholars Sthavira śāk who is mentioned in the *AiĀr* is the Pdk of the *RV*. In the *ṚPr* also we find the mention of Sthavira Śākalya. Besides mentioning the name of Śāk, AiĀr discusses also the three *pāṭhas* viz., Sp, Pp, and *kramapāṭha*. The terms used to denote these *Pāṭhas* are : *nirbhuja, pratṛna*, and *ubhayam antareṇa*. These terms are also mentioned in the ṚPr.[32] This leaves no doubt that the Śāk of *AiĀr* is the Pdk of the *RV*. Yāska[33] and P[34] refer to the Pdk by simply Śākalya. I think śāk of Yāska and P is the same Sthavira Śāk of the *AiĀr*. But, as we have seen in the previous section, it is difficult to say with great certainty that Sthavira Śāk and Vidagdha Śāk are the same person.

Now, the *AiĀr* is placed in the seventh century B.C. by *KEITH*[35] and this date remains almost unchallanged by other scholars. The *ŚatBr* is certainly older than the *AiĀr*.

Therefore, if Vidagdha Śākalya is the Pdk of the *RV*, then the date of the composition of the *Pada*-text of the *RV* can be placed before the seventh century B.C. But, in any case, the *Pada*-text cannot be later than the seventh century B.C. on the basis of the date of the *AiĀr* mentioned above.

I.1.5. The Pps of the other Vedas.

Although the present thesis mainly investigates the principles of isolating the constituents adopted by Śāk in his Pp of the *RV*, still it would be worthwhile to make a few observations about the salient features of the Pps of the other *Saṁhitās*. What needs to be urgently done in this connection is to undertake a comparative study of all the *Pada*-texts which would throw more light on the development of the grammatical thought in India. Before attempting such a comparative study of all the

Pada-texts, I propose that each and every *Pada-texts* should be studied individually first. Then only a final picture of the development of the grammatical thought can be made available to the readers for comparison. The following lines just offer the bare salient features of the other *Pada-* texts in cursory manners.

The *Pada*-text of the *AV* follows the same principles which are adopted for the Pp of the *RV*. Other *Pada*-texts differ from the *Pada-texts* of the *RV* and the AV in many ways:

i) In the Pp of the *TS* and the *VS*, separation is shown by adding *iti* to each separable unit. For example, *Prajā́vatīrī́ti prajā́- vatīḥ* (TS and VS 1.1) whereas in the Pp of the *RV* and the *AV* we have simply *prajā́- vatīḥ*. Opposed to this the Pp of the *SV* does repeat the unit to be analysed without adding *iti* to it, e.g. *havyádātaye havyá-dātaye (1.1.1).*

ii) The Pdks of the *TS* and the *SV* do not recognise *iva-*compounds. For instance, *pitā́/iva (TS. 1.5.6), carma/iva/ (SV 2.9.8).* The other Pdks treat them as compounds.[36]

iii) Excepting the *SV-Pp* and the Pp of the *TS* (in a few cases), all other *Pada* texts show a *Pragṛhya-* vowel by adding *iti* to it. In the Pp of the *RV* and the *TS*, vocative ò is also followed by *iti*, e.g., *Viṣṇo iti (RV 1.156. 1. and TS. 1.1.3).* As opposed to this we have *viṣṇo* only in *TS* 1.2.13, where *o* is not followed by *iti*. It is observed that when a consonant follows a *pragṛhya-* vowel *o*, the *Pada*-text adds *iti* after that.

For instance, *viṣṇo havyam (TS 1.1.3) But, iti* is not added when this *o* coalesces with the following vowel, e.g., *viṣṇa utá (TS 1.2.13).*

The *Pada-text of the VS* adopts a different method for indicating *pragṛhya-vowels*. The unit preceding *iti* is repeated even if the *unit* is not a compound word. For instance, *viṣṇo iti viṣṇo (VS 1.4).*

In the Pp of the *SV* no *iti* is added after a vocative *o* and no repetition is made if the unit before *iti* is a compound word. The separation of the constituent words is shown by an *avagraha* and the *pragṛhya*-vowel is indicated by adding *iti* to it at the end. For example, *viṣurūpe viṣu-rūpe iti (SV 1.8.3.)*

The Pada-text of the *TS* assigns and additional function to *iti*. It is used to indicate that a verb is compounded with the *preverb* and *daṇḍa* is given for isolation of each constituent. Thus, if we have two preverbs *iti* is added to the second one. For instance, in the case of single preverb, the analysis is as follows:

ánviti (TS 1.2.3), and in the case of double preverb :

sám / préti/ yacchati/ (TS 6.3.2).

iv) When the *avagraha*-sign is inserted, no change in accent is shown in the *Pada-* texts of the *RV* the *AV* and the *VS. But in the Pp of the SV* and the *TS* the portion preceding *avagraha* and following it are shown independently and accordingly accent mark is given. For instance, *ghṛtápratīkaḥ (RV* 3.1.18 and *AV* 2.13.1) is analysed as *ghṛtá-pratīkaḥ* with no change in accent. The whole compound is treated as a single word. Similarly, *prajávatīriti prajá -vatīḥ in VS* 1.1. But,

prajávatīríti prajá vatīḥ (TS 1.1.1) and

bṛ̥³hád²dánīkaḥ bṛ̥³hád t ²ánīkaḥ (SV 1.9.10).

In short these are the distinctive salient features of the other *Pada-* texts available to us. There are, of course, good many points where there is no one opinion among the Pdks. The Pp of the *SV* is peculiar in may ways when compared to other Pps. It is interesting to note that there is striking similarity between the explanation of a particular word given through separation of it in the *Pada-* text of the *SV* and the etymology of that word given by Yāska. For instance, *mitram* is analysed as *mi tram* in the Pp of the *SV* 1.5, and Yāska's etymology for this word is *pramītes trāyateḥ (Nir 10. 21)* Similarly, *adya* is analysed as *a dya* in the *Pada*-text of the SV 5.6, *sakhye as sa khye (SV 9.4), samudram as sam udram (SV 27.4), and putrasya as pu trasya* (SV 188.2). Yāska explains them as follows:

adya asmin dyavi (Nir 1.6).

sakhya-samānakhyānaḥ (Nir. 7. 30),

samudra-sam uddravantyasmād āpaḥ (Nir 2.10)

putra- punnarakaṁ tatastrāyate (Nir 2.21).

Many other words which are not analysed by the Pdk of the RV are analysed by the Pdk of the SV. A further study would tell us how many such unanalysable words have been separated in the Pp of the SV following the etymology given by Yāska. This will throw light on the date of the Pp of the SV.

I.2.0 Juncture-features as shown by the Pp

Since the Pp was called *pāṭha,* it is clear that the text is meant for recitation. While reciting, the *sandhis* of the Sp were dissolved and pauses were introduced in order to keep the separate units as distinct as possible. These pauses are of two types: one of a longer duration and the other of a shorter duration. They are traditionally known as *daṇḍa* and *avagraha* respectively. The units separated by either a *daṇḍa* or *an avagraha* are always meaningful units. In other words, these units are utterances consisting either of one morpheme such as *ṛṣi*-or *bhiḥ*-or consisting of more than one morpheme such as, a-dabdha-vrata-or- tamebhiḥ. Thus, these pauses are introduced at the morpheme-boundaries or word-boundaries. Only one pause is allowed within a word consisting of more than two morphemes. If a suffix-morpheme begins with a vowel, no pause is allowed before it.

Taking into consideration these facts we may say that they correspond to what is called *Juncture* in modern linguistics.[37] This poses a problem: Do the juncture-features introduced by the Pp correspond to the phenomena of the spoken language (Sp)? It is difficult to answer this question.

Every body will agree that sentences in spoken form have an external *open juncture* i.e., a juncture occuring at the time of crossing one boundary of a word to the other. Also there is a sharp audible transition within a word while crossing over from the boundary of a stem-morpheme to the initial phoneme of a suffix. The same holds true in the case of a compound. Here also we assume a sharp transition while acrossing over from the last phoneme of the first component to the first phoneme of the second component.

Though there is non-perceptible transition while crossing over from any one phoneme to the immediately following one, this transition is not marked. This is the case before a suffix beginning with a vowel. For instance, *parvatāt, bhavati* etc. That is why the Pdk does not separate a suffix which begins with a vowel. This does not mean that a suffix beginning with a consonant will be perceded by juncture. For instance, *kṛta, bhūta* etc. The Pdk does not show separation in these cases. But the secondary suffixes beginning with a consonant and the components of a compound are separated with the help of pause *(avagraha)* in the Pp. Thus, where juncture is possible in a spoken language, the Pdk will indicate it by *avagraha* and *daṇḍa* in the Pp.

But, one might raise the question whether this juncture or pause in the Pp is phonemic. In other words, does it form any contrast?

In Engish, juncture is phonemic because it forms a contrast with non-juncture or *muddy* juncture. For example, in the utterance of 'nitrate' and 'night-rate' all the segmental phonemes are same; stresses are also same; the difference is only in the manner of transition from [t] to [r]. Because of the this very difference, the speakers of the English language can discriminate 'nitrate' from 'night-rate'. This difference is the *juncture* which is also called *plus juncture*[38]. It is, therefore, phonemic in English. Is is so with the Pp?

Let us have the homophonous pair *avasáya* (10.169.1) meaning 'for the food' and *avasā́ya* (1.104.1) meaning 'having released'. Here also all the distinctive phonemes are the same in both the words. Both of them show accent on the same syllable. But, there must be some criterion to account for the difference in meaning they exhibit. And I think it is only the supraseg- mental phoneme i.e. the *plus juncture* which alone can differentiate these words in meaning. Normally, this differentiation in meaning is done by the accent in the Vedic language. But when a minimal pair, like the one mentioned above is found in the RV it is likely that some such suprasegmental phoneme in addition to the accent might have existed in the language of the *RV*. The Pdk seems to be very alert on such occasions. He inserts a pause by means of *avagraha* or *daṇḍa* wherever it is due.

Now, if we take into account the vulnerable boundary in Sanskrit language as such, we find that it is only on these places of word-boundaries and morpheme-boundaries we get *sandhis*. The later Indian grammarians describe these alternations involved at the junctures in terms of *pada and bha i.e.., non-pada* The Pdk represents the same tradition which we find in the later grammatical works. In the *bha*-environment, the Pdk does not show separation and in the *pada*-environment he shows separation either by *avagraha or daṇḍa*.

From the preceding discussion the following basic questions emerged:

Why does the Pdk attempt the analysis of the units which involve particular type of alternation *(sandhi)*?

Why does the Pdk prefer to separate the finished words or morphemic units which involve alternations resulting from junction-features?

Why does he not separate roots or stems before all inflexional or derivational suffixies?

What is the main intention of the Pdk in limiting his analysis to the *Pada*-units which are exposed to particular morphophonological alternations?

The answer to these equestion lies in the fact that the main motivation of the *Pada*-text is to preserve the Vedic text which must have been in danger in the process of oral transmission, as we have already pointed out earlier.[39]

In large majority of the cases, the word-final position in Sanskrit is relatively weak. For instance, *hariḥ, harir, hariś,hariṣ, haris, or, tasmāt, tasmād,tasmāc, tasmāj, tasmān,tasmāl, etc.* The tendancy to final assimilation is greater at word-justion (*pada*) or morphemic junction (inside *pada*). For instance, *bhārabhṛ́d yathā (8.75.12), or marúdbhyaḥ (1.64.1), but marútaḥ (1/3) (1.23.12).*

The greater weakness at the word-final position may lead to the corruption of the original text or one may miss the basic form. Therefore, the Pdk establishes the basic *avasāna-* forms occuring before pause in this situation. But when a root or a stem is intimately connected with a derivational or influexional suffix as in *Parvatāt (parvata-āt), marutaḥ (marut-aḥ) or bhavati (bhav-ati),* there is no possibility of mispronouncing the text or missing the exact letter in the text.

Therefore, the Pdk does not feel the necessity of seperation of a root or a noun-stem before a derivational or an inflexional suffix beginning with a vowel.

I.2.1 Grammatical Significance of the Symbols 'S' *(avagraha) and I (daṇḍa) in the Pp*

The symbols 'S' and 'I' traditionally known as *avagraha and daṇḍa* respectively have different connotations in the *Pada- text of the RV*. Primarily, they represent pause or juncture while passing from one concatanated unit to the other on the sentence-level. *Daṇḍa* represents intervention by the length of time required to pronounce a short vowel *ekamātrā* between the two finished words: whereas an *avagraha* represents the intervention by the length of time required to pronounce a consonant *(ardhmātrā)* between two phonological units. Both these symbols indicate the juncture-feature i.e. the grammatical *padatva* of a finished word or a stem preceding these symbols. The symbol *daṇḍa*[40] always comes after a finished word. it indicates that the finished word is followed by a pause for the purpose of isolation of *pada* items. For instance.

Sp : *agnımīḷe puróhitam*......1.1.1.

Pp. *agnım / īle/ puráḥ-hitam /*.....

The symbol *avagraha*[40] comes (A) before a few case- suffixes, (B) before a secondary suffix, (C) before the primary suffix-*vāṁs*, and (D) in a compound. For example.

(A) Before a case-suffix

Sp	*Pp*
Śáśvadbhiḥ	*Śáśvat - bhiḥ* 7.93.6.
marúdbhyaḥ	*marút-bhyaḥ* 1.64.1
mahadbhyām	*mahát-bhyām* 3.7.6
mahátsu	*mahát-su* 1.81.1

(B) Before a secondary suffix

Sp	*Pp*
prajā́vān	*prijā́-vān*, 3.30. 18
dyumátā	*dyu-mátā* 6.62.10

(C) Before the primary suffix-*vāṁs*

Sp	*Pp*
tasthivā́ṁsam	*tasthi-vā́ṁsam* 1.72.4
papivā́ṁsam	*papi-vā́ṁsam* 3.43.5

(D) In a compound

Sp	*Pp*
ádabdhavratapramatiḥ	*ádabdhavrata-pramatiḥ* 2.9.1
bṛhádukthaḥ	*bṛhát-ukthaḥ* 5.19.3.

Before a case-suffix the symbol *avagraha* denotes internal *padatva* of the stem on the basis of which *sandhi* is allowed between the final phoneme of a stem and the initial phoneme of a case-suffix. This can be clear from the examples under (A) above.

This symbol is also used to indicate *padatva* of the stem in the case of adding secondary suffixes and compounding. According to P. after the stem the case-endings are supplied and deleted in the case of compouding and adding secondary suffixes. Therefore, according to P. a stem in such cases is regarded as external *pada* though in the surface form case-endings are not seen. For instance, the deep structure of *prajā́vān is prajā + sU+vat. Here sU* is dropped by P.2.4.11 Similarly, *nṛpatiḥ*

(4.20.1) is derived from *nṛ+ām+patiḥ* where *ām* is deleted by *P 2.4.71*. Therefore the symbol *avagraha* represents external *pada* in such cases.

The separation of the suffix-vāṁs by the Pdk is most probably due to his confusing certain *vāṁs* forms with the *vat*-forms and due to availablility of independent usage of certain action nouns derived from reduplicated roots.[41]

It can be further seen that the symbol *daṇḍa* cuts the constitutents of a sentence whereas *avagraha* separates an immediate constituent of a finished word (simple or compound). Therefore, in *adabdhavratapramatih, avagraha* is used after *adabdhavrata'* 'unbroken observances' showing that it conveys a single-integrated meaning with which *pramatih.* superiorminded' forms semantic connection. We will be discussing this aspect of the Pp in detail in I.3 below.

The following diagram will make the picture clear regarding the significance of the symbols *daṇḍa* and *avagraha:*

a.

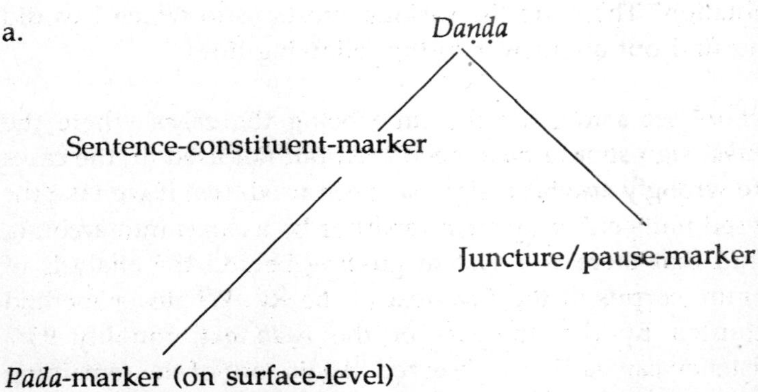

b.

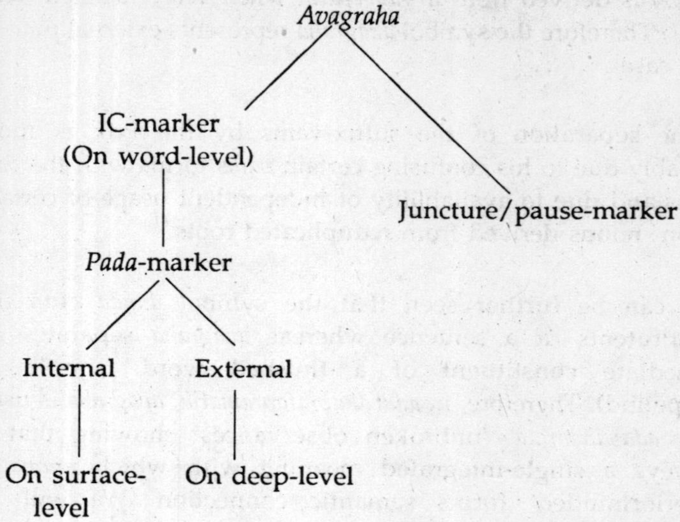

1.2.2 Significance of the term pada in the Pp

Can we account satisfactory for the term pada in the Pp of the RV? If yes, what is the significance of the term *pada* in the Pp? Does it have grammatical connotation or semantic connotation? These are the various questions to which I would like to find out an answer in the following lines.

Let us set aside, for the time being the cases where the *avagraha*- sign should have been used but not used or, the cases where wrongly *avagraha*- sign has been used. Just if we take the analysed units either by an *avagraha* or by a *daṇḍa* into account, we find that there is a system guiding behind the analysis of the entire corpus of the *Pada*-text of the *RV*. Whatever method is adopted by the analyser of the *Pada*-text, roughly 95% consistency can easily be observed. Again, out of the remaining 5% inconsistency 4% cab be justified by assuming few rules which must have in the mind of the Pdk. And the remaining 1% cannot be answered satisfactorily. It is attempted here to find out the basic criteria on which the Pdk has based his method of analysis. Let us see first of all what he has done.

In the *Pada*-text, only a few case suffixes, some secondary suffixes, one primary suffix, and component of a compount are found separated. Moreover, only in certain environments these morphemes are found analysed. Out of case-suffixes, only-*bhiḥ, -bhyām, -bhyaḥ and -su* are subjected for separation. Again, these suffixes are separated if they occur after a short vowel or after a consonant. No case-suffix is found separated after any feminine base ending in ā, ī, and ū. Moreover, if S of su is found cerbralised in the Sp, no analysis is offered in the Pp.

For example,

Sp	Pp
kármabhiḥ	*kárma-bhiḥ 3.36.1*
ṛ́ṣibhyaḥ	*ṛ́ṣi-bhyaḥ* 10.14.15
vásubhiḥ	*vásu-bhiḥ 1.58.3*
pitṛ́bhyām	*pitṛ́-bhyām 1.111.1*
ṛgbhıḥ	*ṛk-bhıḥ 2.35.12*
ṛtayúgbhiḥ	*ṛtayúk - bhiḥ 4.51.5*
marúdbhyaḥ	*marút- bhyaḥ 1.64.1*

Similarly, not all the secondary suffixes are separated from the bases. Only those secondary suffixes which begin with a consonant are separated in the Pp. For example,

Sp	Pp
citrátamaḥ	*citrá- tamaḥ 1.108.1*

dáśátayaḥ	*dáśa-tayaḥ 1.158.4*
kavıtaraḥ	*kavı-taraḥ 7.86.7*
satyátātā	*satyá-tātā 10.111.4*
Sp	Pp
vasútātiḥ	*vasú-tātiḥ 1.122.12*
amṛtatvám	*amṛta-tvám 1.66.6*
martyatvanā́	*martya-tvanā́ 8.15.2*
káṇvamantam	*káṇva-mantam 8.2.22*
gomáyam	*go-máyam 10.62.2*
maghávā	*maghá-vā 1.32.3*
ánnavān	*ánna-vāñ 10.117.2*
cáturvayam	*átuḥ vayam 1.110.3*
ákṛṣivalām	*ákṛṣi-valām 10.146.6*
māyāvınaḥ	*māyā-vınaḥ 9.83.3*

The perfect participale-marker-*vāṁs* is the only primary suffix which is found separated in the *pada*-text. This treatment originates from the fact that the Pdk treats this primary suffix as the secondary suffix out of some confusion.[42] For example,

Sp	*Pp*
tasthivā́n	*tasthi-vā́n 5.85.5,*
cakṛvā́n	*cakṛ-vā́n 5.29.14*

Unlike the treatment of case-suffixes, this suffix is never separated from a consonant-base.

The remaining area where the *avagraha-* sign is used is that of the compounds. It is worth-noticing that the *avagraha* is used only once irrespective of the number of components which constitute a compound. In separating a component of a compound, no restriction of specific environment is laid down as it is done in the case of case-suffixes and the suffix *-vaṁs*. In analysing the *taddhita* -suffixes also no such restriction is laid down that and these suffixes should not be separated after a long vowel. For example,- *vān* (possessive suffix) is separated from *prajā in prajā́vān* (3.30.18). Similarly *Patiḥ* separated from *prajā in prajāpatiḥ* (4.53.2). But, *bhiḥ* is not separated from the base *prajā in prajā́bhiḥ* (2.33.1). The suffix - *vāṁs* also is not separated from *jigī-in jigīvā́n (2.12.4).*

As far as *Daṇḍa* is concerned, it always comes after a finished form. Taking into consideration the facts stated above we are tempted to say that the entire analysis of the Pdk is based on the concept of the term *pada*. Wherever, there is a *daṇḍa* or an *avagraha* the portion preceding the *daṇḍa* or the *avagraha is a pada* according to the Pdk. This explains why śākalya's text is called a *Pada-text.*

Let us now reconstruct śāk's concept of the grammatical term *pada*. Supposing that whatever precedes the symbols *daṇḍa* and *avagraha* is *pada,* we can reconstruct śāk's concept of *pada* as follows:

A.(i) An inflected or a finished word is a *pada*. (Indicated by *daṇḍa)*

B. (i) A stem (both simple and compound) before a case-termination or a secondary suffix which begins with a consonant is a *pada* excepting t and s stems before a matvarthiya suffix.

ii) What precedes the denominative suffix is a *pada*

iii) What precedes the suffix - *vāṁs* is a *pada*.

iv) A constituent of a compound preceding another constituent is a *pada*

When we compare this concept of the Pdk with the Pāṇinian concept of *pada* we find that Pāṇinian concept of *pada* does not agree with B. iii) and partly agrees with B. ii); the rest is exactly identical. Thus, here we get pre- Pāṇinian concept of *pada*. The Pāṇinian concept of *pada* is an imporved version of the same concept.

I.3. The Principle of ICA and Isolation of items in the Complex forms

The aim of the following lines is to point out some similarity between the principles of ICA and those of the Pp of the *RV*. The necessity of such a comparasion between the systems is felt imperative because of the fact that we know very little about the pre-Pāṇinian grammatical conventions which would have thrown sufficient light on our history of study of grammatical concepts in India.

All scholars agree on the point that śāk, the Pdk of the *RV* precedes P.P himself mentions his name in his *Aṣṭā.*[43] But,, unfortunately no grammtical text composed by him is available to us. What we are left with under his name is the *Pada*-text of the *R.V.* from which we get some scanty information concerning the development of grammatical thoughṭs. That is to say, we can reconstruct the grammar known to Śāk from the method which he adopts for isolation of items. The data, with which we are left, clearly indicates that the system adopted by the Pdk is somewhat similar to that of what we understand to-day by ICA.

What the Pdk does is that he beaks first of all a *ṛk by daḍa* into its constituents and dissolves the *sandhis* which occur in the continuous text (Sp.) But, the cuts are not random cuts. A *daṇḍa* always comes after a finished form-in a more appropriate term-after a free morpheme.

The following *ṛk*. will clarify this point:

Agnım iḷe puròhitamam yajñāsya devám ṛtvıjam/

hótāram ratndhā́tamam 1.1.1

The *daṇḍa*. cuts of this *ṛk* in the Pp are as under:

Agnım /iḷe/ puráḥ-hitam yajñásya / devám/

ṛtvıjam / hòtāram / ratna- dhā́tamam//

Thus, *daṇḍa* divides a verse into its constituents i.e., what we can call, words. Such a treatment may be said to be similar to that of cutting an English sentence like 'He goes home' into its word-components: He / goes/ home/ in Constituent Analysis. That is to say, it is something like breaking a lager constituent into smaller ones. Thus, the use of *daṇḍa* can be taken as providing us with a word-level analysis of a particular *ṛk*.

Having come to the word-level, the Pdk attempts to analyse further these words or fee morphemes into their smaller constituents. For this level of analysis he uses the symbol of *avagraha*. Thus, he keeps two distinct levels of analysis apart, such as, the analysis of sentence into free morphemes and the analysis of free morphemes into further constituents, by using two different symbols. A *daṇḍa* always comes between two finished morphemes and never between two constituents of a finished morpheme; similarly, an *avagraha* is used between two constituents if a finished morpheme and never between two finished words.

But, while analysing a free morpheme into its constituent morphemes, the Pdk imposes certain restrictions. The following are such restrictions:

a. No suffix begining with a vowel is separated from a base, e.g. *uṣásam 1.32.4*

b. Only those suffixes which begin with a consonant are separated, eg. *ṛ́ṣi-bhiḥ(1.1.2); ṛṣṭi- mántaḥ* (3.54.13)[44]

c. No primary suffix is separated from a base except the perfect participle suffix *-vāṃs, e.g., gatáḥ (7.58.3),* but *tasthi- vā̊ṃsaḥ (1.33.15)*

d. Only the case-suffixes and the secondary suffixes are separated from the bases, e.g., the examples under b. above.

e. The case-suffixes are not separated after a long vowel and after an affected base, e.g., *pra-jā́bhiḥ (2.33.1); devébhiḥ* (1.1.5).

f. Only one cut is shown even if a word consist of more than two morphemes, *e.g. sutásomavat-bhiḥ* (10.69.11). Such a cut is shown in the following order of priority;

i) An IC of a word is separated first if the above mentioned conditions are fulfilled. Naturally an IC in the Vedic languages is a case-suffix on the word-level. *sutásomavat-bhiḥ.*

ii) If a case-suffix is inseprable, the secondary suffix if any, preceding the case-suffix gets second preference for cut[45] e.g., *prajā́-vatīṣu* (7.1.11).

iii) If there is no secondary suffix preceding an inseperable case-suffix, then IC of a compound gets separated. But if the base is a single unit base, no cut is shown. *pra-jā́bhiḥ.*

(iv) If a compound-base has inflected component as its first member, no cut is shown, e.g., *bṛ́haspátiḥ* (1.62.3).

g. *Devatādvandva-* compounds are not separated, e.g., *agnī́ṣómā* (1. 93.8)

h. No verbal form is analysed. Only prefixes are separated from the verbs by *avagraha* if they are unaccented. eg., *atirat* (1.33.13); *ati-rócate* (10.187.2)

i. Negative particle a or an is never separated from a negative compound, e.g, *ádevah* (6. 17.8).

All these rules show that the Pdk has generally followed the principles of breaking ICs of a word with the above mentioned restrictions reasons for which cannot always be ascertained with certainty. Excepting a few cases like *kava-ambhyaḥ (10.107.3), ratna- dhắtamam (1.1.1)* etc. he is quite consistet in separating the immediate constituents. But, if a case-suffix is not analysable, second priority is extended to the next immidiate constituent. If that also is not analysable, the third priority is given to the still next immediate constituent. This order of priority is almost strictly followed by the Pdk. So far the use of *daṇḍa* is concerned it consistently separates each and every word-constituent of a ṛc. In case of *avagraha,* the order of priority of separation sufficiently reveals that the Pdk must have started analysing the words with the idea of showing immediate constituents of words, although this cannot be the main aim of he *Pada*-text. In the *Pada*-text, the main stress was given on disjoining the *pad-sandhis.* But, the Pp has another purpose to serve; it helps in understanding the meaning of a *ṛk*.. And in this context the principle of ICA proves the best, in his system of analysis. And from the way of seperation adopted by him it is implied that his method of isolation of items is similar to the concept of isolation that we see in ICA in linguistics.

I.4 SANDHI

1.4.0. Introductory Remarks

Sandhi-alternations result from the juxtaposition of words, from the juxtaposition of compound-constituents, and before juncture (i.e., before *pada*-forming suffixes, e.g., the case-terminations like *bhyām, -bhiḥ* etx. and the secondary suffixes which begin with a consonant). These *sandhis* are not applicable to roots or stems before inflexional or derivational suffixes unless they are *pada*-forming suffixes. The internal *sandhi*-alternations which are applicable to roots or stems before inflexional or derivational suffixes also result from the juxtaposition of independent words or from the juxtaposition of compound- constituents. Terminal *sandhis*(i.e., *sandhi* "in pausa" or *avasānasandhi*) do not occur in the Sp unless the word occurs at the end of a hemistich. But these occur in the Pp wherever a terminal position of finished word shows the tendency for a change. For instance, *ṛ́ṣibhir ī́ḍyo*...(Sp) 1.1.2

ṛ́ṣi - bhiḥ/ ī́ḍyah/..

I.4.1 EXTERNAL SANDHI

Both external and internal *sandhis* of the Sp have been dissolved in the Pp. From the treatment of this dissolution of *sandhis* we can doubtlessly presume that the following *sandhi*-rules must have been known to the Pdk

I.4.1. à Vowel + Vowel

A. *Sandhi of the sequence of the two similar vowels*

$$\left|\begin{array}{c}\breve{\bar{a}}\\ \breve{\bar{i}}\\ \breve{\bar{u}}\end{array}\right| + \left|\begin{array}{c}\breve{\bar{a}}\\ \breve{\bar{i}}\\ \breve{\bar{u}}\end{array}\right| \Rightarrow \left|\begin{array}{c}\bar{a}\\ \bar{i}\\ \bar{u}\end{array}\right|$$

e.g.,

Índrā́ /Índra ā́ / 1.3.6; *sávanā́ / sávanā ā́/* 1.4.2;

agnināgniḥ /agninā/agniḥ 1.12.6; *ihā́vase/ihá/ávase/* 1.22.10;

ádhītau / ádhi -itau / 2.4.8;

mṛḷātīdṛ́śe / mṛḷāti/ īdṛ́śe / 4.57.1; *sadhrī́m/ sadhrī́ /īm/*

2.13.2; *sūktásya / su -uktásya /* 2.23.9

It should be noted in this connection that we do not find the sequence: *ṛ+ṛ* in the Sp of the RV. Therefore, there is no illustration for their sandhi in th *RV*[46]

B. Sandhi of open vowel plus close vowel

$$\breve{\bar{a}} \quad + \quad \left|\begin{matrix}\breve{\bar{\imath}}\\ \breve{\bar{u}}\end{matrix}\right| \quad \Rightarrow \quad \left|\begin{matrix}e\\ o\end{matrix}\right|$$

Examples:

sīdatedám/ sīdata / idám/ 2.3.4

éhá / ā́ / inhá / 1.1.2

ém/ā́/ īm/ 1.4.7

tvòtāsaḥ/ tvā́ -uṭāṣaḥ/ 1.8.2

nótáyaḥ / ná/ūtáyaḥ/ 5.54.7

ávosrıyaḥ/ áva/ usrıyaḥ/ 5.59.6

C. *Sandhi of ā plus ṛ*

ā+ ṛ ⇒ āṛ/ ā ṛ

e.g.,

tátha ṛtúḥ/ táthā/ṛtúḥ/ 1.162. 19

vipanyā̃ ṛtásya / vipanyā́/ ṛtásya 4.1.12

D. *Open vowel* plus e, o, ai, au

(a)	+	e/ai o/au	⇒	ai au

e.g.,

aınam / ā́/énam/ 1.123.1

páraitat/ párā/ etat 10.61.8

yàtraúṣadhīh/yàtra/ aúṣadhīḥ/ 10.97.6

praúkṣan/ prá/ aúkṣan/ 10.90.7

D1. *Open vowel a plus e*

a + e ⇒ āe

e.g.,

āminant évaiḥ/aminanta/évaiḥ/ 1.79.2

D2. *Irregular Sandhi*

ā + e/o ⇒ e/o

e.g.,

tatārevá/ tatāra/ evá/ 7.33.3

yáthohiṣe/ yáthā/ ohiṣe/ 8.5.3

E. *Glide-formation rule*

ĭ *ŭ*	+	Vowel (except *ĭ*) Vowel (except *ŭ*)	⇒	y+ v+

e.g.,

máhyā́/ máhi/ ā́/ 3.31.3

nvásya/ nú/ asya/ 3.38.8

tvétā/ tú/étā/ 1.5.1

F. e, o, ai, au in terminal position[47]

e/o	+	vowel (except *a*)	⇒	*a*
ai/au	+	vowel		*a*

e.g.,

vávakṣa ṛṣváḥ/ vávakṣe/ṛṣváḥ/ 4.23.1

agna ihá/ agne/ihá/ 1.22.10

vā́ya ukthébhiḥ/ vā́yo iti/ ukthébhiḥ/ 1.2.2

tásmā ındrāya/ tásmai/ ındrāya/ 1.4.10

sujihvā́ úpa / sujihaú/ úpa/ 1.13.8[48]

F1. *O in terminal position becoming av*[49]

o ⇒ av

e.g. *vāyavā́/ vāyo iti/ ā́/* 1.2.1.

G. *Terminal e/o plus short open vowel a*

e/o + a ⇒ *e′*

e.g.,

vájrahasto′ him/ vájra-hastaḥ/ áhim/ 2.19

sunáve'gne/sunáve/ ágne/ 1.1.9

I.4.1.b *Vowel + Consonant*

a + ch ⇒ ā cch

e.g.,

mā́ cchedma/ mā́/ chedma/ 1.109.3

I.4.1.c Consonant + Vowel

A. *The terminal final stops are voiced before Vowels.*

k/ṭ/t/p + vowel/ voiced stop ⇒ *g / ḍ / d /b* +

e,g.,

arvā́gā́/ arvā́k / ā́/ 4.32. 15

havyavā́ḍ juhvā́syaḥ/ havya - vā́ṭ/ juhú- āsyaḥ/ 1.12.6

havyavā́ḷagnıḥ/ havya - vā́ṭ/ agnıḥ/ 5.4.2.[50]

yádaṅgá/ yát/ aṅgá/ 1.1.6

triṣṭúbihá / triṣṭúp/ ihá/ 10.130.5

triṣṭúb gāyatrī́/triṣṭúp/ gāyatrī́ 10.14.16

B.

Short vowel	+	*ṅ*	+	Vowel	⇒	-*ṅṅ*-
"	+	*n*	+	"		-*nn*-

e.g.,

kīdṛn̐nındraḥ/ kīdṛn/ ındraḥ/ 10.108.3

abhavannasya/ abhavan/ asya/ 4.17.6

c. *ā/ī/ū+ n + vowel ⇒ ā̃ / ī̃ / ū̃ / +*[50A]

e.g.,

sárgā̃iva/ sárgān/iva/ 8.35.20

D. *ī /ū/ṛ + n + vowel ⇒ī̃ / ū̃ / ṝ̃ / + r*

e.g.,

*paridhī̃ ráti/ paridhī̃n / áti/*9.107.19

abhī́śū̃ riva / abhī́śūn - iva / 6.57.6

nṝ̃ rabhı nṝn abhı / 5.54.15

1.4.1.d *Consonant + Consonant*

A. *The replacement of h by the voiced aspirate corresponding to the preceding stop*

k				*g*	*gh*
ṭ	+	*(h)*	⇒	*ḍ*	*ḍh*
t				*d*	*dh*

e.g.,

madryag ghuv/āanáḥ/ madryak/ huvānáḥ/ 3.41.1

àvāḍḍhavyā́ni / ávāṭ / havyā́ni / 10.15.22

B. *Lateral assimilation*

$$t + l \Rightarrow l\ l$$

e.g.,

áṅgāl lómanaḥ/ áṅgāt/ lómnaḥ/ 10.163.6

B1. *Assimilation to the following initial*

$$(t) \quad + \quad \left|\begin{array}{c} c \\ ch \\ s \end{array}\right| \quad \Rightarrow \quad \left|\begin{array}{c} c\ c \\ c\ ch \\ c\ ch \end{array}\right|$$

e.g.,

táccákṣuḥ/ tát/ cákṣuḥ/ 7.66.16

yácchardiḥ / yát / chardiḥ/ 8.67.6.

rochicchyāvā́ / rohit / śyāvā́ / 1.100.16[51]

B2. *Assimilation to the following initial*

$$t + j \Rightarrow j\ j$$

e.g.,

yájjigāsi/ yát/ jigāsi/ 10.73.3

C.

$$\left|\begin{array}{c} ṭ \\ t \\ n \end{array}\right| \quad + \quad (ś) \quad \Rightarrow \quad \left|\begin{array}{c} ṭ \\ o \\ n \end{array}\right| \quad + \quad (ch)$$

e.g.,

rohıcchyāvā́/ rohıt/ syāvā́ 1.100.16

vajrinchnathihi/ vajrin/ śnathihi/ 1.63.5

vıpāṭchutudrí/ vıpāṭ/ sutudrí/ 3.33.1

It is worth-noticing that *RPr* 4.16 provides a rule that (*ṅ* + sibilant) becomes *(n + k +ch sibilant) and Uvaṭa quotes arvā ṅkchaśvattamam* (3.35.6) and *pratyaṅk sa viśvā* (9.80.3) as the examples of this phenomenon. But no printed edition reads these examples with inserted *k*. This *sandhi* is noted by P also (P 8.3.28).

D.

$$(a + n) \quad + \left|\begin{array}{c} y \\ r \\ v \end{array}\right| \quad \Rightarrow \quad (a) \quad + \left|\begin{array}{c} y \\ r \\ v \end{array}\right|$$

e.g.,

dadhanvā̃ yáḥ/ dadhavā́n/yáḥ 9.107. 1

dadvā̃ / dadvān / vā/ 10.132.3

pı́voannā̃ ráyivṛdhaḥ / pı́vaḥ - annān / ráyi-vṛdhaḥ/ 7.91.3

E. Sandhi of r-insertion

$$(\imath/u) + n \quad + \left|\begin{array}{c} y \\ v \\ h \end{array}\right| \quad \Rightarrow \quad (\imath/u + r) \quad + \left|\begin{array}{c} y \\ v \\ h \end{array}\right|$$

e.g.,

paṇī́r hatam / paṇī́n/ hatam/ 1.84.2

dásyū̃r yónau/ dásyūn/yónau/ 1.63.4

paṇī́r vácobhiḥ/ paṇī́n/ vácaḥbhiḥ/ 6.39.2

F. Assimilation of n to the following initial

$$(n) + \left| \begin{matrix} c \\ j \\ \acute{s} \end{matrix} \right| \Rightarrow (\tilde{n}) + \left| \begin{matrix} c \\ j \\ \acute{s} \end{matrix} \right|$$

e.g.,

vajrinchanathihi / vajrin/ śnathihi/ 1.63.5

ūrdhvā́ñ caráthāya/ ūrdhvā́n/ caráthāya/ 1.36.14.

tā́ñjuṣethām/ tān/ juṣethām/ 5.51-6

G. *Insertion of a fricative between the nasal and the stop.* The nasal is dropped and the preciding vowel is nasalised.

i) a + n + c ⇒ *ã ś c*

e.g.,

tā́ścit / tā́n / cit / 10.154.1

ii) a + n + t ⇒ ã s t

e.g.,

āvā́dástvam/ ā-vádan/ tvám/ 2.43.3

H. *Insertion of a visarjanīya before the stop p.*

The nasal is dropped and the preceding vowel is nasalised.

nṝ́ḥpā́tram/ nṝ́nn / pā́tram/ 1.121.1

svátavā̄ḥ pāyúḥ/ svá - tavān/ pāyúḥ 4.2.6[52]

I. *Insertion of a stop before a fricative*

n + s ⇒ n t s

e.g.,

ahantśhasā/ ahan sáhasā/ 1.80.10

J. *Nasality in the form of anusvāra*

		r				*r*
		s				*s*
(m)	+	*ṣ*	⇒	*(ṁ)*	+	*ṣ*
		s				*s*
		h				*h*

e.g.,

hótāraṁ ratnadhā́mam / hótāram/ ratna - dhā́ mam/ 1.1.1

várdhamānaṁ své vā́rdhamānam / své / 1.1.8

mitrā́ṁ huve / mitrám/ huve/ 1.2.7

J1. *Nasality (anusvāra) of m before the initial voiced and voiceless stops*

m + *voiced/ voiceless stop* ⇒ *ṁ* + *voiced/ voiceless stop*

e.g.,

bhadráṁ kariṣyási/ bhadrám / kariṣyási/ 1.1.6

ahám̐ ca / ahám /ca/ 8.62.11

bhadrám̐ naḥ / bhadrám/ naḥ/ 10.20.1

śiśyám̐ tvā/ śiśayám/tvā/ 10.42.3[53]

K. *Anusvāra of n before I* [54]

n + I ⇒ *m̐*+l

e.g.,

jigīvā́m̐ lakṣám / jigivā́n/ lakṣám/ 2. 12.4

L. *Insertion of a fricative between the two stops*

cit + skambhanena ⇒ citkambhanena

e.g.,

citkámbhanena/ cit/ skámbhanena 10.111.5.

It is to be noted that although the Pdk restores *s* in the above mentioned example, he does not do so in the case of *úttahitm (10.149.2) and úttabhitā (10.85.1)*

These are analysed as *útthitam/* and *úttabhitā/* respectively.

1.4.l.e *visarga - Sandhi*

A. *Upadhmaniya -modification of ḥ*[55]

ḥ + p ᳵ+

e.g.,

svátavā̃ ᳵ pāyuḥ/ svatavān/ pāyuḥ/ 4..2.6

B. *ḥ + k/ p ⇒ s/ ṣ+*

e.g.,

diváspári /diváḥ/ pári/ 1.121. 10

pátnīvataskṛdhi/ pátnī -vataḥ/ kṛdhi/ 1.14.7

mātúṣpadé/ mátúḥ/ padé/ 4.5.10

C. *r-modification of visarga*

ḥ + p ⇒ r +

e.g.,

pūrpatim/ puḥ- patim/ 1.173. 10

svarpatiḥ/ svaḥ-patiḥ/ 8.44. 18

D. *Assimilation of ḥ to a following stop*

i) *ḥ + c ⇒ ś +*

e.g.,

devāscakṛmá /devāḥ/ cakṛmá/ 10.37.12

pū́śca/ pū́ḥ/ ca/ 1.189. 2

ii) *ḥ + t ⇒ s +*

e.g.,

yáste / yáḥ/ te/ 1. 4.4

iii) *ḥ* + t⇒ *ṣ ṭ* when ḥ, is preceded by a vowel other than *a, ā*

e.g.,

duṣṭáraḥ/ duḥ- táraḥ/ 3.24.1

E. *r.-modification of visarga before fricatives*

ḥ + s ⇒ r ṣ

e.g.,

dhūrṣádam/ dhūḥ - sádam/ 10.132.7

svarṣā́/ svaḥ - sā́n/ I.91.21

F. *Dropping of visarga*

ḥ + *s*+ voiceless stop ⇒ + *s* +

e.g.,

mandıbhi stómebhiḥ/ mandı-bhih / stómebhih/ 1.9.3

But VSM-edition does not show this *sandhi,* rather ḥ is always retained in all these cases. P does not deal with this *sandhi*. Kātāyana ofcourse, under P 3.8.36 puts a *Vārttika* to be operated optionally : *kharpare sari vā visargalopo vaktavyaḥ*

G. *Diphthongisation of visarga*

i) *a*+*ḥ* + *a*/ voiced stop ⇒ + *o* +

e.g.,

yó asmai/ yaḥ/ asmai/ 8.31. 2

devó devébhiḥ/ deváḥ/ devébhiḥ 1.1.5

Also, *mahó ādityā́ / maháḥ / ādityā́n/ ā́/* 10.63.5

ii) a + ḥ + voiceless stop/ fricative ⇒ + o +

e.g.,

itó ṣiñcitā/ itáḥ/ siñcitā/ 9.107.1

ádo pito/ adáḥ/ pito ıti/ 1.187.7

H. *Dropping of visarga*

i) a + ḥ + vowel (excepting a) ⇒ a +

e.g.,

yá ındrah/ yáḥ ındrah/ 8.12.1

ii) ā + ḥ+ vowel/ voiced stop ⇒ ā+

e.g.,

sutāimé/ sutā́/ imé/ 1.3.4

vırūpā diváḥ/ vı- rūpāḥ / diváḥ/ 3.53.7

iii) *Irregular dropping of ḥ and crasis*

svádhitāva/ svádhitiḥ -iva/ 5.7.8

bhū́myā́dade/ bhū́miḥ/ ā́ dade /9.61.10

I. *Peculiar sandhi*

		dabha-		*dūḷabha-*
(dur)	+	*nasa-*	⇒	*dūṇāsa*
		dhy		*dūḍhy*

e.g.,

dūḷábhaḥ/ duḥ - dábhaḥ/ 3.2.2

dūṇā́śā/ duḥ - náśā/ 3.56.8

dūḍhyaḥ/ duḥ - dhyaḥ/ 1.94.8

This irregular feature is noted by Kātyāyana in his *Vārttika: duro dāśanāśadabhadhyeṣū tvam uttarpadāḥ ṣṭutvaṁ ca,* (on P 6.3.109).

J. *Dropping of visarjanīya of pronominal stems*

eṣaḥ				*eṣa*	
saḥ	+	*(Consonant)*	⇒	*sa*	+
syaḥ				*sya*	

e.g.,

eṣá kavih / eṣáḥ/ kaviḥ/ 9.27-1

sá vājī́/ sáḥ/ vaji/ 4.36.6

syá vājī́ / syáḥ / vājī́/ 4.40.4

Peculiar cases are :

só cit/ sáḥ/ cit/ 1.191.10

sā́ nú/ sáḥ/ nú/ 1.145.1

K. Dropping of ḥ and crasis in the case pronoun tad

*saúṣadhīḥ/ sáḥ/ óṣadhīḥ/*8.53.9

séndra/ sáḥ/ indra 2.13.11

sédu/ sáḥ/ ıt/ ū̃ıti/ 1.32. 15[56]

L. *Avoiding geminate rr and lengthening of the preceding vowel*

vowel + *ḥ*+ *ṛ* ⇒ vowel (lengthened) + r

e.g.,

prātā́ rátnam/ prā́taḥ/ rátnam/ 1.125.1

agnī́ rákṣā́ṁsi/ agnıḥ/ rákṣāṁsi/ 7.15.10

I.4.2 INTERNAL SANDHI

Only those internal *sandhis* are analysed by the Pdk which are similar in nature to the external *sandhis* i.e., *sandhis* which are determined by juncture or morphenic boundary. This type of *sandhi* can be termed as internal *pada-sandhi.* This occurs before case- endings which begin with *bh-*, and *s-* (of locative *su*), and secondary suffixes, beginning with a consonant. Both these suffixes are *pada*-forming suffixes. Therefore, the Pdk analyses these cases of *sandhi*.

If we compare the Pp which isolates *padas,* it will be clear that the Pāṇinian concept of internal *pada* is more or less based on that of the Pdk since in pāṇinian system also only above mentioned two types of suffixes are regarded as *pada*-forming suffixes. Only before these juncture -forming suffixes *sandhi* takes place, which seems to have been the main criterion to decide *padatva* of a stem before these suffixes. This is the reason why P gives the name *padá* to stems before these suffixes. In Sanskrit the general principles involved in external *sandhi* and in the *sandhi* of stems and juncture- forming suffixes are the same.

The Pdk finds the following internal *sandhi* rules which are identical with external *sandhi* rules discussed in the previous section.

i) *k* (< *c, j*)/*ṭ* (< *ṣ*)/*t* + voiced stop ⇒ *g*[57]/*ḍ*/ *d* +

e.g.,

ṛgbhiḥ/ *ṛk-bhiḥ*/ 2.35.12

ṣaḍbhiḥ/ *ṣaṭ - bhiḥ*/ 2.18.4

bṛhádbhyaḥ/ *bṛhát - bhyaḥ*/ 4.54.5

pṛ́ṣadvat/ *pṛ́ṣat- vat*/ 7.2.4

ii) *d + nasal ⇒ n+ nasal*

e.g.,

mṛnmáyam/ *mṛt*[58] *-máyam*/ 7.89.1.

That the main criterion to decide *padatva* of a stem was *sandhi* is confirmed by the treatment of the forms like *pṛ́ṣadvat* mentioned above. Here, since *t of pṛṣat-* is changed to *d* before *-vat,* the Pdk takes *pṛṣat* as a *pada* and analyses it. Otherwise, i.e., if it had not been changed to *d* as in the case of *marutvat*-etc., he would have left it unanalysed.

ṣaḍbhiḥ is analysed as *ṣaṭ-bhiḥ* showing that the *pada-sandhi* is between ṭ and *bh*. That the ṣ of the stem ṣaṣ -is changed to ṭ owing to *padatva* is not indicated by the Pdk, since this is not the main aim of the Pp.[59]

iii)

$$\left|\begin{array}{c} \breve{\bar{i}} \\ \breve{\bar{u}} \\ \text{r} \end{array}\right| + (s) \Rightarrow \left|\begin{array}{c} \breve{\bar{i}} \\ \breve{\bar{u}} \\ \text{r} \end{array}\right| + (ṣ)$$

e.g.,

sīṣādhāti/ sīsadhāti/ 6.49.8

siṣicatuḥ/ sisicatuḥ/ 7.33.13

suṣupuḥ/ susupuḥ/ 7.18.14

suṣumā/ susuma/ 1.101.9

In all these examples the change of *s* to *ṣ* is not a *pada-sandhi*. As a matter of fact, the *sandhi* which is not a *pada-sandhi* is mostly kept undissolved. For example, the s of the future marker *sya*, or of the locative case-ending - *su*, when cerebralised, is never restored.[60] Thus, *kariṣyati* (1.164.39) or *bhaviṣyati* (10-86.7) or deveṣu (1.1.4) is not analysed as *karisyati* or *bhavisyati* or *devesu*. But in the example types mentioned above, the Pdk is consisent in restoring *s* when it is cerebralised. This is something peculiar on the part of the Pdk to go against the main criterion of *padatva* for dissolving a *sandhi*. Probably, this is the next stage in the development of the *Pada-text*. The later layer of the *Pada*-text may aim at giving comments on the earlier Pp.

I.4.3 CEREBRALIZATION

The cerebralization of *n* and *s* in the *RV* is possible at two levels:

i) at the level of word-formation, and ii) at the level of the continuous recital i.e., at the level of the Sp. Cerebralization at the word-formation level is not touched by the Pdk excepting a few cases discussed under the preceding section.[61] Since cerebralisation within a single word is not taken into account by the Pdk, he does not analyse the forms like, *agnıṣu* (1.108.4), *kariṣyati* (1.164.39), *kṛṇoti* (1.18.8), etc.

But, the cerebralization at the *saṁhitā*- level is consistently removed in the Pp and the original *n* and *s* are restored.[62]

Thus, *abhī́ ṣú ṇaḥ sákhīnām* is analysed as *abhi/sú/naḥ/sákhīnām/* 4.31.3; *pari ṇetā matīnām* as *pari/ netā/ matīnām/; góróheṇa* as *góḥ/ óhena/*[63], *nirgamāṇi as niḥ/ gamāni/*[64]; *indra eṇa as indraḥ/ enā/*[65] *indra eṇam/ indraḥ/ enam/*1,163.2; *agnéraveṇa/ agnéḥ/ ávena/ 1.128.5; śakrá eṇam/ śakráḥ/enam/* 8.1.19 etc.

In the cases of *dūṇā́śaḥ (7.32.7), dūṇā́śam (1.176.4) and dūṇā́śā* (3. 56.8) of the Sp. the Pp reads as *duḥ-náśaḥ duḥ-náśam,* and *duḥ náśā* respectively. The cerebralization of *n* is due to the *r* of the prefix dur and the lengthening of *u* of *dū* is due to dropping of this *r*. It is interesting indeed, that the Pdk could visualise the whole historical process of derivation. It appears to me that this type of nicities might have been introduced in the Pp in a later stage. At the early stage of the *Pada*-text these forms might have remained unanalysed as the forms like *abhī́śavaḥ (1.38.12) etc.* In the case of *abhī́śavaḥ,* the lengthening of *ī* is due to the elision of *a* of the root *aś*. But the Pdk does not show it. Whereas, *dūṇāśaḥ* etc have been explained.

What is stated above holds true for the following examples:

dūḷabha/ duḥ-dabha/ 2.28.8

dūḷabháḥ/ duḥ - dábhaḥ/ 3.2.2

dūḷábham/ duḥ - dábham/ 1.15.6

dūḷábhāsaḥ duḥ - dábhāsaḥ/ 3.56.8

dūḍhyaḥ/ duḥ - dhyaḥ/ 1.94.8

dūḍhyā/ duḥ-dhyā/ 9.53.3

dūḍhye/ duḥ - dhye/ 1.190.5

In addition to these above mentioned cases, the cerebralization due to compounding in compound removed words is consistently in the Pp. For instance, *goṣā́ḥ go - sáḥ/* 9.2.10; *nṛṣā́ḥ/ nṛ-sā́ḥ/* 9.2.10

goṣṭàm/ go -sthàm/ 8.43.17;

vanarṣàdaḥ/ vana-sádaḥ/ 2.31.1; *vanarṣádam/ vana-sádam/* 10.132.7[66] etc.

I.4.4. PROHIBITION OF SANDHI

No *sandhi* is allowed with a *pragṛhya*-vowel. The following cases are cosidered as *pragṛhyas*:

i) Vocative o, *vıṣṇo áśvinā/ vıṣṇo ıti* 8.27.8

ii) *O* which is a word by itself

ò hı/ ó iti/ hı. 10.117.5

iii) *O* resulting from the *sandhi* of *a* or *ā* of a noun/ pronoun or of a particle and the particle *u.*

eṣó uṣā́ḥ/ eṣó ī́ti/ uṣā́ḥ/ 1.46.I

átho ındrāya / átho ıti/ ındrāya 1.28.6

iv) Dual *ī, ū, e*

hárī ṛ́kṣasya/ hárī ıti/ṝ́kṣasya/ 8.68.15

ındravāyū imé/ ındravāyū ıti/ imé/ 1.2.4.

ródasī ubhé ṛghāyámānam/ ródasī ıti/ ubhé ıti/ ṛghāyámānam/ 1.10.8.

v) Locative *ī, ū*

*sómo gaurī́/ ádhi/śritáḥ/sómaḥ gaurī́/ ıti/ ádhi/ śritáḥ/*1.151.4

svā́yāṁ tanū́ ŕtvye nā́dhamānam/

svā́yām/ tanū́ ıti/ ṛtvye/

nā́dhamānam / 10.183.2

vi) *asme, yuṣme, tve,*[67] *amī*

asmé ā́/ asmé ıti /ā́ 8.5.15

yuṣmé ıt/ yuṣmé ıti/ ıt/ 8.18.19

tvé ıt/ tvé ıti/ıt/ 1.26.6

amī́ patáyantaḥ[68]*/ amī́/ ıti/ patáyantaḥ/* 1.24.6

vii) The particle *u*. It is lengthened and nasalised in the Pp.

u aṁśave/ū̃ ıti/ aṁśáve/ 1.46.10

Every where the Pdk has indicated a *pragṛhya-vowel by adding iti* to it.[69] Generally no *sandhi* should e allowed after a *pragṛhya*-vowel. But, in the Sp, we find that sometimes these *sandhi*- prohibition rules are violated. For instance, *nṛpátīva nṛpátī iváti nṛpátī - iva/* 7.104.6; *ródasīmé ródasī ıti/ imé ıti/* 7.90.3; *dámpatīva/ dámpatī ivétī dámpatī-iva/* 2.39.2, etc.

One interesting point in this connection is worth-noticing. In the case of *nṛpátīva, dámpatīva,* etc, of the Sp, the Pp reads as *nrpátī ivá ti nṛpátī -iva; dámpatīvéti dámpatī -iva,* etc., which indicates that either the Sp should read *nṛpátī iva, dámpatī iva, etc., as in the case of hárī iva* (1.28.7), or it may be merely the Pdk's suggestion.

Other cases of the violation of the *sandhi*- prohibition rule are:

upadhī́ va/ upadhī́ ivéty upadhī́ - iva/ 2.39.4

pradhī́va/ *pradhī́ ivéti pradhī́ iva*/ 2.39.4

viśpátīva/ *viśpátī ivéti viśpatī -iva*/ 7.39.2

Perhaps, the Pdk does not approve of these *sandhis* in the Sp and therefore, he indicates them in his *Pada-* text by putting *iva* separately and then by giving its regular compound- treatment by *avagraha*. This treatment of the Pdk further suggests that a fairly good range of time must have elapsed between the redaction of the Sp and the Pp. By the time of the Pdk, the irregular *sandhis* might have been given up and strictness about *sandhi*-rules might have come into force.

I.5 ŚĀKALYA'S THEORY OF AVSĀNA-SANDHI

The rules of external euphonic combination, *i.e. padānta*-rules, are, in general, applied to internal *pada* (*avāntara-pada*). But the rules applicable to a finished word before pause are never applied to an internal *pada*. It appears that śāk does not adhere to this practice in order to achieve the purpose of the Pp. To illustrate this point I shall discuss here two such rules which are exclusively external, but are allowed to be operated by śāk internally also in the Pp of the *RV*.

We know that an unaspirated unvoiced stop followed by a voiced stop changes into its corresponding voiced. This *sandhi* is applied externally as well as internally. Thus *k* of *vāk* in *yádvāgvádanty avacetanā́ni* (8.100.10) and that of *usik* in *pánantośigbhyo nā́mimīta várṇam* (2.4.5) are changed to g. Same thing holds true for ṭ of *ṣaṭ in utó sá máhyam ındubhih, ṣáḍyuktān* (1.23.15) and in *ā́ catūrbhir ā́ ṣaḍbhır hūyámānaḥ* (2.18.4); final *t* of *tanukṛ́ti* in *tanukṛ́d bodhi prámatiśca kāráve* (1.31.9) and in *tvám soma tanukṛ́dbhyo dvéṣobhyaḥ* (8.79.3) ; and *p* of *triṣṭup in triṣṭúb gāyatrī́ chándāṁsi sárvā tā́ yám ā́hitā* (10.14.16). The same principles are applied to compounds also, e.g. *ṣáḍvidhānāḥ* (7.87.5)/ *ṣát- vidhānaḥ*/; *ṛdhádrayaḥ*/*ṛdhát-rayaḥ*/*8.46.23; and adjā́m*/ *ap-jā́m* / *7.34.16*

Again, voiced stops are never changed to voiceless sound before a voiced stop of a vowel. But, before a *surd* or *pause* they are changed to the firsts of the corresponding series, e.g., *padbhyā́m* (10.90.12), *patsú (5.58.11), samidhā (1.95.11), samıtsu, samıt (5.6.9), triṣṭúbham (8.7.1), triṣṭúp* (1.121.4), *śarádbhiḥ* (1.86.6) and *Śarát (10.90.6).*

We come across about hundred stems in the *RV* which end in voiced consonants. The Pdk has converted a few of them into unaspirated surds before a *pada*-forming suffix or before a constituent of a compound beginning with a voiced sound. And therefore, the problem arises why and how the Pdk adopted such a method. In other words why *d* of *ud, pad*-'foot', nad-'river' *śarad 'autumn'* and *hṛd* -'heart' is changed to *t* in analysing *udvataḥ/ut-vátaḥ/, nadbhyáḥ/nat-bhyáḥ, padbhyā́m/pat-bhyā́m/, śarát-bhiḥ/* and *hṛdbhī́ḥ, hṛt-bhıḥ/?*

The other problem is about he *visarjanīya. In pausa,* final s and *r* of a word are converted to ḥ i.e. *ḥ* stands at the end of a finished word. This is where a *visarga* occurs in final position, (e.g., *Índraḥ vadhaḥ* etc.). S is also changed to ḥ internally before a hard consonant of a pada-forming suffix e.g., *rájaḥsu* (7.34.6) etc. but in such positions r cannot change to *ḥ* e.g., *gīrṣú* (8.92.7).

But in the *Pada-text* we find *s* or *r* of the *saṁhitā* occurring at the end of a stem are changed to *ḥ* before any *pada*- forming suffix or a constituent of a compound just as these are turned into ḥ occurring at the end of a finished word. Thus *aharvıdaḥ* has been analysed as *ahaḥ - vıdaḥ* (1.2.2). Similarly, *gnā́spátiḥ as gnā́ḥpátiḥ*[70] *jyotirjarāyuḥ as jyótiḥ- jarayuḥ* (10.123.1), *áns̈īrdām* (10.27.1) as *ánāSiḥ-dām, gīrbhıḥ (1.9.9) as gīḥ-bhıh*[70a], *catúrbhiḥ (1.155.6) as catúḥ-bhiḥ, pūrbhıḥ* (1.58.8), as *pūḥ-bhıḥ agnériva* (2.25.3) as *agnéḥ-ıva, Vástor vastoḥ* (10.40.1) as *vástoh -vastoḥ* and *daurgahé* (8.42.8) as *dauḥ - gahé.*

So far as the first case is concerned, no ancient commentator of the *RV* has thrown any light on it. *RPr* does not say any thing in this matter. It has made some general remarks about a *sandhi in pause.* In *RPr* 1.15-16, two views are quoted regarding the voiced and unvoiced unaspirated stops in *pausa*. According to the school of Gārgya the thirds of the consonantal series can stand at the end of a word in *pausa,* wheras according to the school of *Śākaṭāyana, the firsts are allowed.*[70b] *In this connection, the author of the RPr* does not commit himself to any of the views. *RPr* 12.1, again, gives us the idea with regard to the permitted finals indirectly. He enumerates those phonemes which do not occur at the end of *pada.* The remaining phonemes automatically become permitted finals. He says:

uṣmānaḥ (h s,ṣ, s, jihvāmūlīya, upadhmānīy and *ṁ) antahsthāḥ (y, r,l,v), ṛ, soṣmānaḥ (kh, gh, ch, jh, th, dh, th, dh, ph, bh)* and the *c-* class do not come at the end of a word[71] Thus *ṛ k,g,ṭ,ḍ,t,d,p,b* and nasals (except n) can occur at the end.

Now, by this enumeration, it becomes clear that he allows both unaspirated voiced as well as unvoiced stops as permitted finals. Moreover, ṛ and ṇ are also taken to be final. But in the *Saṁhitā-* text neither voiced stop nor ṛ nor ṇ occurs in *pausa.* Uvaṭa in his commentary on this rule has cited examples for each of the finals from the *Pada*-text.[72] But no example has been provided by him to show that unaspirated voiced stops occur at the end of a *pada* in *avasāna.* One more point is worth-considering. He has cited *nṛ- bhiḥ* and *vṛṣaṇ- vān* to show that *ṛ* and *ṇ* occur as permitted final. Now, if *RPr* 1.12 refers to the *Saṁhitā-text, how* ṛ *and* ṇ *of nṛ-bhiḥ* and *vṛṣaṇ-vān* respectively can taken as final phonemes in *pausa.* Again, if at all, the final position here refers to the final position of internal *pada,* what was the harm in showing the unaspirated voiced stop occurs at the end of a *pada* in *hṛdbhiḥ saradbhyaḥ etc.* where *d* belongs to the stems? Moreover, if this rule refers to the *pada-text* and if by *pada* he understands both internal and external *pada-* as he usually does -why does Uvaṭa not cite any example to prove that voiced unaspirated stops occur at the end of a *pada*?

The difficulty before Uvaṭa is this that the *Pada*-text does not analyse *hṛdbhiḥ* of the *Saṁhitā* as *hṛd- bhiḥ,* but as *hṛt-bhiḥ* and although the *pada-text gives hṛt-bhiḥ* the *Saṁhitā*-text consistently gives *hṛdbhiḥ.* So Uvata did not take the risk of committing himself to a view that unvoiced letter occurs before voiced one by citing the *Pada*-text. But, according to the Pdk neither at the end of internal *pada* nor at the end of external *pada* there exists any third consonant. If this is so, then why does Saunaka call *g,* ḍ, d and b as permitted finals and includes them in *RPr* 12. 1? This gives rise to the following question : does the author of the RPr refer to the internal *pada* of the *Saṁhitā*-text here ? But in that case the permitted finals before the *pada*-forming suffixes cannot be considered as occurring in *avasāna* The main difficulty is that the *RPr* does not define the term *avasāna.*

Other Prs give a bit better description of the fact. According to *VP*r. 1.85, the firsts of each consonantal series except *c* stand in the final position of a word.[73] The statement concerning the enumeration of the thirds does not occur in this *Pr*. The word standing in the final position in *VPr* refers to the final position of external *pada,* because in another rule[74], the cases of internal *pada*-finals are taken into account separately according to which ṛ and ṇ occur at the end of a word only before *avagraha.*

APr agrees with *VPr* on this point. According to this *Pr*[75] also, firsts and fifths stand at the end of words, except c-class.[76] But *APr* does not seem to have discriminated the internal and external *pada*-positions because in *APr* 1.4, it is prescribed that any vowel except ḷ can occur at the end of a *pada.*[77] But no specific mention of the two *pada*-levels is made. Whereas, VPr clearly states that ṛ and ṇ as *pada*-final can occur only before *avagraha.* But what is remarkable in the *Apr* is, it takes note of the opinion of śaunaka's school according to which only thirds of each series can occur at the end of a *pada,* and discards it on the ground of their not being authorised usage.[78] Thus, according to *APr* only unvoiced unaspirated stops can stand at the end of a *pada.* But the question is : does this *pada* include internal *pada* of the *pada*-text also? It is not clear from the statements of this *Pr*. But when it discards voiced consonants from being *pada-* final it implies that the author of this *Pr* is talking in terms of external *pada-* level.

TPr does not take this problem into account. But from its rule VIII.I, it appears that the final mute is an unaspirated surd.[79] But whether this 'final' includes internal *pada*-final also is not clear here. The *pada*-texts of the *AV* and the *VS* follow that of the *RV*. But the *pada*-text of the *TS* presents many a time improved analysis compared to the Pp of the *RV*. But so fat this case is concerned namely, the occurrance 'of first sounds before a *pada*-forming suffix, the Pp of the *TS* also offers the same analysis. Here also *śarátbhiḥ* (4.3. 13.5), *sáradbhyaḥ* (7.1.15.1) etc. are analysed as *śarátbhiḥ* and *sárat - bhyaḥ*

P also does not decide the point whether the first or the third sound occurs in the final position of pada in pause. He simply incorporates in his system both the views of his predecessors. Otherwise, when there is not a single instance of sonant coming in *pausa* why should he insert *vā* in *vāvasāne (P 8. 4. 56)*? According to P 8. 2. 39, sonants stand at the end of a *pada*. But again P 8.4.56 prescribes surd and sonant both at the end of a word in *pausa*. The only difference between these two *sutras* is the difference in conditioning i.e., in P 8.2.39 *ante (i.e., padānte)*[80] which allows the third even when *pada*-final is followed by another sound, but before pause (*avasāna*) both are allowed. In P 8.4.56 *avasāne* is used to determine the application of the rule. Now, what is the diference between *padānte* and *avasāne*? The term *padānte* stands for both the *padas* external and internal, whereas *avasāne* stands only for external *pada* followed by pause. So theoretically we get both *hṛt* and *hṛd* before pause in Pāṇinian system, even though we do not come across *hṛd* in *pausa* P's *vāvasāne* is applicable only in *Pausa* and never before any *pada*-forming suffix.

Coming to the non-Pāṇinian schools of Grammar one finds that almost the same views are carried over about the permitted finals. According to *Kātantra*[81] the first mutes come at the end of a word. It phrases the rule without mentioning the condition *avasāna*. As per *Cāndravyākaraṇa* 6.3.67, sonant mutes are replaced in place of any consonant except semi-vowels and nasals at the end of word (padante)[82] Again, in 6.4.149 (vā virāme) both voiced and unvoiced unaspirated consonants are allowed if *virāma* follows. Thus, practically there is no difference between the views held by P and *Cāndra*, *Cāndra* also does not commit himself to either of the two alternatives mentioned by the predecessors namely, voiced unaspirated or unvoiced unaspirated. The same is the case with *Jainendra*.[83] Later grammarians like *Bopadeva*[84] etc., also follow the same principle. *Sārasvata*[85] does not mention *avasāna*.

The same is the case with *visarjanīya* which comes internally in the *pada*-text. For instance *gīrbhıḥ* is analysed as *gīḥ-bhıḥ*. How can it be possible unless the Pdk considers that *r* of *gīrbhiḥ* and of *gīr* (1/1) occur in final position of a pada followed by a pause?

It is observed in the ancient phonetic texts that the grammarians start with ḥ. According to the *RPr*, *ḥ* assumes o, r, and /s/ś/ṣ indifferent environments.[86] There appears no different conditioning for the two levels of *pada*-sandhi so far ḥ is concerned. According to this *Pr*, *ḥ* can be of two types: *riphita/rephī (i.e.,* those which are changed to r before vowel or a sonanat occlusive) and *ariphita/ arephī* (i.e., those excluding riphitas). But in any case in euphonic combination it is ḥ which undergoes a change. The same is the case with other *Prs*. They too start any *sandhi*-alternation with *ḥ* and prescribe different changes or subsitutes for ḥ[87]

But there is marked difference between P and the *Prs* regarding *visarjanīya*. The so called repha- *sandhi* of the *RPr* (i.e., ḥ < r before a vowel (except a, *ā*) and (a voiced stop)[88] is not a *visarga-sandhi* accoding to P, rather it is a combination of final r with the following vowel or sonant. Pāṇian system never prescribes *r* for ḥ In other words, there is no such rule which prescribes replacement of r in place of ḥ in Pāṇinian system.

Similarly, in *aṅgirobhiḥ* that *o* is an immediate result of *aḥ* is the view of the *Prs*, but according to P the process is different. According to him the *s* of the stem *aṅgiras* first takes rU before -bhiḥ by the rule *sasajuṣo ruḥ* (8.2.66) and then *r* is changed to *u* by *haśi ca* (P 6.1.114) and afterwards by gunation, we get *aṅgirobhiḥ*. In Pāṇinian system *s* or *r* can be changed to ḥ if a hard consonant or pause follows. Under no circumstance *o* of *aṅgirobhiḥ* can be dissolved into ḥ if *saṁhitā* (i.e., continuous utterence) is maintained. He clearly discriminateds between the two levels of *sandhi* which were not kept apart by the author of the *Prs*.

Let us have the survey of non-paninian as well as leter grammarians's views. Katantra-school[89] follows the views of the *Prs*. Cāndra[90] and Janinendra[91] follow P. Later grammars like Mugdhabodha[92] and Sārasvata[93] follow the process as given in the *Prs*. According to them also *o* of *aṅgirobhiḥ* will be considered as immediate result of *aḥ* before *bhiḥ*. Some will prescribe that the whole *aḥ* will become *o* or *ḥ* will take *u* first and then by gunation it will be *o*.

The same principle is followed by MACDONELL[94], among modern scholars. He also prescribes *r, s,* or *zero* for *ḥ*

But in any case we must not forget that all these rules of either permitted finals or of *visarga* are meant for *Smhitā* i.e., for a sequence of continuous utternce only. Whereas, the Pp offers us a sequence with pauses inserted after each *pada*-final. So practically there is no *Saṁhitā* or continuity between two phonemes in the *pada*- text before and after either *daṇḍa* or *avagraha*. *Daṇḍa* and *avargraha* both indicate pauses.

Now, what is the function of pauses inserted in the *pada*-text? Before arriving at certain conclusion let us, first of all, raise some apparent doubts. If-*aḥ* is the original sound for *s, o,* or *r* then should we think that the Pdk gives the original stem and thus he presents a stem-suffix analysis? We cannot hold this view, because had it been so he should have analysed *rājasu* as *rājan-su* and not *rāja-su* as he does. Moreover, the forms *hṛdā́* (1.61.2)3/1, and *hṛdı* (1.32.14) 7/1 *śarádi* (2.12.11) 7/1, *nadàm* (1.32.8) 2/1, *padā́* (1.22.18)3/ and *padı* (4.12.6) 7/1 definitely indicate that the original stems are *hṛd-*, *śarad*, -nad-, and pad-. We do not find any form like *hṛtā*, *śarati*, *natam*, *or patā* which would have given us stems ending in *ṭ*. Thus, we cannot think of this possibility.

Again, when all the stems ending in unvoiced unaspirated stop become ending in corresponding voiced stop, does the Pdk take *d* of stems ending in *d* as a result of *t*? That is to say wherever *d* occurs before a voiced stop of a *pada*-forming suffix or of a second constituent of a compound, does he assume *d* coming from original *t* ? Thus, should we assume that just as in *bṛhádbhiḥ* (2.11.15), *d* is a resultant change of *t*, so also in *śarádi*? But before arriving at this wrong hypothesis, we must find out, it possible, some consistent and sufficiently explanatory formula to fit in the case under discussion. Moreover, there is no reason for the Pdk to get confused with stems ending in voiced consonant and unvoiced consonants. Because, if the stem ends in t that gives *-tā* in 3/1 like *mahatā*, but, if it ends in *d* it gives *-dā* as we actually get in *hṛdā́*.

Again, if in *hṛdbhyā́m*, *d* < *t* is allowed due to *pada-sandhi* only then *d* of *hṛdā* should also be taken as a phonetic change due to its being at the end of a *pada* and it should have also been analysed by the Pdk as *hṛt -ā*. But it is not done. Because, he knows that the stem here is *hṛd* - and not *hṛt*. So, there is little scope for this type of analogous anomally in this case.

Similarly, one may say that the Pdk simply dissolves the *sandhi* of the Sp and offers before us just immediately preceding steps. This statement may hold true in the case of *visarjanīya*. Because if we apply *Pr*-process of *visarga-sandhi, r, or o,* while dissolving them, it may give us ḥ as just immediately preceding steps. But still *hṛt-bhiḥ, śarat-bhiḥ* etc. will remain unexplained, because in these cases *t* cannot be justified as being the original stem-sound.

Then, what is the way out? I feel the *Saṁhitā*-text consists of sets of continuous utterences of different corpuses which were split up into *padas* in the *Pada*-text. Now, when the *Saṁhitā* is dissolved, pause which was at the end of a hemistich was extended to end after each free item. Then, again, it was extended to inside the word before a *pada*-marker suffix as well as before a component of a compound[94a] -in which case there remained no immediate contact between two phonemes immediately preceding and following the *avagraha* or the *daṇḍa.*[94b] The stops which come before the *avagraha* also assumed the status of *pada*-finals.[94c]

Thus, an environment for (stop + pause)-*sandhi*[26] was created by *avagraha* also. This *sandhi* is nothing but an avasāna-sandhi. What happened here is that the *avasāna-sandhi*-rules are extended to be operated in internal *pada*-finals also by just creating pause after those finals.

To explain in linguistic terminology, it is a phenomenon of assilimilation between a stop and an immediately following pause. The assimilation between a stop and an immediately following pause. The assimilation of voiced stop with pause always weakens the stop[96] i.e., the voiced stop first becomes devoiced and then there remains a chance of further weakening, so much so that in course of development of language it is either assimilated to silence i.e., dropped by the law of progressive assimilation or when in verge of dropping it takes some vocal support in order to protect the dropping. In both these cases, the theory of neutralization i.e., keeping of the articulation sound in nertral position for a paricular unit of time, is most operative.

This process of weakening of final stop by regressive and progressive assimilation with the following pause is well-established by a fact in MIA[97].

Kātyāyana[98] refers to two definitions of *avasāna: (1) virāma 'end of utterance'* and *(2) abhāva 'followed by an absence of letters'. śāk probably follows the second definition. Taking into account this notion* śāk *applied avasāna-sandhi* rules to even internal *pada*-finals. But if we follow the second defination we cannot apply *avasāna-sandhi* to the internal *pada*-before *pada*-forming suffixes, because *hṛd* in *hṛdbhiḥ* is not followed by absence of letters. According to the Pdk, the term *avasāna* or *virāma* is also applied in the case of theoretical or artificial pause, before *avagraha.* This practice of showing *virāma* in the case of internal *pada* is still followed by traditional Vedic recitors : *hṛt-bhiḥ*.

But this type of *avasāna-sandhi* has scope only in the Pp-*sandhi* and that too because it is recited. This kind of *sandhi* has no chance else where either in the *Saṁhitā* or in the spoken form of language. In both these cases we have continuous text without a pause between *pada* and *pada*-forming suffixes. The main task of the Pdk is to separate a stem from a *pada*-forming suffix or from another constituent of a compound. Since there is a separation, the pause is intorduced between a stem and a suffix. Since there is a pause, there is *avasāna.* And since there is *avasāna, avasāna-sandhi* is applied.

I.6 PĀṆINI AND ŚĀKALYA

Indian tradition knows śāk as the Pdk of the *RV.* That he was a great grammarian of his time has been recognized by P in his *Aṣṭā* P refers to śāk four times by name. At 1.1.16 P records vocative *o* as a *pragṛhya*-vowel which is indicated by *iti* in the Pp of śāk e.g., *viṣṇo ıti* (1.156.1). P 6.1.127 describes that 'according to the opinion of śāk, the simple vowels excepting ā, when followed by a non-homogenous vowel, retain their original forms; and if the vowel is long it is shortened optionally.' The *Kāśikāvṛtti* offers the example *cakrī atra cakri atra*. But I do not get any such example in the *RV*.

P 8.3.19 describes the 'v and y occuring at the end of *pada* preceded by *a* or *ā* are elided before voiced letters, according to the opinion of śāk'. For instance, *agna indra* (5.46.2) from *agnay indra* / *agne* / *indra* / ; *ubhā́v u (10.106.1) from ubhā́v u* / *bháu* / *ū̃ ıti*/

P 8.4.51 states the opinion of śāk that no where we have reduplication of phonemes. Therefore, we have *arkáiḥ* (1.33.2) etc.

Apart from these four *sūtras* which mention śāk by name, we find the following rules in *Aṣṭā* which are supported by the analysis in the Pp of the *RV*.

P 1.1.13 describes that e of the suffix *śe* is a *pagṛhya*. For instance, *asmé indra* (8.97.8)/ *asmé ıti*/; *yuṣmé itthā́ (6.18.5)/yuṣmé ıti*/;*tvé agne* (2.1.14)/ *tvé-ıti* /. In all these cases the pdk has marked *e* as *pragṛhya* by adding *iti* to these forms. p's this rule has its implication in the treatment of the Pp.

P 1.1.17-18 describe that 'the particle *u* is called *pragṛhya* and it is replaced by *ū̃*. The expression śākalyasyetāv anārṣe continutes from the previous rule 1.1.16. This rule, as a matter of fact, directly refers to the analysis that is found in the Pp of śāk, for instance,/ *ū̃ ıti*/1.24.8.

P. 1.1.19 also is supported by the Pp. It means : 'the final ī and ū of words denoting the sense of locative are called *pragṛhya*'. For instance, *the Saṁhitā*-text *sómo gaurī́ ádhisritáḥ* (9.12.3) is commented by the Pdk as / *gaurī́*/ *ıti* / .... *Similarly, svā́yāṁ tanū́ as* = / *tanū́* / *ıti* / *10.184.2.*

P. 6.1.126 means that 'for the adverb ā, the nasalised *ā̃* is substituted in the *Chandas* when a vowel follows and it retains its original form i.e., *sandhi* is allowed'. The word *saṁhitāyām* continues from P 6.1.72. Here *saṁhitāyām* refers to the continuous utterrence. The following examples can be cited from the RV:

ā̃ apáḥ (5.48.1) and *ā̃* úgraputre (8.67.11). śāk in his *Pada*-drops this nasalisation because in the Pp we do not have continous utterence. He puts it as simply / *ā*/.

P.6.1.128 is another instance to prove that P takes the Sp versus the Pp. It means that 'before ṛ the simple vowels retain their original form and if the vowels are long they are shortened. For instance, *tátha ṛtúḥ* (1.162.19). Here also *saṁhitāyām* (P6.1.72) means 'in the continuous text'. The Pdk analyses the above example as / táthā/ ṛtúḥ/.

P 6.1.129 directly refers to the Pp. It describes that 'a *pluta*-vowel (of the Sp) is treated as an *apluta*-vowel when followed by an *anārṣa iti i.e.,* the *iti* of the the Pp'. But we have only three cases of *pluta*- vowels in the RV and in all these cases the written *Pada*-text shows *plutatva* of the preceding vowels by putting the figure '3' after them[99] e.g., */āsī 3 t,/vindatī, 3/ etc. Aparently P6.1.129 does not refer to the Pada- text of the RV.*

P. 6.1.139,151 and 153 are doubtlessly applicable to the *Saṁhitā-text* of the RV. In the *RV,* we have *pariṣkṛṇván* (9.39.2), *súścandra* (5.6.5) and *háriścandraḥ* (9.66.26). The Pdk analyses them as */ pari kṛṇván, /, / sú-candra /, and / hári - candraḥ/* respectively. P included cases like *práskaṇva* (1.44.6) and *táskara* (6.28.3) etc., under P 6.1.153 and 157. But the Pdk has left both these examples unanalysed. This is the case of more inconsistency on the part of the Pdk.

Similarly, P 6.3.128,131,133,134,135, prescribe the lengthening of the final vowel of the first member in certain conditions and are applicable in the continous text. The examples are, *viśvā́ vasuḥ* (10,139.5), *somāvatīm* (10.97.7), *symbolśvāvataḥ* (1.122.8), *viśvā́devyāvatā* (10.170.4), *tū́* (4.32.1), *nū́* (1.10.9), *ghā́* (1.5.3), *makṣū́* (1.39.7), *bharatā* (10.176.2), *átrā* (1.62.4) *uruṣyā́* (8.71.7), *abhī́* (4.31.3), *vidmā* (1.10.10) and *evā́* (1.8.8). There are analysed in the *Pada*-text as /*viśvá- vasuḥ* /, *áśva*-vataḥ/, viśvádevya-vatā/, tú/, nú/ gha/, /makṣú/, bharata/, /átra/, /uṛuṣyá/, /abhı/, /vidma/ and *evá*.

P.6.3.128, 6.3.129, and 6.3.130 prescribe the lengthening of the final vowel of the first member in the following cases,

aṣṭāpadī, viśvānara, viśvāmitra, oṣadhībhiḥ dadhīcah etc. These were left unanalysed by the Pdk.

Apart from these direct or indirect references of the treatment of śāk, we find that P's concept of the term pada is based on that of śāk's *pada*-analysis. śak's isolation of finished words corresponds to the concept of *padatva* stated in P 1.4 .14 This is indicated by a *daṇḍa*. The *avagraha*-analysis corresponds to the concept of *padatva* mentioned in P 1. 4.15 - 17.[100]

Of course, a strict correspondence cannot be shown between śāk's *avagraha*-sign and the internal *pada*-status defined by P. To explain more fully, for the separation of constituents of a compound the Pdk used the same sign i.e., *avagraha*. But, according to P's system the *Pada-saṁjñā* for the constituent of a compound is applied by P 1.4.14 because according to Pāṇinian grammatical theory the constituents of compounds are case-inflected words whose case-endings have been dropped by P 2.4.71. In P's system internal pada as well as external *pada* are called by the name *pada*. But when the Pdk wants to show that *pada* unit is a constituent of a larger complex form he uses *avagraha* otherwise *daṇḍa*.

Some improvements are made by P with regard to the concept of *pada*. For instance, before the denominative suffix-ya only the stems ending in *n* are called *pada*, The purpose of the designation *pada* is to have *lopa* of *n* of stems ending in *n*. This dropping of *n* is restricted to the *pada*-final position. But elsewhere before the denominative suffix *ya*, juncture features are not seen. For instance, in *tapasyati* we do not see *padasandhi* which we see before *bhiḥ in tápobhiḥ* (7.1.7). But the Pdk has not noticed probably this fact and before the denominative suffix-ya he makes separation very often in connection with the stems other than *n*- ending. Similarly, before the case-ending beginning with y, the stem is called *bha* (i.e., non- *pada*) according to P. But the Pdk very often treats the stem as a pada-unit before case-ending beginning with *y*, even if no where *pada-sandhi* is applied. For instance, *sādhu-yā́* (1.46.11), *ā́śu-yā́* (4.4.2), etc.

There is another fact worth-noticing in P's grammar. According to the commentators the definitions of *pada* are applicable to the stems preceding a secondary suffix. Thus, in *prajā́vān, prajā is a pada* by P 1.4.14 as well as by P 1.4.17. But the pada sandhis are allowed by the name *pada* which is applicable by P 1.4.17. In other words, the designation *pada* by P 1.4.14 has been restricted before the certain secondary suffixes by P 1.4.17. The Pdk has separated - *vān* from *prajā* Therefore, it is clear that he considers *prajā* as a *pada*. But it is not clear whether the Pdk took *prajā* here as *subanta*. It appears that the Pāṇinian commentators gave a very sofisticated technique of analysis for the derivation of such secondary stems considering *prajā* - in *prajavān as subanta*. And this theory might not be known to the Pdk.

P also improved upon the Pdk's concept about the perfect participle suffix-*vāṁs*.The Pdk took this suffix to be a secondary suffix, whereas P takes it as a primary suffix.

The above discussions sufficiently demonstrate that P did have thorough knowledge of the Pp of the *RV* as against the view of B.K. GHOSH[101] It is not true P 'copies' many of -sutras from the *RPr as GHOSH has tried to establish.*[102]

There is no need to devide P's *uñaḥ ū̃* into two *sūtras* as *Kātyāyana*[103] has suggested and as Patañjali interprets. It is to be noted that the application of P 1.1.17-18 has no scope out side the Pp of the *RV*. Therefore, it is not proper to interpret P 1.1.17-18 having optional operation.[104] We do not get *viti* any where in the Sanskrit literature. Here *iti* means nothing else than the *iti* of the Pp.

One may raise a question here : Why should a descriptive grammarian like P who deals with the actual language include in his grammar a phenomenon which is peculiar to an artificial text like the *Pada*-text? The problem is understandable and could be answered by saying that we should not take P as a descriptive grammarian in the sense a modern linguist understands, P considered the *Pada-* text as a separate text of grammatical improtance and thus included it under his data for description. P's gratness lies not in selecting materials, but in building up a technique of description of lingustic facts.

I.7. INCONSISTENCIES IN THE Pp

Looking at the treatment of the Pdk as a whole we find that there are a few cases in the Pp which are not covered by his normal rulers of analysis. Cases of such deviation from the normal rules are found on both the levels of analysis, namely, (A) the level of the treatment of individual types to items as well as (B) the level of over-all guiding priciples of analysis of the Pp as a whole.

Cases of devitation on level (A) have been pointed out while describing the treatment of individual type of items in Part II of the thesis. The deviations can be sammarised as follows.

i) The case-suffix-*bhyaḥ* is a separable suffix and it is separated from the stem if the stem ends in a short vowel. But in *kavārıbhyaḥ* the suffix *-bhyaḥ* is not separated although the stem ends in short i. Similarly, the locative plural suffix- *su* is also a separable suffix if it is not cerebralized. But, in *dhūrṣú-su* is found separated even though it is cerebralized, (see II. i.i.)

ii) A secondary suffix that begins with a consonant is a *pada*-forming suffix and as such, it is separated in the Pp. The suffix-*tya* is separated in *āviṣṭyaḥ as āviḥ-ṣṭyaḥ:* but the forms *ápatyam, amā́tya, and niṣṭyaḥ* are left unanalysed, although they contain the same suffix, (see II. 1.2.b.3).

The suffix-*ma* is separated from *upa* in *upamáḥ* but not in *adhámáḥ, apamásya, avamáḥ, caramáḥ, paramáḥ, madhyamáḥ, aṣṭamám, navamám, and daśamé* (see II. 1.2.b.6).

Similarly, the suffix-*van* is separated from *vibhā́-in vibhāvā* but it is not separated in *somapā́vā, (see II.1.2.b.8).*

Likewise, in the forms *pūrváthā* and *viśváthā* the adverbial suffix- *thā* is separated. But it is not clear why it is not separated in *anyáthā, (see II. 1.3.b.2)*

Similarly, the adverbial- suffix-*dhā*- is separated *in caturdhā́ as catuḥ -dhā́, but not in dvidhā, tridhā, purudhā́, bahudhā́ and viśvádhā,* (see II.1.3.b.4).

iii) Since compound forms like *vanarṣádam* are analysed as *vana-sádam,* it is not clear why *vanargúḥ* is not analysed. The *ráthaspátiḥ jā́spátiḥ, and gnā́spátiḥ* are analysed as *ráthaḥpáthiḥ, jā́ḥpátiḥ,* and *gnā́ḥpátiḥ* respectively, but *Vánaspā́tiḥ* is kept as it is without changing s to ḥ, (see II. 2.1.).

Likewise, the prefix ā is separated by the *avagraha in ā́hataḥ, ādā́ya, and ā́yatiḥ,* but it is not separated in *āhanaḥ, ā́dāma and ā́yudham.*

Similarly, in *pravā́saḥ pra* is not separated although it is separated in *pravā́cyaḥ (see II.3.6).*

iv) *Śāk takes iva* alongwith the form after which it comes and considers the whole from to be a compound. The particle *iva* is separated by an *avagraha*. But in the form *gartārúgiva* the particle *iva* is not separated, (see II.2.2).

v) The Pdk always indicates a *pragṛhya* vowel by *iti*. But *Índrāganī* (7.94.8) is not indicated as *Indragnī iti,* although in the same *sūkta* in rest of *ṛks* it is marked so.

Also a ḥ of the Sp resulting from r of a root is marked by *iti* and the form is repeated in order to distinguish such ḥ from a ḥ resulting from r of a nominal stem. For instance, *akanty akaḥ and prātánti*. This is true in almost all cases. But it is not clear why *iti* is added to *vaneḥ, vark, and te (3.33.10))*. They appear in the Pp as *vananti vaneḥ, vargiti vark* and *ta iti te*[105]. Similarly, we do not know why *iti* is added to *syuḥ* (Opt. 3/3) and it is analysed as *syunti syuḥ* in the Pp. The same is the case with praṇapāt which is shown as *pránapāditi prá- napat*.

One cannot argue that since these forms come at the end of a *pāda,* the Pdk puts *iti* after them, and repeats them after *iti*. This is not true because the form *pranapāt* occurs in the middle of the *pāda*. Moreover, the form *vark* occurs at the end of the *pāda* in Rv 6. 26.3, but *iti* is not added there.

Similarly, *te* occurs at the end of a *pāda in RV* 1.30.5, but no *iti* is added in the Pp. We cannot argue either that when such words come at the end of the fourth *pada* or at the end of a *ṛk,* the Pdk marks them with *iti* because *vaneḥ* occurs at the end of the second *pāda* and still the Pdk says *vananti vaneḥ*. We cannot say either that these words are found in the last *mantra of a sūkta* and therefore the Pdk indicates the end of a chapter. This is not the case because there are eight *ṛks in RV.* 2.6, but *vaneḥ occurs* in the very first *mantra of the sūkta*. This holds true for the other forms also. Therefore, we are unable to formulate a principle behind these instances, (see II.4).

vi) The form *páriṣk-ṛtaḥ* is analysed as *pári-kṛtaḥ* but *sáṁskṛtaḥ* (8.33.9) is left unanalysed. One expected deletion of s in this case also (see II. 2.1)

vii) The forms *Jamádagninā and Dīrghátamāh, Bharádvājaḥ* are analysed as *Jamát-agninā, Dīrghá-tamāḥ and Bharát-vājaḥ* respectively, although they are proper names, but Gótamaḥ is left unanalysed, (see II.2.1)

Cases of deviation on the level (B) are the following :

a) Lengthening of a syllable which is not due to *pada- sandhi* should be left as it is. This is the general rule followed by the Pdk. Thus, *-bhyām* is not separated in *hástābhyām as hasta-bhyām*, because the change of a to ā in hastā- is not caused by any *sandhi*. According to P also here the change a to ā in hastā is not a *pada*- change, but an *aṅga*-change. The Pp is not supposed to show *aṅga*-changes (P 7.3. 102). But, forms like *ṛtāyate, ṛtā́vā, putrī yàntaḥ and the like are analysed as ṛtá-yate, ṛtà- vā, putri-yàntaḥ* respectively, even though lengthening of a to ā and i to ī is not caused by any *pada-sandhi* rule.

(b) As pointed out earlier, the Pdk while analysing a compound form follows the principle of ICA. That is to say on the level of compound-word-analysis, he first sees whether it is an *iva*-compound. If it is so, he separates *iva* by means of an *avagraha*. For instance, *prajā́natī-iva*. If it not an *iva*-compound, he sees whether there is a pada-forming case-suffix. If finds one, he separates that, for instance, *śatábhuji-bhiḥ*. But if he does not find any, he sees whether there is any pada-forming secondary suffix. If he finds a *pada*-forming secondary suffix, he separates it, for example, *prajā́- vān*. if it is not there, then his next step is to divide the constituent of compound, *e.g., pra-jā*.

Now, let us take the case of *ratnadhā́tamam*. It is not an *iva-compound,* therefore one has to see whether the case-suffix is separable. Here-*am* is the case-suffix which is not a *pada* forming suffix. Naturally the next step is to separate the secondary suffix-*tama*. But the Pdk has analysed the form as *ratna- dhámam,* which goes against his normal rule of ICA. Moreover, when the Pdk analyses *vibhávā, vibhávam* and *vibhávarī* as *vibhá - vā, vibhá- vam* and *vibhá - varī* respectively, one fails to understand why *ratnadhátamam, somapátamaḥ somapávā* and *yatumávān* should not be analysed' as *ratnādhá - tamam, somapá-tamaḥ, somapá-vā and yatumá - vān* respectively.

c) *Taking for granted that his concept of pada and non- pada* prompted śāk to divide *vṛṣaṇvān,* and *prapathıntamam* as *vṛṣṇa-vān* and *prapathın-tamam* we do not see any reason why the denominative suffix-*ya in brahmaṇyántaḥ and vṛṣaṇyati* is not separated. Or, if we argue that since the *n* is retained in the forms *brahmaṇyántaḥ* and vṛṣaṇyati,-ya cannot be taken as the pada-forming suffix and therefore the Pdk avoids separation, then the division of *vṛṣaṇvān* etc. will go against this hypothesis. Because in these forms also *n* is retained.

d) Single accent is the main formal judging whether the form in question is a compound or not. This principle is consistently followed by the Pdk. But in a few vocatives he keeps the constituents separate by means of *daṇḍa* and not by means of *avagraha*. This means that he does not take these sequences to be compounds. For example, *divo duhitar, divo naraḥ, brahmaṇaskave, brahmanaspate, and śubhaspatī* are analysed as / *divaḥ / duhitaḥ/, divaḥ/ naraḥ/ brahamaṇaḥ/ kave/./ brahmaṇaḥ/ pate/* and/ *śubhaḥ/ patī iti/* respectively. In all these cases, the entire sequence i.e.. *divo duhitar* etc is unaccented. This implies that these cases should be treated as compounds. Otherwise, the non-appearance of the accent in the genetive forms *divaḥ brahmaṇaḥ, and subhaḥ* cannot be explained. Moreover, the Pdk treats *bṛhaspátiḥ* as one word although its first component is inflected (6/1 of *bṛh*) and it show two accents. However, if this word used in vocative, it should lose both the accents and we have actually *bṛhaspate* without any accent in the *RV*. Similarly, the Pdk should have treated *divo duhitar, etc.* as compound forms.[106]

Out of these inconsistencies, some of them are purposeful, but most them seem not explainable. Thus, in the case of *kavārıbhyaḥ and gartarúgiva* the normal rules are violated in order to explain the *sandhi between Kava plus ari, and garta plus āruk* so that one should not be in doubt about the division of the constituents. Devitation from the normal rule is found elsewhere also whenever the Pdk wants to explain certain *sandhi,* (see II.3.I).

But in the rest of the cases we do not see any reason for deviating from the general rule on the part of the Pdk.

I.8. THE PADA-TEXT AND THE RGVEDIC EXEGESIS

It is evident that no text can be grammatically analysed unless the structure of the text under analysis is properly undertood. No one denies that the grammatical analysis certainly presupposes the knowledge of the structure of the language in which the text is composed. This knowledge of the structure of the the language, again, presupposes semantic knowledge about the language. Now since the Pdk does not offer random analysis of the *ṛks* which would involve isolation of meaningless items, it will not be wrong to suppose that the Pdk must have understood the *Saṁhitā-* text semantically in a general way before he began to isolate it.

Pdk's isolation mainly attempts to analyse various types of junctures which involve *sandhi-* alternations. Broadly speaking, the technical term *pada* can be equated with juncture.

We can think of a hierarchy of analysis in the Pp. The first step must have been the word analysis and then the analysis of word-constituents. These two levels have been maintained by using two different symbols, namely, *daṇḍa and avagraha.* Both these symbols are in complementary distribution. That is to say, *daṇḍa* always comes after a finished word[107] and never within a word[108]

Similarly, an *avagraha* never comes after a finished form or phrase, rather it always occurs within a finished form. All this gives us an idea of hierarchy in a constituent analysis: Sentences are analysed in their constituents i.e., words and the words are further analysed in their constituents with certain criteria put for this purpose. Not necessarily all the constituents are separated. While offering the analysis of a word which may consist of more than two morphemes only one is separated from the rest. This method of analysing words further creates curiosity. It can be seen from the analysis that except for one set of items[109] an *avagraha* always separates the immediate constituent of a word if the portion preceding the *avagraha is a pada*. This correspond clearly to the principle what is called ICA in linguistics. This ICA is applied only to the analysis of words with certain restrictions discussed earlier. No effort seems to have been made towards applying this ICA to sentence- analysis and showing the hierarchy of the constituents of a sentence. In fact, this was not possible, because the text is in verses where no method can be consistently made operative. In other words, one cannot draw line to divide subject and predicate without changing the order of words in a verse. Since the purpose of the Pdk was not to offer ICA of a sentence, no attempt is made to achieve this goal. His purpose seems to have been not to disturb the order of words in the Sp, because the main aim of the Pp is to preserve the *Saṁhitā-text* as it is.

Coming to the main point we can say without hesitation that the structural understanding of the Ṛgvedic verses has been made very easy by the Pdk. Nowhere in the *Pada-text,* the structure of composition of verses remains unexplained. We can draw this conclusion on the basis of the following reasons:

i) Wherever there is a *pada-sandhi* in the Sp, it has been dissolved and we get all constituents of sentences separated. This dissolution of *sandhi* certainly helps in grasping the word isolates of Vedic verses.

ii) Secondly, while dissolving the *pada-sandhi* stem- suffix analysis is attempted in case of certain case- suffixes and a few secondary suffixes which we have already discussed earlier. This helps in understanding the text.

iii) Thirdly, the Pdk divides a compound into its components which again supplies further help to a reader, as it gives the idea about meaningful units of a compound. Sometimes the Pdk does not split the combined word and makes thereby indirect comment on semantic unity and one accent of a compound word. For instance, *mo, no, atho,* etc. which are combinations of mā+u, na+ u, and atha+u. They are followed by *iti* to show that *Sandhi* is not allowed with a following vowel. It should be noted that these forms are not treated as compound forms. Had they been so, the Pdk should have put *avagraha* between their components. But he does not do so. This should be taken to mean that since all these forms noted above give only one meaning and not a compound meaning, he treats them as mono-morphemic words.

iv) Fourthly, the Pdk restores the original forms by removing the metrical lengthening and shortening of the Sp. For instance, *srudhī hávam of the Sp is analysed as srudhi/hávam/ and mitra vayám as/ mitrā/vayám/*. This is a direct help.

v) Fifthly, the Pdk uses the device of affixing *iti* after certain forms. This *iti* indicates the *pragṛhya-* vowels with which there can be no *sandhi. Iti* is also used to indicate that r not coming from s does not allow o-sandhi. Thus, one can easily understand that *pṛthivī́* without *iti* in the Pp is in nominative sg. and with *iti* it is nom/. acc. dual. We can also make distinction between *āvaḥ* derived from *āvas* (root av) and *avar* derived from the root *Vṛ*

vi) Finally, it should be noted with great interest that what a minute semantic and accentual knowledge was necessary on the part of the Pdk to differentiate between the forms in the following minimal pairs and to treat them differently:

SP	Pp
a)*avasáya*	/ *avasáya* / *10.169.1*
avasáya	/ava-sáya/ 1.104.1
b) ávasthāḥ	/ávasthāḥ/ 3.32.11
avastháḥ	/*ava-stháḥ*/ *5.19.1*
c) *nidānáḥ*	/*nidānáḥ*/ *4.5.12*
nidánam	/ *ni -dánam* /*6.32.2*

In 10. 169.1 *avasáya* is derived from *avasa-* (root av), whereas in 1. 104. 1 it is derived from *ava+root sā to let go;. In 3.32.11 ávasthāh* is a verbal form (aor. 2/1) from root vas 'to cover', but in 5.19.1 it is from *ava+root sthā*. Similarly, *nidānāḥ* is from root *nind* 'to condemn, whereas *ni-dānam* is evidently *ni* plus *dāna* 'rope for tying up cows.'

All the above mentioned facts confirm that the Pdk must have been well-acquainted with the structure of the Vedic language and his text helps a lot in order to understand the structure of the Ṛgvedic language. But it should be borne in mind that this help of the Pdk is limitted to the understanding of the structure of the language only and beyond that it does not help directly in offering semantic interpretation of the Vedic verses. The Pdk's text does not give semantic paraphrase of the *Saṁhitā* text, rather it gives word-isolates of the continuous text which is a purely formal analysis. How it gives indirect semantic analysis can be shown by the example, *ádabdhavratapramatiḥ*. The Pp shows the immediate constituents of the compound as *adabdhavrata-pramatiḥ*. The Pp should be looked upon as a grammatical commentary rather than an interpretative commentary like sāyaṇa's.

The *Pada*-text does not tell us the lexical meaning of a particular word.

I.9 STAGES IN THE COMPOSITION OF THE Pp

Taking into consideration the various devices used by the Pdk one may feel inclined to recostruct a few stages in the development of the *Pada*-text which might have undergone at the hands of redactors of the text. Though it is not possible to prove with great certainty that the present *pada*-text has several layers composed by different persons, it is not, however, difficult to show that the present pada-text has incorporated in its body the new devices discovered in the filed of grammatical science in course of time.

The name itself suggests that the Pp has been handed down orally first and while isolating the words, the *sandhi* due to the saṁhitā has been dissolved in the Pp. This is the primary aim of the Pp. This holds good for single words as well as compound words. This isolation was indicated by shorter or longer pauses interposed between two words. This can be considered to be the starting point in determining the main aim of the Pp.

The Principle adopted for isolation of words is that the unit technically called *pada* is isolable. The concept of *pada* is more or less same as that found in the *Prs i.e. arthaḥ padam.*

This indicating of the junction-features applied to the words in the continuous text can be taken as the starting point and thus the first stage in the composition of the Pp.

II

Once the *sandhi* of the continuous text is dissolved and the words were separated by pauses, the Pdk must have proceeeded further to analyse each and every word which can be changed due to the *pada-sandhi*.The principle adopted for such analysis is the dissolution of juncture- *sandhi* occurring in one and the same finished word. In fact, the juncture-*sandhi* applicable to nounstems before inflexional or derivational suffixes are largely identical with *sandhi* alternation which result from the juxtaposition of words or that of compound- constituents. Therefore, the term *pada* which means junction-feature is extended to the internal word. I am of this opinion that the later grammarians like P and others borrowed and introduced in their treatises this very concept of the Pdk's internal *pada*. The main aim of the Pdk in isolating the words internally as well as externally is to show junction-features between the units concerned. This stage of dissolving the internal *sandhi* is further analysis below word-isolate level can be taken as the second stage in preparing the *Pada-text*.

Although the main idea behind isolation was to indicate junction-feature, the Pdk made it a point to isolate unit before *bhiḥ-bhyām, -bhyaḥ, and -su* even when they do not cause any *sandhi* alternation in the stem. For instance, *ṛ́ṣibhiḥ* is analysed as ṛ́ṣi- bhiḥ. This is the analogical extension of isolation. It indicates that the Pdk calls *ṛṣi-in- ṛṣibhiḥ a pada* even though there is no possibility of *pada-sandhi*. This artificial analysis was probably later introduced.

III

Dissolving the *sandhi* provides the starting point for the next step i.e., the attainment of the right method which shows that the certain vowels in certain situation do not coalesce with the following vowels. This device is known by the term *itikaraṇa* This device of adding *iti* appears to be grammatical comment., One may consider this as the third stage in the information of the Pp. This stage shows all the *pragṛhya*-vowels.[110]

IV

The general principles involved in an external *sandhi* are found in the *sandhi* of compounds. Therefore, the Pdk extended his principles of analysis in compounds also. But this scientific procedure finally becomes generalised. First aim of separation was to indicate juncture. Finally it resulted into constituent analysis. Ultimately this separation was meant to indicate the maximally independent unit of words, for which we have the term ICA. For example, in the case of *dáśapramatim* (1.141.2), there are three units *daśa, pra, and mati,* If only one cut is to be shown, should we adopt the analysis *dáśa-pramatim, or dáśapra-matim*? The Pdk adopted the first and not the second because the second analysis does not show the semantic linkage between the constituents of compound.

V

Apart from simply indicating junction feature the Pdk appears to be intended in indicating the basic form. It appears that the Pp is not simply concerned to establish a word - unit liable to *sandhi* alternation, but seems to be concerned to explain in which way a word units is liable to *sandhi*-alternation. The final ḥ comes, as we have seen above, from two different sources *s* and *r*. The terminal forms with ḥ provide different sandhis. In order to indicate the sources of final ḥ, the Pdk make a distinction between ḥ coming from r and ḥ coming from s if it is not indicated in the Sp. To indicate this difference the Pdk adds *iti* to ḥ coming from r. This stage of *iti-karaṇa* can be considered as the further development in the composition of the Pp.

VI

Further the Pdk wanted to distinguish ḥ derived from r of a verbal form from ḥ derived from r of a normal form. To do this, he simply employed the device of repeating the form after *iti*. Therefore, akaḥ of the Sp is analysed as *akarıty akaḥ*. This method of explaining the form can be schematized as follows :

X as found in Y comes from Z

(akaḥ) (Sp) *(akar)*

Now, one can raise a question regarding the method adopted by the Pdk. Usually, the word *iti* is exployed to quote the form as found in the Sp first. The subsequent portion should indicate the grammatical comments about the *sandhi*. In other words, the quotation should remain on the left-hand side of *iti* and his comment should appear on the right hand side of *iti*. That is to say , we except the *Pada*-text as *akaḥ iti akar*. However, the text is *akanty akaḥ* This gives us a solid clue to the fact that the method of repeating the Sp form after *iti* is a later development. As has been indicated above that the Pdk must have marked first all the ḥ derived from r without any discrimination whatsoever. Thus in the early stage both *prataḥ* and *akaḥ* of the Sp probably have been analysed as *pratariti* and *akariti*. It is in the next stage that the discrimination between a verbal form and a nominal form was introduced. This was done simply repeating the Sp form after *iti*. That is why we get *akar* on the left hand side and *akaḥ* on the right hand side of *iti*. Here *iti* means *it gives or originates from the preceding*.

There are however, a few cases where *iti* is added and repeatition is done for which no specific reason is known, (see II.4).

VII

The Pp provides a frame-work on which the phonological theory, and to certain extent the grammatical analysis, is based. We find gradual development in concepts and methods which is achieved by assigning different function to the employment of the various devices. The original aim of adding *iti* was to indicate *pragṛhya* vowels. Then changes in the scientific attitude compelled the Pdk to give the constituent analysis. This innovation led to further elaboration and demanded a radical recasting of the method of description. The result is the Pdk has to indicate both absence of junction-feature *(pragṛhya)* and the constituent analysis. Thus, *vasumatī (3.30.11) is analysed as vásumatī ıti vásu -matī. Similarly praṇetaḥ became pranetanti pra-netaḥ*

The theory and mode of description must be used with scientific accuracy and consistency.The use of *iti* should indicate the preceding vowel is *pragṛhya*. But in the analysis *áśveivéty áśve- iva* consistency is violated. The proper analysis should be *asve iti iva asve-iva*. But the use of *iti* after *áśve* would give the idea that the morpheme *áśve* is an independent unit. To avoid this, the Pdk assigns somewhat new function to the use of *iti*. In the case of *nitya* compounds, *iti* may not necessarily follow the *pragṛhya-* vowel.

VIII

The Pdk in the last stage of development is not merely content with showing junction-features or *pragṛhya-* vowels or constituent- analysis. He enters upon restoring the original words. Every branch of sciences finds out the new things and in turn wants to teach others. To handle this new situation , the Pdk again uses the word *iti*. To describe this new data the Pdk does not find any additional spoken sign but sticks economically to the use of the word *iti*. For instance, the word *sī* and *ī* in the Sp has been commented as *sīm iti* and īm iti in the Pp.

The each stage in the Pp provides a starting point to the next stage. The next states of the Pp wanted to handle the situation exhaustively, but within the frame-work of the Pp. The frame-work of the Pp is to indicate various things by pauses or by use of the word *iti*. In successive development the same practice is followed by assigning new functions to the word *iti*. In the last stage the semantically bound units which were intervened in the Sp were brought together, for example. *súnaścicchépam is analysed as súnaḥśépam/ cit/.*

Similarly, *dukṣan* is analysed as *dhukṣan,*[111] *dūḷá*bha as *duḥ-dábha dūṇāṣa,* as *duḥ-náśa, varuṇa* as *varuṇā, mıtra* as *mıtrā* etc. But for none of these comments *iti* is used. This certainly indicates that these comments are later comments. But in any case these comments are before the period of the ṚPr since it has taken note of these peculiar treatments.

REFERENCES

1. See A.A. MACDONELL, *A History of Sanskrit Literature,* Indian Reprint 1962, p. 41: ".......precautions soon began to be taken to guard the canonical text ......The first step taken in this direction was the constitution of the *pada* or 'word' text.
2. See SATAVALEKAR, S.D. Edn. of the *RV* p.794.

2a. See section I.1.3 here

3. See the section I.1.3. of this Introduction.
4. See ROTH, *KZ,* vol.26, pp. 46-64; P.D.NAWATHE, PAIOC, 1969, pp. 247-50; K.V. ABHYANKAR, ABORI, 1972, pp. 211-14; K.L.SHARMA, *Charudeva Shastri Felicitation Volume Delhi, 1974, pp. 133-48.*
5. *NAVATHE (1969)* thinks that the analysis of the word *gartārugiva as garta-ārugiva* is an 'error' on the part of the Pdk for which to "plausible reason can be given". That normal analysis of the word should have been *gartāruk-iva* is true. But this rule is violated in order to help the recitor avoid confusion regarding the actual stem. This type of help is provided by the Pdk elsewhere also. See, the section II.2.2 of this thesis. Likewise, some of these so-called dis cripancies can be explained if we have before us the entire treatment of the Pdk. Some others offer simply overall observation and make some passing remarks. See WEBER. *The History of Indian Literature,* 1882.p.23 fn. 14; Winternitz. *A History of Indian Literature,* vol. 1. 1927, p. 283, MACDONELL, *Ibid,* p. 41.
6. "Prolegomena to the *Vedapadapāṭha" ABORI, Vol. 54, 1973, pp. 9-44.*
7. *AiĀr 3.2.6: Atha yad vayam anusamhitam ṛcó dhīmahe yacca Māṇḍukeyyam adhyāyaṁ prabhrūms tena no ṇakāraṣkārā upāptāv iti ha smāha sthaviraḥ śākalyaḥ*
8. *Te yad vayam anusaṁhitam ṛco' dhimahe yacca māṇḍukeyīyam adhyāyaṁ prabrūmas tena no ṇakāraṣakārā upāptāv iti ha smāha hrasvo Māṇḍukeyaḥ "Hrasva Māṇḍukeya* says "If we repeat the

verses according to the *Samhitā*, and if we say the teaching of Māṇḍukeya, then the letters ṇ and ṣ are obtained for us".

9. *Sa yo haitau ṇakārasakārav anusaṁhitam ṛco veda sabalāni saprāṇāni saṁhitaṁ veda (AiĀr 3.2.6).*

10. *Śāṁkh Ār. 7.16 : Jāyā pūrvarūpaṁ patir uttararūpaṁ putraḥ saṁhitā retaḥ sandhiḥ prajanaṁ sandhānam iti Sthaviraḥ śākalyaḥ: 8.1:prāṇo vaṁsa iti ha smāha Sthaviraḥ śākalyaḥ.....trayam tv eva na etat proktam iti ha smāha Hraso Māṇḍukeyaḥ*

11. 11.6.3.3; 14.6.9.1; 14.6.9.20; 14.6.10.17

12. *Ikārayośca praśleṣe kṣaiprābhinihiteṣu ca/udāttapūrvarūpeṣu śākalyasyaivam ācaret//* One should, according to *śākalya,* proceed in the same way (I.should regard the result of combination as circumflex) in the contraction of two short vowels and so-called "hastened' and 'absorbed" combinations if the first element (in the different combinations) is acute."

13. *Pracaya-svara ācāraḥ śākalyānyatareyayoḥ* (This practice with regard to the 'accumulated accent' is according to śāk.'

14. It becomes so according to the father of śāk,. cf. *ṚPr* IV.5.

15. *Chakāramtayor udayaḥśakāro, na śākalyasya'* S following those two (i,e *n* and *c*) becomes *ch;* but not so according to śāk.'

16. *Samāpādyaṁ nāma vadanti ṣatvaṁ tathā ṇatvaṁ sāmavasāṁśca sandhin/ upācāraṁ lakṣaṇataśca siddham ācāryā Vyāli-Śākalya-Gārgyāḥ//* The teachers *Vyāli śakalya* and *Gārgya* give the name *samāpādya* (i.e. requiring restoration in the *Pada* text) to (the changes into) ṣ ṇ, the so-called *sāmavasa* combinations and sibilation of *visarjaniya* supported by a rule.

17. *Prācya-pāñcāla upadhinibhodayāḥ śākalyasya Sthavirasya* 'According to the Old śākalaya (the hiatuses) in the Prācya and pāñcāla (*padavṛttis)* have their following vowels resembling their preceding ones.'

18. See fn. 9. above.

19. *Nir VI. 28* śāk is mentioned here and he is qualified by the adjective *padakāra*

20. P. i. I. 16 mentions śāk's name but does not qualify it with the word *padakāra.* But undoubtedly śāk mentioned here

refers to the Pdk of the *RV*

21. *Prolegomena* p. 380. fn 2: "An die Identitat dieses śākalya oder seines Sohnes mit dem Vidagdha śākalya des śatapatha scheint nicht zu denken."
22. I.2.33-34; *Devamitraśca śākalyo jñanāhaṁkāragarvitaḥ/ janakasya sa yajne vai vināsam agamed dvijāḥ.*
23. 60. 59-63: *Atha sannoditam prasnāni Yājñavalkyena dhimatā/ śākalyas tam avijñāya sadyo mṛtyum avāpnuyāt//*
24. Vedische Studien III, pp. 144-46.
25. "The Problem of the Gaḷantas in the Ṛgvedapadāpāṭha" *PAIOC, 13th session , 1946, Nagpur, p. 45 (Vedic Section).*
26. 14.2. 2.31.
27. See the section I.1.3. above
28. *Ibid*
29. *Aitareya Āraṇyaka,* pp. 239-40, fn.1
30. See the section I.1.3 above.
31. *Ibid.*
32. *ṚPr I.3.4: sandher vivartanaṁ nirbhujaṁ vadanti/ sauddhākṣaroccāraṇañca patṛṇam // ubhayamantareṇobhayam vyāpatam/*
33. See the section I.1.3 above
34. *Ibid*
35. *Aitareya Āraṇyaka,* Introduction , pp. 15-26.
36. It is to be noted that P does not say that *iva* forms a compound. It is only Kātyāyana who prescribes that *iva* forms a compound. (See *Varttika* III on P 2.1.4). A reason in regarding an expression consisting of a word standing for the *upamāna.* followed by *iva* as a compound is that the cps like *piteva* has one accent and they have fixed word-order i.e., the word standing for the *upamāna* is followed by the word *iva* invariably.
37. For the concept of *Juncture, see* TRAGER and SMITH. *An Outline of English Structure, 1951, para 1.62; and HOCKETT, A Course in Modern Linguistics,* 1958, pp. 54-61.
38. See TARGER AND SMITH, *Ibid.* p.38
39. See the section I.1.0 above
40. In this thesis the symbols *daṇḍa* and *avagraha* are

respresented by the oblique-sign (/) and the dash-sigh (-) respectively for the convenience of typing.

41. See the section II. 1.5 in Part II of this thesis.
42. See the section II. 1.5 in Part II of this thesis.
43. See P. 1.1.16: 6.1.127;8.3.19;4.51
44. For further restrictions, see the chapter II.1.1.
45. But this rule is violated in those cases where the preceding stems are roots in a long vowel. In that case the next IC is separated, e.g., *ratna-dhā́tamam* (1.1.1): *bhūri-dā́vnaḥ* (2.27.17), etc.
46. *Irregular sandhi : dhánarcam/ dhána - arcam/* 10.46. śatárcasam/ śatà -arcasam/ 7.100.3, *dhànvarṇasaḥ/ dhànva -arṇasaḥ/* 5.45.2.
47. When *e,o, ai, au,* occur in non-terminal position the question of restoration of their original form does not arise.
48. P says *e,o, ai, au* are converted into *ay,av,āy, and āv* respectively before a vowel. Then he states that *y* and *v* are omitted according to śākalya when they occur in terminal position.
49. Śākalya knows : *e == ay == a, ai == āy == ā. Y* is regularly omitted. But in the case of *v*, practice varies. Sometimes, *o == av.V* is retained.
50. The intervocalic ḍ is replaced by*ḷ*. For instance, *saṭ - ūrvīḥ* The intervocalic *ḍh* is changed into *ḷh*-Cf. *RPr* I.52.

50A. This *sandhi* is allowed in the same *pāda*. Therefore, in *yajatrānā* this rule is not applicable because *ā* belongs to the next *pāda*

51. This alternation is optinally prescribed by P. śāk also accepts this (RPr 4. 13), śāk's father does not admit this *sandhi (RPr* 4.14).
52. The VSM-edition reads the Sp as *svatavā̄* ꣳ *pāyuḥ*
53. *m (of īm)* + Consonant === Consonant. e.g., *sámīgā́vah/ sám/ īm iti/ gā́yaḥ* 9.72.6. It should be noted that the Pdk has indicated the peculiar *sandhi* by adding *iti* to it, *RPr* 4.83 takes care of this case.
54. In fact, according to the *RPr* 4.8, the *sandhi* of n + l should be *l l;* but VSM-edn. shows *ṁ I. Similarly, the sandhi* of the sequence *(m+y/v/l)* according to the ṚPr, should be y~y, v~v, l~l,

respectively. But the printed edition (VSM) does not show this *sandhi,* and in all cases *m* is converted into *ṁ* e.g., *yáṁ yaṁ yújam/ yám / yam / yújam /* 2.25.1; *táṁ vaḥ/tám/vaḥ/* 6.48.14; *bhadráiṣāṁ lakṣmī́ḥ/ bhadrā́/eṣām/ lakṣmī́ḥ/* 10.71.2; *The ṚPr.* 4.7 states *antasthāsu rephavarjaṁ parāsu tāṁ tāṅ padādiṣvanunasikāṁ tu//.*

55. The *jihvāmūliya-* modification is not found in the printed edn. of the *RV*. Cf. *viṣṇoḥ karmāṇi* (1.12.19).
56. This Pecular phenomenon is noted by P 6.1.134.
57. The Pdk's process of derivation is c --- k --- g, and not *c* --- *j* --- *g,*
58. *d* is changed to *t* because it is followed by a pause inserted by the Pdk.
59. P also treats all these *sandhis* as *pada- sandhis.* This internal *padatva* is defined by P by his rule: *svādiṣv asarvanāmasthāne'* When the affixes beginning with *su* (P4.1.2) and ending in *kap* (P 5.4.151), follow not being sarvanāmasthāna (p1.1.43), then that which precedes is called *pada'* VASU's *tr.*
60. *dhūrṣú* (1.100.16) is the only exception which is analysed as *dhūḥ-sú.*
61. *Internal sandhi* section I.4.2.
62. Many a time this cerebralization causes cerebralisation of the immediately following *t* into *ṭ*. The Pdk restores these cases also consistently. For example, *kū́ṣṭho/ kū́-sthaḥ/* 5.74.1 etc.
63. *RV* 1.180. 5
64. *RV* 4.18.2
65. *RV* 10.19.2
66. It should be noted that in both these examples *vanarṣádaḥ* and *vanarṣádam,,* the Pdk drops *r* which is quite unique treatment because normally he keeps *r* of *r-* stems i.e., either he does not analyse forms ending *r* or changes *r* to *ḥ*. For instance, *vanargúḥ* (1.145.5) is not analysed and *pū́rpátim* is analysed as *Pū́ḥ-pátim* (1. 173.10). He, perhaps, does not know the stem *vanar*
67. But, *tve* when unaccented or when part of a word, is not called *pragṛhya.*

68. In the *RV* the word *amī* does not occur before a word which begins with a vowel. But the Pdk always adds *iti* to it wherever it occurs. Similarly, vocative *o* allows *sandhi* within a *pāda* when it is followed by a vowel, e.g., *viṣṇavévayāvah*/ *viṣṇo iti*/ *éva* - *yāvaḥ*/.1.90.5.

69. Excepting one case i.e., *indrāgnī* (7.94.8). Here, although the form end in dual *ī*, *iti* is not added in the Pp. It is put as simply/indrāgnī/.

70. It is to be noted that, here, no *avagraha*-sign has been used. Similarly, *ráthaspáti,-jāspáti-, and ṛtaspáti-* are also analysed as *ráthapáti,- jāḥpáti-*, and *ṛtaḥpati-* without *avagraha*. There are certain other compounds with *pati,-* as the second member, which are neither analysed by *avagraha* nor sibilant coming in between the constituents is turned into ḥ as in the above cases. They are *bṛhaspáti-* and *vánaspáti-*,

70a. The Pp of the TS does not analyse *gīrbhiḥ* (1.4.15.1). This is an improvement over the Pp of the *RV*.

70b. *Tasmād anyamavasāne tritiyam*/, *Gārgyaḥ prathamaṁ śākṭāyanaḥ*//

71. *Uṣmāntaḥstharsoṣmacakāravargā nāntam yānty anyatra visarjanīyāt*//

72. They are : *eva, tayā, nṛbhyaḥ, abhi, devī, vasu, bāhū, agne, vāyo, vai, tau, vāk, arvāṅ, viṭ, vṛṣaṇ-vān, yat, devān, triṣṭup, indram.*

73. *Prathamottamāḥ padāntiyā a- canau.*
'With the exception of c *and n* the firsts and the fifths of the class-consonants may occur at the end of words 'Trans. *RASTOGI* Indumati, Chowkhamba Sanskrit Series office, Varanasi, 1967.

74. *VPr* 1.88: *nakārarkārāvagrahe*, 'Ṇ and ṛ (may occur at the end of words) only in *avagraha*'. *RASTOGI*

75. *APr* 1.6 :*sparśāḥ prathamottamāḥ* 'Of the mutes, the first and the last of each series (are allowed finally)' Trans. WHITNEY, Chowkhamba Sanskrit Series Office, Varanasi, 1962.

76. *APr* 1.7 : *na ca-vargaḥ* 'C-class consonants do not come at the end of a word'.

77. *Anḷkāraḥsvaraḥ padyḥ* 'Any vowel excepting *ḷ* may occur as final. The term *padya* is defined in rule 1.3 as *padāntyaḥ*

padyaḥ : 'A letter capable of occurring at the end of a word is called *padya*. It is notable in this connection that the word *padya* in this particular sense is used only in this *Pr.* The *RPr* uses it in the sense of 'a member of a compound'. *VPr* or P does not use this term.

78. *Prathamāntāni tṛtīyāntānīti śaunakasya pratijñānaṁ na vṛittiḥ//*
79. *Atha prathamaḥ* 'Now for changes of first mutes.'
80. *Jhalāṁ jaso'nte : 'A corresponding j, b, g* ḍor *d* is replaced in place of all consonants (with the exception of semi vowel and nasals) at the end of a word.'
81. *Vargaprathamāḥ padāntāḥ*
82. Jhalo jas : Vṛtti: jhalo jhali padānte jas bhavati
83. Jai 5.4.131 : *virāme vā*
84. *Mugdhabodhavyākaraṇam,* Calcutta, 1911, *sutra* 65. *jhap-jhasoḥ khasjhavo scapjabante ca.*
85. The author of the *Sārasvata-vyākaraṇa* is *Anubhūti-svarūpācārya.*
86. -(a)ḥ>o*cf.RPr*4.2:*ovisarjany o– hrasva–prv*

- ḥ > r cf. *RPr4* : *sarvopadhastu svaraghoṣavat puro repham.....*

-*ḥ* >s/s cf. *RPr* 4; *yathādiṣṭaṁ nāmipūrvaḥ sakāram ṣkāram anyo riphitaḥ kakāre....*

87. VPR 3.6 : *visarjanīyaḥ*

3.7 : *Cachayoḥ śam*

3.8 *tathayoḥ sam etc.*

APr 2.40 : *visarjanīyasya parasasthāno' ghoṣe, visarjanīya,* before a surd consonant, becomes of like position with the following sound'.

2.42 : *nāmyupadhasya rephaḥ'* If preceded by an alternate vowel, it becomes *r* before a vowel'.

2.43 : *ghoṣavati ca* 'As also before a sonant consonant.'

TPr 8.5 : *atha visarjanīyaḥ.*

8.6 : *repham eteṣu, where eteṣu* means *svaraghoṣavat-uttameṣu pareṣu.*

8.7 : *Okāram aḥ* '*Aḥ* the whole of it, when followed by a becomes o'.

9.8: *ghosavat paraṣca*

88. *Sarvopadhastu svaraghoṣavatparo rephaṁ rephī te punā repha-sandhyayaḥ (RPr 4.27) 'A rhotacized visarjanīya,* however,

which is preceded by any (short or long vowel) becomes *r*, if followed by a vowel or sonant consonant. These are called *r modification (repha-sandhayaḥ);*

89. *Kātantra*, ed. EGGELING, Calcutta, 1876.
1.5.1 *visarjanīyas ce che vāśam*
1.5.14 : *raprakṛtiranāmiparo' pi*
1.5.7 *umakārayor madhya*
90. Cand 6.3.98 : *sasajuṣor Uḥ*
6.4.20 : *virāme visarjnīyaḥ*
6.4.21 : *khari ca*
For 6.4.20-1, P gives only one: *kharavasānayor visarjanīyaḥ (8.3.15).* Thus the process of derivation of the word *payskāmyati* is as under:
payas + kāmyati - Stage I
payar + kamyati -Stage II
r < *ru (u being redundant)*
payas + kāmyati -State III
And not like that of the *Prs* i.e,
Payaḥ + kāmyati -I
payas + kāmyati -II
91. *jai 5.3.76: sasajuṣo ri*
5.4.19 : *virāme visarjanīyaḥ*
4.3.100 : *reraddhasoḥ* (cf. P 6.1.113)
5.4.23 : *śari saśca* (cf. P 8.3.36)
92. Rule No. 103 : *srorviḥ phe*
pha means hasóntah phaḥ (rule 86)
70 : *ato'ddhavyuḥ* 'if *a and hab* follow ḥ preceded by a is substituted by *u'*.
73 : *rīco'be : 'ḥ preceded by vowels except a,ā* and followed by *ab, becomes r.*
74 : *ro'caḥ'ḥ preceded by a and* followed *ab changes to r.*
93. Sāras. *svarātapullinga-prakaraṇam,* rule no.4.
sror visargaḥ (cf. P 8.3.15).
Sandhi-prakaraṇa, rule 5 : *ato'tyuḥ*
'ḥ preceded by a and followed by at becomes u'.
6 : *habe'* ḥ changes to *ū* before *hab'*.
10 : *nāmino raḥ 'ḥ* preceded by vowel other than *a, ā* becomes r.

94. *Vedic Grammar for Students*, Oxford University Press. 1962, pp. 34-35.

94a. The *TPr* 22.13 tells us four kinds of *virāma: ṛgvirāmaḥ padavirāmo vivṛttivirāmaḥ samānapada-vi-vṛttivirāmaḥ trimātro dvimātra ekamātro ardhamatraḥ ityānupūrveṇa.*

RPr 1.28 prescribes one *mātrā* to avagraha : *mātrāhrasvas tāvad avagrahāntaraṁ dve'* Short vowel has one mora; that much is an interval of an *avagraha'*.

VPr 5.1 ; *Samāse avagrahaḥ hrasvamātrākālaḥ padavicchedo saṁhitaḥ*

94b. *VPr* 1.156 : *padavicchedo' saṁhitaḥ* 'short vowel has one mora; that much is an interval of *an avagraha'*.

94c. *VPr* 1.153; *avagraha padāntavat.*

95. The position of this type of assimilation is in *TRUBETZKOY'S* terminology, a 'position of neutralization *(Aufhebungsstenung). cf. p. 97 of W.S.* Allen's *Sandhi*, Multon and Co.'s - Gravenhage, 1962. For reference of *TRUBETZOKOY'S* work see fn. 3 on the same page.

96. The *RPr* deals with the question of incomplete articulation of sound and this named as *Abhinidhāna*, where weakening of the final stop followed by *avsāna* is demonstrated. But this theory has been extended to consonant clusters also. The *APr* and *Cārayṇīya śikṣā* also have discussed this phenomenon. For a detailed study see Siddheshwar VARMA, *Critical Studies in the Phonetic Observations of Indian Grammarians*, Delhi, 1961.

97. Sukumar SEN, *A Comparative Grammar of middle Indo Aryan (MIA)*, Deccan College, Poona, 1960. p.97.

98. Under P 1.4.110. According to the *kāśikā* on P 1.4. 109 even, in the *Saṁhitā* -text, there is a deviation of half a *mātrā* between the various phonetic elements, even between two consonants or between a vowel and a consonant, which however, is quite imperceptible; cf, *paro yaḥ sannikarṣo varṇānām ardhamātrākālavyavadhānaṁ sa saṁhitāsaṁjño bhavati. Siddhānta Kau.* on Pl.4.110 : *varṇānām abhāvaḥ avasānasaṁjnaḥ syāt. Ṛktantra.* 35: virāmo mātrā.

99. *adháḥ* svid āsī̄ 3 t upári svid āsī̄ 3 t (10.129.5); and bhī́riva vindatī 3 (10.146.1).

100. See the sections I.2.1 and I.2.2. above.
101. IHQ 10:669: ".....But it is very unlikely that Pāṇini had personal *knowledge of the Padapāṭha.....*"
102. IHQ 10: 665-70.
103. See under P 1.1.17-18 : Uña iti yogavibhāgaḥ and *ū̃* vā Śākalyasya.
104. See Śākalyasyacāryasya matena *ū̃* vibhāsā yathā syāt / *ū̃* iti ū iti / anyeṣāmācāryāṇām matenav iti / under p 1.1.17-18.
105. That the ē of te is not *prgṛhya* vowels is made clear by the Pdk by allowing *sandhi* between te and *iti.*
106. It is interesting to note in this connection that both the Pdk and P have the same treatment with regard to two different sets, (A) *vánaspáti, ráthaspáti, bṛ́haspáti* etc where the genitive form cannot be easily guessed, and (B) *brahmáṇaspáti, divásрitar, śúbhaspáti* etc. where the genitive is clearly visible. In the first set they show cp-forms with double accent where first constituent does not appear to be case- inflected and in the second set they say that since both words are case-inflected and since both show independent accent, it is better to treat them as uncompounded word- groups. But even in the second set of examples appearing in the vocative, P has to treat them as semantically single unit having one acent. But while phrasing the rule he does not treat them as compound forms but says that as far as accentuation is concerned they are treated as one word. This type of inconsistency which we find in the Pp is carried over to P's treatment.
107. A finished word may consist of more than two morphemes.
108. The compounds like *dive-dive* etc. are treated as one-word items
109. *ratnadhā́tamam, somapā́van,* etc.
110. See section II. 4 of this thesis.
111. Other form of this type is *jugukṣataḥ* (8.31.7). It is shown in the Pp as/ *jughukṣataḥ*/. Here too no *iti* is added to it.

PART II
ŚĀKALYA'S TREATMENT OF THE PADAPĀTHA AND ITS ANALYSIS

Chapter II

Śākalya's Treatment and its Analysis

II. Śākalya's Treatment and its Analysis

II.1.1.CASE - ENDING

Introductory Remarks:

In the Pp, our of the twenty one case-terminations, only- *bhiḥ* (3/3), *-bhyām* (3-5/2), *-bhyaḥ* (4-5/3) and *-su* (7/3) have been separated by the *avagraha* -sign. Also the suffix- *ā* an allomorph of *-nā* (3/1) has been separated from the oblique base ending in *u, e.g.*, / *sādhu yā́* /, /*dhṛṣṇu- yā́*/,/*āśu-yā́*/ etc. Other case-suffixes begining with a vowel have not been separated from the bases. The nominative ending cannot be separated.

All these above mentioned suffixes have been grouped in two sets on the groud of voicedness and voicelessness of the initial phoneme. Therefore, *-bhiḥ- ,bhyā* and *-bhyaḥ* from one set, and *-su* forms the other. In the case of first set, the treatment given is as follows: (A table is given at the end which will clarify the treatment.)

1.1 Treatment in the case of vowel stems

1.1.1 The case-suffixes beginning with *bh* are separated if the oblique stem ends in a short vowel, but not after oblique stems ending in long vowels. This holds good for cp.-stems as well as non-cp. -stems. For instance *dhenu-bhiḥ*.[1] The counter example is *nadībhiḥ*[2]. For cp.-stems the treatment is as follows:

Sp	*Pp*
dravátpāṇibhiḥ	*/dravátpāṇi-bhiḥ/*[3]
tridhā́tubhiḥ	*/tridhā́tu - bhiḥ/*[4]
nṛbāhubhyām	*/nṛbāhu - bhyām/*[5]
dáśābhīśubhyaḥ	*daśābhīśu- bhyaḥ/*[6]

Here the Pdk follows the principle of ICA. That is to say, he separates the immediate constituents and not the cp-constituents. It has only one exception namely, *kavā́rībhyaḥ.*[7] *Here although the oblique base offers a separable envrironment i.e., kavāri,* the suffix *-bhyaḥ* is not separated bu the base has been analysed as */kava-arībhyaḥ/*

The counter examples are *devakarmébhiḥ, àpodakābhiḥ ṛksāmā́bhyām, dàśayoktrébhiḥ,* etc. which are analysed as *deva-karmébhiḥ/*[8]

/apa - udakābhiḥ/[9], */ṛk -sāmā́bhyām/*[10] */dàśa-yoktrebhiḥ/*[11] etc. Here the compound base does not end in a short vowel.

1.2. Treatment in the case of a consonant-stem:

1.2.1 These three suffixes i.e., *-bhiḥ, bhyām,* and *-bhyah* are always separated after consonantal base. At the same time if the oblique bases are modified by *sandhi,* they are restored to their original forms.[12] The Pdk follows this practice consistently.

2. For-*su*, the following analysis is adopted:

2.1 *In the case of a vowel-stem*:

No analysis is given if the vowel-stem ends in either a short or a long vowel.

2.2. In the case of a consonant-stem:

Su is always separated from the stem if it is not affected by any phonetic change i.e., if it is not cerebralised.

There is a single exception to this rule, namely, *dhūrṣú*[13] This has been analysed as */dhūḥ-sú/*[14]. *Here although the -s* of *su* is cerebralised, it has been separated and shown in its original form. This is not his usual treatment as evidenced in */pūrṣú/*[15],*/gīrṣú/*[16] etc. It is not clear why the Pdk has not followed this practice in the case of *dhūrṣú*.

3. The Pp of the other Vedas.

In *Av* and *VS* the same method has been adopted by the respective 'Pdks in the case of words ending in the four case-suffixes under discussion. Here also the other case-terminations are not separated.

4. *The Pp and the Prātiśākhyas*

The ṚPr. formulates no rule regarding the separation of the case- endings in the Pp of the *RV*. It is merely records some cases where the *avagraha* has not been used.[17] However, the other *Prātiśākhyas*, namely, *VPr.* and the *APr.* have phrased rules by way of enumeration. The formulation of these rules is purely based on the data before them. They simply enumerate the cases. They do not state why such a method for word-analysis has been adopted.

4.1 The *VPr* offers the following description regarding the separation of case-terminations:

(a) *Hrasvavyañjanābhyāṁ bhakaradhu vibhaktipratyaye*[18] '*(avagraha)* is put before a case-termination beginning with *bh*, if it is preceded by a short vowel or a consonant.'

As an exception to this word *asmabhyam* as a non- analysed form has been given in a separate list[19] However, *tubhyam* has not been recorded here, perhaps by oversight[20]

(b) *Sviti cānatau*[21] 'Also (before tne case-termination) *su*, if it is not cerebralized, (*avagraha* is put),

4.2.APr offers the four following rules. The first two rules deal with the *bh*-endings.

(a) *Bhirbhyāṁ bhyashsu* : 'Before *-bhiḥ, bhyām, and -bhyaḥ (an avagraha* is put)'[22]

The condition for such a separation is not mentioned in this rule. But it is hinted at indirectly in the rule:

(b) *na dīrghāt: (Avagraha* is) not (put in the case of an oblique base ending) in a long vowel.'[23]

(c) So far the-su ending is concerned APr formulates the following rules:

sau ca: '(avagraha is put) before *su*[24] *and vināme-ca;* 'Also if it is not retroflexed.[25]

Thus the observations made by the *VPr* and the *Apr* hold true for the Ṛgvedic Pp. But ṚPr does not make specific statement about *avagragha* concerning the case-endings.

5. Statement of the problem:

Now, the problem before us which has neither been tackled by the Prātiśākhyas nor by present-day scholars is to find out the intention of the Pdk in adopting this analysis. With regard to this the following questions can be raised:

(a) Does the Pdk by means of *avagraha* or separation intend to give morphemic or stem-suffix analysis?

(b) If this is intention of the Pdk, then why out of twenty one case-suffixes only four are subjected to separation and not all?

(c) Why is the stem-suffix analysis given after bases ending in short vowel or ending in a consonant and not after other bases?

(d) Why is the reason behind adopting a different method in the case of the *bh*-suffixes on the one hand and - *su* on the other?

6. Answers:

We will discuss these problems one by one.

(a) The Pdk intends to give some kind of morphemic analysis of the Ṛgvedic *ṛks*. The analysis however, is not a morphemic analysis in the strict sense of the term as it is understood to-day by modern linguists. In a morphemic analysis each word is segmented into its consituent meaningful units. Thus, not only four case-terminations but all twenty one of them as well as the compound- stems should be separated. But the Pdk does not adopt this practice. He separates only four case-suffixes and in the case of the cp-stems he does not give the complete analysis but gives only one cut. Therefore, this is not a morphemic analysis in its strict sense.[26] But in any case, in presenting his analysis the Pdk must have some notion about what the stem is and what the suffix is. Since the suffixes are separated from the stems by means of *avagraha* we can say that the analysis of the Pdk amounts to stem-suffix analysis.

(b) The reason why only the four case-terminations are selected for segmentation appear to be as follows:

i) It should always be kept in mind that the Pdk intends to analyse words into *padas*.

ii) According to the Pdk, the stems preceding *bhiḥ,-bhyām, -bhyaḥ* and *-su* i.e., suffixes beginning with consonant can alone be termed as *pada* but not the stems preceding a case-suffix which begins with a vowel. This concept of *pada* is the same as that used in the Pāṇinian grammar.[27] P., however, states that before the consonant y the stem is *bha* (non-*pada*).[28] This is the improvement made by P. But the Pdk separates the stem from the suffix beginning with *y*, for instance, */sādhu-yā́ /ā́śu-yā́/ etc.*[29] *But since before yā* no *pada* changes are found, P refers to call it *bha*.

Thus, the Pdk indicates separation generally in those cases in which the difinition of *pada* as stated by P applies. He does not indicate separation in the other cases i.e., in the case of non-*pada* stems i.e., *bha*. But he avoids this separation when the stem ends in a long vowel enven though it is *pada* technically. In selecting the suffixes-*bhiḥ,- bhyām* and *-bhyaḥ* the Pdk has one more point in his mind. He wants to restore the original consonant which undergoes change due to *sandhi*. It is quite clear that in the stem ending in a consonant such euphonic changes occur before-*bhiḥ bhyām* and *bhyaḥ* only. But stems ending in consonants followed by suffixes beginning with a vowel do not undergo any phonetic modification. That is to say, where the stem is called *pada* the final sound undergoes phonetic change. In these cases the Pdk finds a scope for his analysis, e.g.,

Sp	Pp
/dadbhıḥ	*/dat-bhıḥ/*[30]
/paḍbhıḥ/	/paṭ - bhıḥ/[31]
/tàpobhiḥ/	tàpaḥ - bhiḥ/[32]

(c) In answer to the third question we may state the following:

i) The Pdk does not see any *pada*-change in the lengthened feminine bases in *ā, ī*, and *ū* Therefore, he does not separate them. But in the case of the secondary suffixes even if there is no *sandhi-* change, still he prefers to separate. He should have adopted that practice here also. Perhaps, the reason is that with regard to the case- terminations only the *prātipadika*-bases are separated. The feminine stems are not the *prātipadikas* (i.e., original stems)[33] Therefore, he does not separate. Or, we may say that legnthening is one basic factor which prevents the Pdk from the separation.

ii) The change a > *ā* before- *bhyām* as in *hástābhyām, devā́bhyām* etc, and a > *e* before- *bhiḥ* and- *bhyaḥṣ* as in *devébhah, karmè*bhiḥ etc. are not caused by the *pada-status, but this lengthening is morphologically conditioned, P puts the rules for a >* ā *and a > e* in the *aṇga*-section and not in the *pada* section [34] Wherever the stem undṇergoes the morphological changes (in Pāṇinian term *āṇga* changes), the Pdk avoids separation.

Thus, in *dhītıbhiḥ*[35]. *nidhıbhiṇ*[36], *tántubhiḥ*[37], *náma-ukatibhyaḥ*[38], *aktúbhyaḥ*[39] *etc.* the bases preceding the case -suffixes are padas and at the same time *prātipadikas*. Therefore, the Pdk separates those forms. In *tápobhiḥ marúdbhaḥ*[40] etc. We see *pada*-change, therefore, he has separated. In *rájabhyaḥ,*[41], *hastıbhiḥ*[42], *aśvıbhiḥ*[43], *etc , the final n is dropped due to the pada* status. Therefore, he separates these. But in the case of hástābhyā[44], devébhiḥ,[45] nadıbhiḥ[46] etc. he does not separate because these changes are not *pada-* changes but *aṅga*-changes.

iii) In *góbhiḥ*[47] *and naúbhiḥ*[48] the Pdk does not show separation. Probably in order to maintain symmetry with other long bases mentioned above he may not have separated these cases.

(d) The reply to the fourth question, namely, why does the Pdk not separate *su* even after short vowel-bases can be put as follows:

From the data given in the table, it is clear that the Pdk does not separate-*su* when it is retroflexed. In *tápobhiḥ* the change as > o is a *pada*-change. To indicate this, separation is made. It appears that the Pdk's *avagraha* comes whenever he wants to restore the stem-form affected by the *pada* change. His main purpose is to indicate that stem has undergone *sandhi* due to *pada*-status. He is not concerned with the changes affecting the suffixes. So whenever he wants to indicated the original stem or constituent of a compound which has undergone retroflexion, he will indicate it. But he will not do so if the ṣ belongs to the suffix. Therefore, *puruṣṭuta* has been analysed as / *puru -stuta/*[49], *suṣutásya* as /*su- sutásya/*[50] *suṣupaṇaṃ* as / *su-supānam/*[51], *bárhiṣadaḥ* as / *bárhi- sadaḥ*[52] and so on. This shows that his use of the *avagraha* is limited to indicating the original form of a stem which has undergone *sandhi* change due to the *pada*-status.

7. Conclusion

(a) So far the analysis is concerned, whatsoever method he has adopted is almost consistently followed.

(b) The Pdk's analysis is not a stem-suffix analysis in the strict sense of the term, but a *pada*-analysis. Had it been stem-suffix analysis, then in *nā́mabhiḥ yuvábhyām, rā́jasu, kármasu* separation should have been shown as *nā́man - bhiḥ, yuván-bhyām, rā́jan -su, kárman - su* etc. But what we find is *nā́ma-bhiḥ*[53], *yuvá bhyām*[54], *rā́ja -su* [55] *kárma - su*[56]

(c) From investigation of the *pada*-text it has become clear that the main aim of the Pdk is to show the *pada*-changes in the stem. This is possible before the four suffixes only. Therefore, the Pdk has introduced separation before these four suffixes only.

(d) The Pdk in his treatment of the consonantal stems is more consistent than in his treatment of vowel-stems. The reason is that he can show the *pada*-changes in the consonantal stems better than in the vowel stems. Moreover, it seems that the lengthening always put the Pdk in difficulty. He is not sure whether the lengthening is due to the pada or phonological or morphological or metrical.

(e) We find that the Pdk sees that particular changes occur in certain environment, in compounding, before morphemic boundary or before certain phonemes. These changes the Pdk takes to be *pada*-changes. So to him the *pada* is a unit which shows particular changes in the particular environment. This concept of *pada* is taken over by P who, however, refines this concept by clear definitions. But in the case of changes which are not due to the *pada*- status the Pdk is silent. But P again refines and introduces changes under the names : *aṅga* or *bha*.

We may end our discussion by the following remarks. The work done by the Pdk is not merely of lexical importance but it has basic value for linguistics. Many linguistic phenomena become explicit in his works which were only vague in the previous works. The work done by the Pdk forms the basis of the further works in linguistics. The Pdk does not state the rules according to which he analyses. He gives the analysis keeping the rules in his mind . From the analysis given by the Pdk we must formulate the rules known to the Pdk. This work is not only concerned with phonology but it tells also that the Pdk knows about suffixation, primary and secondary and compound formation. His analysis also helps the interpretation of the *RV* by giving ICA type of analysis.

TABLE-A

– *bhiḥ*

Stem	Oblique stem	Treatment[57]	Example
a	*e*		*/devébhiḥ/*
ā	*ā*		*/prājabhiḥ/*
i	*i*	✔[57]	*/ṛṣi- bhiḥ/*
ī	*ī*		*/nadī́bhiḥ/*
ū	*u*	✔	*/táru- bhiḥ/*
ū	*ū*		*/tánūbhiḥ/*
ṛ	*ṛ*	✔	*/nṛ-bhiḥ/*

Stem	Oblique	Treatment	Example
o	o		*/góbhiḥ/*
au	au		*/naubhiḥ/*
an	a	✔	*/nāma -bhiḥ/*
as	o	✔	*/tapaḥ-bhiḥ/*
t	d	✔	*/marut -bhiḥ/*
j	g	✔	*/ṛtajuk-bhiḥ/*
ir/is	ir	✔	*/gīḥ- bhiḥ/; haviḥ-bhiḥ/*
ur	ur	✔	*/pūḥ-bhiḥ/; / catuḥ -bhiḥ/*

TABLE- b
-bhyām

Stem	Oblique stem	Treatment	Example
a	*ā*		*/hastābhyām/*
ā	*ā*		*/daśa-śakhābhyām/*
ī	*ī*		*/kṣoṇībhyām/*
u	*u*	✔	*/nṛbahú - bhyām/*
ṛ	*ṛ*	✔	*/pitṛ -bhyām/*
at	*ad*	✔	*aṣṭhivat- bhyām/*
an	*a*	✔	*/yuva-bhyām/*
in	*i*	✔	*/aśvi-bhyām/*

TABLE-C
bhyaḥ

Stem	Oblique stem	Treatment	Example
a	*e*		*/devebhyaḥ/*
ā	*ā*		*/prajābhyaḥ/*
i	*i*	✔	*/ṛṣi- bhyaḥ/*
ī	*ī*		*/oṣadhībhyaḥ/*
u	*u*	✔	*/aktu- bhyaḥ*
ū	*ū*		*/tanúbhyaḥ/*
ṛ	*ṛ*	✔	*/pitṛ- bhyaḥ/*
o	*o*		*/góbhyaḥ/*
ut	*ud*	✔	*/marut-bhyaḥ/*
an	*a*	✔	*/dhā́ma-bhyaḥ/*
as	*o*	✔	*/aṅgiroḥ-bhyaḥ/*

TABLE -D
-su

Stem	Oblique stem	Treatment	Example
a	*e*		*/ā-haveṣu*
ā	*ā*		*/pathyāsu/*
i	*i*		*/ṛṣiṣu/*
ī	*ī*		*/nadī́ṣu/*
u	*u*		*/purúṣu/*
ū	*ū*		*/tanùṣu/*
ṛ	*ṛ*		*/nṛṣu/*

Stem	Oblique Stem	Treatment	Example
o	o		/góṣu/
t	t	✔	/nivat- su/
an	a	✔	/ádhva-su/
am	aṁ	✔	/daṁ-su/
as	aḥ	✔	/rajaḥ -su/
ir	īr	✔	/gīrṣú/
is	iṣ		/haviṣṣu/
ūr	ūr	✔	/dhūḥ-su/

II. 1.1a *-yā* **(Case- termination 3/1)**

It is always accented and is added to *a, u, i* and *s*-stems. It is always separated from the base which shows that the Pdk takes this suffix as a *pada*-marker unlike P. According to P 1.4.18, the stems before the suffixes beginning with y are termed *bha* and not *pada*. The denominative suffix *ya* after n- stems is taken to be *pada* marker (Pl. 4.15) which is the only exception. But the Pdk takes it always as a pada- forming suffix except after s-stems as can be seen in *namasyati* where no cut is shown. If he does separate s-ending stems before *ya,* we will have *namoyati* instead of *namasyati*. Therefore, in the case of *duvoyá* (5.36.6), even though *duvas* is a s-stem, *yā* is separated because here *sandhi* has taken place i.e., s of *duvas* is changed into *u* due to the *pada-status.* Thus, it is clear that the main criterion of separation is the *pada-sandhi*. The Pdk refrains from separation where it would lead to wrong *sandhi* not appearing in the Sp.

It can be seen from the classified list given at the end, that the suffix-*yā* fulfils the functions of the instrumental singular according to the forms attested in the *RV*. Usually those forms are adverbially used.

There are about 20 forms derived with this suffix in the *RV*. According to Sāy. Out of these two are in 1/1, one in 1/2, three in 1/3, thirteen in 3/1, one in 4/1, one in 7/1, and one doubtful case which can be in 1/3 as well as in 3/1 both. Some of Sāy's treatments are given below :

1/1, Sādhu -yā́ (1.23.11)

1/2, aryayā́ (5.75.7)

1/3, raghuyā́ (2.28.4)

3/1, áśvayā́ (8.46.10)

4/1, vīrayā́ (7. 90.1)

7/1, naktayā́ (4.11.1)

But formally all these are instrumental forms which express in most of the cases the adverbial sense. GELDNER always translates these forms as adverbs.

The suffix-*yā́* has its allomorph - *iyā́* to be attested in *sukṣetriyā* (1.97. 2) and in *urviyā́* (1.92.9), which being a *svarādi* suffix has not been separated. That's why in *sukṣetriyā, iyā́* being an inseparable suffix, the next immediate constituent ***su*** is separated. This suffix has been recorded by the *Vārttika* : *iyādiyājokārāṇām upasaṁkhyānam* under P 7. 1.39.

DATA

-a + yā

abda - yā́ (5.54.3), áśva-yā́ (8.46.10), nakta - yā́ (4.11.1), ṛta - yā́ (2. 11.12), gavya - yā́ (8.93.17), hiraṇya-yā́ (7.66.8), vira-yā́ (7.90.1), eva -yā́ (5.41.16), arya-yā́ (5.75.7), sumna - yā́ (10.101.4) ratha-yā́(8.46.10).

-i +yā

su - kṣetriyā́ (1.97.2).

-u +yā

raghu - yā́ (2.28.4), vasu -yā́ (1.97.2), sukratu- yā́ (1.31.3), dhṛṣṇu- yā́ (1.23.11), āsu - yā́ (4.2.2), sādhu - yā́ (1.46.11), sugātu - yā́ (1.97.2).

-ḥ + yā

duvaḥ - yā́ (5.36.6 Sp duvoyā)

II. 1.2. SECONDARY SUFFIXES

Introduction:

There are 54 secondary suffixes mentioned by MACDONELL[58] and 57, by WHITNEY.[59] According to MACDONELL [60] 17 suffixes begin with vowels and 37 with consonants. Whereas according to WHITNEY[61] there are 18 secondary suffixes beginning with vowels and 39 with consonants. These two lists differ because MACDONELL does not record *-āna and -kaṭa* as secondary suffixes, and because WHITNEY does not mention *-ā,-yin and -sa* as secondary suffixes. WHITNEY mentions a few more suffixes like *alu, āla* etc. which occur only in the later language and not in the *RV*

Because the stems before a secondary suffix begginning with a consonant are taken to be *pada* the secondary suffixes are separated by the Pdk and not the primary suffixes which do not give the status of *pada* to the preceding stem. The entire treatment of the secondary suffixes by the Pdk can be classified in three groups:

a. The suffixes which are separated consistently without any exception;

b. The suffixes which are separated with certain exceptions;

c. The suffixes which are not separated at all.

The suffixes under group a. are *-taya, -tāt, tāti, -tva, -maya, -vala, and -vaya.*

The suffixes under group b. are *-tama, -tara, -tya, tvana, -ma, -mant, -va, -vat-van-vant, vani, -vin, -vari, and -vana.*

The suffixes under group c. are *ka, -ta, tana, -tna, -tā -tvatā, -tha, na, -bha, -man, -min, -mna, -ya, -yin, -ra/la, -va, -vana, -s and -śa*

The discussion of the treatment of each suffix follows hereafter:

II.1.2.a.1 *-taya*

There is only one stem in the *RV* after which this suffix is added. The stem is *daśan-*. The suffix is used in the sense of 'consisting of so many parts.' The examples which are found in the *RV* are *dáśatayaḥ* (1.58.4) and *dáśatayasya* (1.122.12) meaning 'tenfold'

In the *AV* also we have one example : *catuṣṭaya* 'fourfold'. This shows that the use of the suffix is restricted to numeral bases only.

In the *Pada-* text of the *RV* both the forms are separated because the Pdk finds *pada-sandhi,* namely dropping of *n*. If this is so then he knows numeral stems ending in *n*. But in *saptatha,* he does not separate.

II. 1.2.a.2 *-tāt / -tāti*

The suffixes *-tāt and -tāti* seem to be related to *-tā*. They have the same meaning as that of *-tā*. There are ten forms derived by adding *-tāti,* and five forms by adding *-tāt*. All these forms are analysed by the Pdk without any exception.

Here it is clear that the Pdk knows that all these stems are used independently and therefore, *-tāt or -tāti* must be suffix. It looks strange that the Pdk does not separate *-ka* while he does so in the case of *tāt/tāti.*

DATA : *-tāt*

-ā -tāt

uparā́-tāti (1.151.5), devá-tātā (1.3.5.), devá-tāte (9.96.3), satyá-tātā (10. 111.4), sarvá-tātā (1.94.15).

DATA : -tāti

-a -tāti

ariṣṭá- tāti (10.137.4) ásta -tātim (5.7.6), gṛbhītá-tātaye (5.74.4), jyeṣṭha-tātim (5.44.1), devá-tātaye (1. 127. 9), devá- tātim (1. 141. 10), vasú-tatiḥ, (1.122.12) śam-tāti (8. 18.7), sātya-tāte (4.4.14) sarvá-tātaye (1.106.2).

II. 1.2.a.3 -tva

More than thirty neuter abstract substantives are formed with the suffix-*tva*. It has got the same meaning as *-tā*. The accent is always on the suffix. Because the suffix is a *pada* marker since we find *pada-sandhi*. The Pdk has separated the forms derived with this suffix.

In *anāgāḥ-tvám (1.94.15), anāgāḥ-tvé (1.104, 6), and anāgāḥ-tvéna (10.37,9),* the final syllable of the stem is lengthened; whereas, in *sadhani-tvám* (4.1.9) it is shortened. In *suprajāstvám,* the analysis offered by the Pdk is *suprajāḥ-tvám,* changing *-s* to -ḥ-. Here the stem is suprajas which is a *bahuvṛhi* compound. P specifically notes that the word *prajā* when it occurs as a final member of a compound takes *asIC* (P.5.4.122). So the compound stem is *suprajas.* The Pdk cannot analyse it as *su- prajāstvám* either, because - *prajāstvam* is not a semantically single unit[62]

This suffix is added to stems ending in *a, ā, i, ī, u, ṛ, t, and ṣ.* In all the forms- *tva* is separated from the stems, e.g., *amṛta -tvám (1.66.6) suprajāḥ-tvám, sakhi-tvám (1.4.10), strī-tvám (8.45.5), bhrātṛ-tvám (8.20.2), maghvat-tvám (6.27.3), and rakṣaḥ-tvéna (8.18.13)*

DATA: *-tva*

-a -tva

amṛta-tvám (1.66.6), amṛta-tvásya (10.90.2), amṛta-tvā́ya (1.72.9), amṛta-tvé (1.31.7), subhaga-tvám (2.21.6), deva-tvám (1.68.2), pāpa-tvāya (7.32.18), vṛṣa-tvébhiḥ (1.91.2), sudīna -tvám (2.21.6).

ās-tva

suprajāḥ-tvám (10.62.3)

sakhi-tvám (1.4.10) taraṇi-tvéna (1.110.4), pati-tvám (1.119.5), aditi-tvé (7.51.1), jani- tvám (10.18.8), jami-tvám (1.166.10), kavi tvā́ (10.124.7), mahi-tvám (1.8.5), sadani- tvám (4.1.9)

-ū-tva

strī -tvám (8.45.5)

-u-tva

caru-tvám (10.70.9), dīrghāyu -tvám vasu -tvā́ (10.61.12), śatru -tvám (8.45.5)

-ṛ-tva

bhrātṛ-tvám (8.20.22), svasṛ-tvám (10.108.10)

-t-tva

maghavat-tvásya (6.27.3)

-as -tva

anāgāḥ -tvám (1.94.15), anāgāḥ -tvé (1.104.6), anāgāḥ-tvéna (10.37.9) rakṣaḥ -tvéna (8.18.13).

II. 1.2.a.4 -tvana

The suffix *-tvana* is an extension of *tva with na.* It has the same meaning as *-tva*. This suffix is added to some eight bases. It forms neuter abstract nouns. The stems to which this suffix is added are:

martya-,vṛṣa,-sakhi-,pati-jani-,mahi-, vasu-, and kavi-.

The accent is always on the final syllable of the suffix. All these forms are analysed by the Pdk without any exception.

All of these stems except *martya tvana* have beside them the corresponding abstract form with *tva*

This is a *pada* forming suffix according to P. The Pdk, although he has no evidence of *pada-sandhi* to prove that-*tvana* is a *pada forming suffix, still offers separation. Perhaps, vṛṣatvana* might be the example of *pada- sandhi* if he takes this form from the stem *vṛṣan*

DATA: -tvana

-a -tvana

martya-tvanā́ (8.92.13)

-i-tvana

jani-tvanā́ya (8.2.42), pati -tvanám (10.40.9) mahi -tvanám (1.166. 12), mahi-tvanā́ (1.85.7), sakhi-tvanā́ya (6.51.14)

-u -tvana

vasu -tvanám (7.81.6), vasu -tvanā́ (8.50.6)

II. 1.2.a.5 *-maya*

There are nine stems in the *RV* after which this suffix is added. Out of these, one is the prefix *su-*. This suffix is used in the sense of 'consisting of', 'derived from', or 'abounding in'. Excepting s- stems all other stems are separated from the suffix. Stems ending in s-remains unchanged before this suffix. Since *pada-sandhi* is not there, no analysis is offered by the Pdk. But when d, which, to the Pdk, is to the original stem, changes to n the Pdk has offered the analysis. He changes n to t. For example, *mṛnmayam* (8.71.1) is analysed as *mṛt-mayam*. Actually, the stem here is *mṛd-* But *d* is changed to *t* here because the morphemic boundary gives rise to the *avasānasandhi* according to the Pdk. For the Sp *sūmayam* (8.77.11) the Pp reads *su-mayam*. Here the ū of sū is shortened. This means that the Pdk takes the lengthening to be of a secondary nature i.e., metrical lengthening.

In the case of *aśmanmaya* the analysis offered is *aśman- maya-* Thus, the suffix *-maya* is separated from the n-stems even if n is retained in the form.

DATA : *-maya*

-a -maya

śaka-máyam (1.164.43)

-u -maya

su -máyam (8.77.11)

o-maya *go -máyam (10.62.2)*

-d-maya

mṛt-máyam (7.89.1)

-n -maya

asman-máyāni (10.63.3), asman-máyīnām (4.30. 20), asman -máyībhiḥ (10.101.10)

II. 1.2.a.6 *-vaya*

Only one example of this suffix is found in the *Rv*. The form is used as an adjective, e.g., *caturvayam* (1.110.3) 'fourfold'. It is analysed in the Pp as *catuḥ -vayam*. It is a very rare suffix. In the *AV* we come across one form : druvaya- meaning 'wooden dish'. We do not have any other example of this suffix. In origin the suffix-*vaya* is probably a noun.

II. 1.2.a.7 *-vala*

There is only one stem in the *RV* i.e., *kṛṣī* 'tillage' to which *-vala* has been added as a secondary suffix. The inflected form found in the *RV* is *kṛṣīvalām (10.146.6)* 'peasant '. The *VS* gives another form derived with this suffix namely, *naḍ-valā* 'reed-bed'.In the *RV* the Pdk has analysed the form as *kṛṣī -valām*. In origin this suffix like the suffixes-*kaṭa;*[63] *-vaya* etc. is probably a noun.

II.1.2.b.1 *-tama*

The secondary suffix-*tama* forms superlatives as well as ordinals. As the superlative marker it comes after substantives, adjectives and the perfix *ud, e.g., puru- támaḥ (3.62.2), very many'; madhúmat-tama (1.47.1) 'very sweet'; rathi -tama/Sp rathītama* 'best charioteer'; ut-tamám (1.24.15) 'highest'etc.

As the ordinal -marker the only available stem in the *RV* is *sata* and the actual forms are *śata -tamám (4.26.3), and śata - tamā́ (7.19.5)*

As a superlative marker it occurs after stems ending in a, ā, i, ī, u, ṛ, j, t, n, m, and s. For example, *citrá-tamaḥ (1.108.1), ratna -dhātamam (1.1.1)*[64], *kavi-tamaḥ (3.14.1), nádī -tame (1.41.16), cāru-tamaḥ (5.1.9), bhiṣák -tamam (2.33.4), nṛ-tama (5.4.6), prapathın-tamam (1.173.7), angiraḥ -tama (1.75.2), tuvī́ḥ -tamaḥ/ Sp tuviṣṭamaḥ/ (1.186.6), and ut -tamā́ (3.56.8)*

The suffix is added to compound stems also. For instance. *madhusut-, hiranyavasimat-,dirghasrut, devasrut-, dyumat-, kratuvid-, gātuvid, pūrvabhid-etc*

In all these examples *-tama* is separated, because the preceding part is a *pada*. But there are only two stems in which this is not separated namely, *go-*, and *ka-* The forms with *go*-form the name of the seer of some *suktas* of the *RV*.Since it is a proper name the Pdk does not give any analysis. *Ka*-is a pronominal stem showing many morphophonemic changes. Therefore, the Pdk is not sure about the stem. Moreover, this type of stems with morphophonemic changes does not occur used independently. As such the Pdk does not show any cut and keep these forms as they are.

DATA: *-tama* **A (analysed)**

-a -tama

avṛká -tamaḥ (1.174.10), ā́misla -tamaḥ (6.29.4), iná -tamaḥ (3.49.2) *ındra-tamā (1.182.2), ındravāta-tamāḥ (10.6..6) gurta tamāḥ (1.167.1),, gosa -tamāḥ (6.33.5) citrá-tamaḥ (1.108.1), citrá-tamā (4.23.6), júṣṭa-tamaḥ (1.163.13), júṣṭa - tamāsaḥ (1.87.1), jyéṣṭha -tamā (6.67.1), tosá-tamāḥ (1.169.5), dasma - tamaḥ (2.20.6), dīrghá-tamāḥ (1.58.1), devá- tamaḥ (4.22.3), devá-tamāya (2.24.3), devavāta - tamāḥ (6.29.4), dyukṣa- tamaḥ (9.108.1), nediṣṭha tamaḥ (9.98.5), nésa-tamaiḥ (1-141-12), kaṇva -tamaḥ (1.48.4), panya - tamāya (3.59.5), puruseka-tamā (6.62.5), práyakṣa-tamam (1.62.6).*

-ā-tama

ratna -dhā́tamaḥ (1:20.1), ratna -dhā́tamam (1.1.1)

-i -tama

ámbi-tame (2.41.16), kavi-tamaḥ (3.14.1), kavi -tamam (5.42.3) kavi-tamasya (5.85.6), tuvikūrmı -tamaḥ (6.37.4), tūrni-tamaḥ (4.4.3), dévi-tame (2.41.16)[65] *dyumnı -tamaḥ (8.92.16), dyumnı -tamam (8.19.6).*

-ī -tama

nádī -tame (241.16)

ū -tama

cā́ru -tamaḥ (5.1.9), cā́ru -tamam (1.62.6), puru -támaḥ (3.62.2), makṣú tamasya (8.19.12)

-ṛ -tama

nṛ́ -tama (5.4.6), pitṛ -tamaḥ (4.17.17).

-j -tama

bhiṣák-tamam (2.33.4)

-t -tama/-d -tama

ut -tamám (1.24.15), ut -tamā́ (3.56.8), ut -tamā́ni (1.91.18), ut-tamébhiḥ (6.60.3) kratuvit -tamaḥ (9.108.1), gātuvit-tamāḥ (8.19.16), gātuvit- tamaḥ (8.103.1), dīrghaśrút-tamaḥ (8.102.11), dīrghaśrút-tamam (5.38.2), dīrghaśrút-tamā (5.65.2), devaśrút-tamam (9.62.21), dyumát-tamaḥ (9.65.19), dyumát-tama (1.53.3), dyumát-tamam (1.28.5), pūrvabhit-tamam (8.53.1), balavat-tamām (10.145.1), maghavat-tama (8.54.5), madhúmat-tama (1.47.1), madhusút-tamaḥ (3.58.9), hiranyavāsīmat-tama (1.42.6).

-n -tama

dasyuhan-tamam (6.16.15), dyumnin-tamaḥ (1.127.9), prapathin-tamam (1.173.7), matsarin- tamaḥ (6.63.2) madin-tamaḥ (8.64.11).

-as -tama

aṅgirah-tama (1.75.2), apā́ḥ-tama (1.160.4), apā́ḥ-tamā (6.61.13), aṅgiraḥ-tamā (7.75.1), uruvyácaḥ-tamam (8.26.4), girvaṇaḥ-tama (8.68.10), girvaṇah-tamaḥ (6.45.20), girvanaḥ-tamā (5.86.4), gurtávacaḥ-tamaḥ(10.61.12), citráśravaḥ-tamaḥ (1.1.5),citra- śravaḥ-tama (1.45.6), citráśravaḥ-tamam (3.59.6), tavā́ḥ-tamaḥ (2.33.3), tavā́ḥ -tamā(1.109.5). tuviśravaḥ -tamaḥ (3.11.6), tuviśravaḥ tamam (5.25.5), devápsaraḥ -tamaḥ (9.105.5), devápsaraḥ-tamam(1.75.1), devavyácaḥ-tamaḥ (5.22.2), prathamáśravaḥ-tamaḥ (4.36.5), bráhmavāhaḥ -tamam (6.45.19)

-is -tama / Sp iṣṭama/

tuviḥ -tamaḥ (1.186.6), tuviḥ -tamā (5.73.2), tuviḥ -tamāya (1.130.2).

DATA: tama B (unanalysed)

katamát (10.81.2), katamā́ḥ (8.43.1), katamásya (1.24.1), katamā́su (4.51.6) katamā́m (1.35.7), katamā́su (10.40.14), gotama (1.79.10)

II. 1.2.b.2 *-tara*

The suffix *-tara* is used to form comparatives. The base to which this suffix is added can be either adjective or substantive or the preposition *ud*. This suffix is found after stems ending in *a, ā, i, ī, u, t,s, e.g, pūrva -tarām (1.113.11), dıvā-tarāt (1.127.5), kavi- tarah (7. 86.7), rathi -taraḥ/Sp- thī (1.84. 6), dhánu-tarau (4.35.5), ut-tarāni (8.41.9), druham -taráḥ (1.127.3), Sp hantara- , /tavaḥ -taram (1.30.7), nahuḥ -taraḥ / Sp -ṣṭ- / (10. 49.8), ádasuḥ -tarasya/ Sp -ṣṭ-/ (8.81.7).*

In all these cases, analysis is shown by the Pdk. Long vowels preceding this suffix are shortened in the Pp. This indicates that the Pdk considers the lengthening to be of secondary nature i.e., metrical.

There are only two stems in connection with which the suffix-*tara* is not analysed. One is *ud* in twoforms only and the other is the pronominal stem *ka*. It is interesting to note that the nominative form úttaraḥ (4.18.9), is analysed as *út-taraḥ* whereas the ablative forms *uttarā́t* (6.19.9) and *uttarāttāt* (10.27.15), are left unanalysed. What made the Pdk refrain from giving separation in these forms is the difference in accent. In *uttaraḥ* meaning 'higher' *ut* is accented. Whereas in *uttarā́t* from the northern direction *ā* is accented. So apparently, the Pdk does not take *tara* as a comparative suffix and prefers not to give separation. It is a good example to show that the analysis of the Pdk is not a mechanical one. He takes into account the meaning of the word also.

I can cite another homophonous pair where one form is analysed and the other is not, namely, *avasānam*. This form is analysed as *ava-sānam* (10.14.9) whereas, it is left unanalysed in the Pp at 3.1.6/ avasānaḥ/. The reason for this treatment is the difference in meaning. The first form *avasānam* is derived from the prefix *ava* plus / *sā*, whereas the second *avasāna* is derived from *a-vasāna-*

Obviously, unless the Pdk takes meaning of these words into consideration, he cannot offer a separation. This further suggests that the Pp not only shows merely phonological changes at the *pada-* level but it also offers help in Vedic exegesis. By not separating these pairs he has given a clue that these words are of different connotations. It is only by separation or non-separation that he can indicate difference of meaning in homophonous pairs.

In the case of *uttarāttāt* there may be another difficulty to the Pdk. Most probably, the Pdk is not sure about the derivation of the forms showing double suffixation[66] and therefore, he might have avoided analysis.

With regard to forms *katarā (1.185.1) and kataraḥ (6.69.8)* the Pdk has difficulty in indicating the stem. Therefore, he has not separated *ka-* from- *tara.* Moreover, he does not find independent use of the base *ka-* in the *RV*. It can be observed that the pronominal bases suffer a great deal of change. Therefore, the Pdk many a time avoides separation.

DATA : *tara*

-a-tara

júṣṭa- tarasya (8.96.11), para- tare (10.95.1), pūrva -tarām (1.113.11)

ā -tara

parā-tarám (10.59.1), dıvā -tarāt (1.127.5)

-i -tara

kavı -taraḥ (7.86.7), kauli-tarám (4.30.14).

-u -tara

dhanu -tarau (4.35.5)

-t/ d -tara

amavat- tarebhyaḥ (10.76.5), út- tarabhyaḥ (10.145.3), út-tarāṇi (8.41.9), út-tarasmin (10.98.6), út-tarā (1.32.9), út-tarasmāt (10.42.11), út-taram (1.50.10), út-tarām (1.50.11), út-taraḥ (4.18.9) út-tare (10.145.30), kṣatravıt-taraḥ (10.25.8) gatuvıt-tarā (8.25.9), bhagavat- tarebhyaḥ (10. 60.12), bhuridāvat-taraḥ (8.5.39), varivovı titarasya (8.48.1).

-n-tara

rathı-taraḥ (1.84.6)

-m -tara

druham -taráḥ (1.127.3), / Sp, druhantaráḥ/

/Sp, surabhıntaraḥ/ surabhım -taraḥ (9.102.2).

-as -tara

taváḥ -taraḥ (1.30.7)

-uṣ -tara

áviduḥ -tarāsaḥ (10.2.4) *nahuḥ -taraḥ* (10.49.8)

-ūs-tara

ádaśūḥ- tarasya (8.81.7)

DATA : -tara B

Uttarā́ttāt (10. 27. 15), *katarā́* (1.185.1), *katarā́ḥ* (6.69.8) *uttarā́t* (6.19.9)

II.I.2.b.3 -tya

The suffix *-tya* is added to prepositions and adverbs to form adjectives and substantives. The following are the stems in the *RV* to which this suffix is added:

apa-, amā-, 'at home', āvis-'openly' nis- 'out', and sanu-[67]

The Pdk separates this suffix only after *avis-*. All other forms are left unanalysed. The reason why this suffix is separated only after *āvis* and not after *apa, amā, nis, and sanu-* could not be discovered.

In the case of *sanutya*-one can argue that since there is no independent use of *sanu* in the *RV*, the Pdk does not analyse *sanutya*. But what about the remaining forms? All *apa,amā, and nis* are independently used in the *RV* and therefore separation was excepted. Here, we will have to admit that the Pdk is inconsistent in his treatment of the suffix-*tya*

DATA : *tya* *A*

āviḥ-tyaḥ (1.95.5), *āviḥ-tyam* (10.100.7)

DATA : *tya* *B*

ápatyam (1.174.6), amātyam (7.15.3), aptyásya (1.124.5), āptyám (10.120.1) āptyáḥ (1.105.9), āptyānām (10.120.6), āptyāya, (8.47.14), āptyé (8.12.16), niṣṭyaḥ (6.75.19), sánutyaḥ (2.30.9), sánutyena (6.62.10).

II.1.2.b.4 *-ma*

The suffix forms superlatives and ordinals. It is added to prepositions and cardinals for 'eight', 'nine', and 'ten', in the *RV*. For instance *adhama-, apama-, avama-, upama-; aṣṭama-, navama-, dasama* etc.

Curiously enough, the Pdk has separated this suffix only after *upa-* All other forms are left unanalysed. It seems that the Pdk is not consistent in analysing these forms. Since all the stems to which this suffix is added are found independently used, the Pdk should have analysed all these forms.

DATA : *-ma A*

upa -máḥ (9.86.35), upa -mám (1.61.3) upa -mā́n (10.8.1), upa -mā́ni (8.99.2), upa -mā́saḥ (5.58.5), upa -mé (8.82.4), upa -mébhiḥ (1.33.2)

DATA : *-ma B*

adhamáḥ (1.33.5), adhamám (1.24.15), adhamā́n (4.28.4), adhamā́ni (1.25.21), apamásya (10.39.3), avamáḥ (4.1.5), avamásya (6.21.5), ántamaḥ (3.10.8), avamáḥ (3.30.16), ántamam (8.33.15), antamébhiḥ (1.165.5), caramáḥ (8.20.14), caramám (7.59.3), paramáḥ (5.30.5), paramám (1.22.20), paramásya (4.12.3), paramā́ṇi (4.1.16), paramé (1.62.7), madhyamáḥ (1.164.1), madhyamám (1.24.15), madhyamé (5.60.6), madhyamébhiḥ (3.32.13):

aṣṭamám (2.5.2), daśamé (1.117. 12) navamam (5.27.3).

II. 1.2.b.5 *-mant/mat*

It is secondary suffix meaning 'possessing.'The forms ending in *-mat* are derived like other secondary derivatives out of syntactic pattern, which is put by P as *tadasyāstīti*, i.e., one who has this. For instance, one who has or who is possessed of Kaṇva (*gotra) is Kaṇvamat* (8.2.22)'a descendent of Kaṇva'. This is the reason why this suffix is separated after all vowels, short or long unlike case suffixes which are separated only after short vowels.

But why has such a distinctive method at all been adopted?

The reason is the secondary suffixes show somewhat compound structure, that is to say, they are added after inflected forms. At the surface structure eventhough they do not show inflection, but at the deep structure there is inflection. It is, therefore, very interesting and at the same time amazing that how the Pdk could make distinction between these two types of formation of words i.e., the relation between a case-suffix and a stem and a secondary suffix and a stem, which is inflected at the deep level. This treatment of the Pdk is another support to a theory that compounds are derived out of sentences i.e., sentence patterns. The Pdk's treatment of secondary suffixes further reflects the position of grammatical concepts during his time. It is this concept of derivation of words which explains why the Pdk separates *-vān* from *prajávān* (3.30.18), but not-*bhiḥ* from *pra-jābhiḥ* (2.33.1).

The treatment of *-mat* is as follows:

It is separated after *a,i,ī, u, ū,ṛ, o, and t*. For example , *kanva màntam* (8.2.22), *abdi-mấn* (5.42.14), *taviṣī mantam* (5.58.1), *dyu-màt* (1.74.9), *vadhú- mataḥ* (6.27.8-), *tváṣṭṛ-mān* (6.52.11), *go-mān* (4.2.5), *kukút-mān* (10.8.2) *respectively.*

Mat is never separated after a stem ending either t or a sibilant, if t is not changed into d or n in the sp, or a sibiliant into ḥ or o in the Sp, e.g., *divitmatā* (1.26.2), and *jyotiṣmat* (1.136.3). But if t is found as d/n in the Sp, separation is made e.g., *kukúdmān* (10.8.2). However, if a stop is not turned into a voiced stop in the Sp before this suffix, then there would be no separation, for instance, *virúkmān* (6.49.5).

This treatment of the Pdk amounts to the fact that the suffix-*mat* is a *pada*-marker as far as the change of g to k is concerned. But it is not a *pada*-marker as for the change k to g or ṅ is concerned. Here the Pdk is in difficulty: should he separate or not ? He prefers not to separate.

Moreover, there is no independent form *viruk* found in the *RV*. The independent occurrence of a form sometimes, becomes the criterion for separation. Since in *hırīman* (10.105.7), *hirī-* is not found to be used independently, the form is kept without separation.

It is, however, interesting to note in this connection that the idea of the Pdk about *pada* and non-*pada* is exactly same as that of P. p 1.4.19:: *tasau matvarthe* tells us that a stem ending in t or s and followed by possessive secondary suffix is called *bha*. That is to say, it is a non-*pada* stem. Since it is a non *-pada* stem, t or s is not changed to *d/n or ḥ/ o* respectively, which is the main reason for calling a stem, *pada*. If a stem is called *pada* then *pada-sandhi*, for instance, elision of final consonant like n, voicing of consonants etc. is allowed. If the *pada- sandhi* s are not applied, the suffix is considered to be a *bha*-marker i.e., the stem preceding the suffix is not a *pada*.

The Pp of the *AV* and that of the *VS* show the same method of separation. According to Apr. IV.17: *matau* the suffix-*mat* is separated by an *avagraha*. No condition for a particular type of stem is mentioned here. The exceptions to this rule are further noted in IV.47: *na takāra-sakārābhyām* 'the suffix *-mat* and its variants are not separable after a stem which ends in either t or s.' Examples for the first rule supplied by the commentators are *madhu-mat (AV 1.34.3) and go-mat (AV 28.3.61)* and examples for the second rule to show non- separation of the suffix are *garutmān (AV 4.6.3) etc.*

The *VPr* presents the description precisely. According to *VPr V.8: tadvati taddhite nyāya -saṁhitaṁ cent* "if a derivation is followed by a secondary possessive suffix, the stem is separable, unless there is no *sandhi* according to the rules of grammar. Now, external *sandhi* can take place between finals and initials of a stem and a suffix respectively only when the stem is considered to be *pada* or in other words only when the suffix is a *pada* forming suffix. Thus, here the author of the *VPr* states the principles of separation clearly. The examples offered by Uvaṭa under this *sūtra* are *madhu -mat* for seperation and *marutvantam* for non- seperation.

DATA : *-mat A*

-a-mat

kanva-mantam (8.2.22)

-i-mat

anji -mántaḥ (5.57.5), abdi -mā́n (5.42.14), abhiṣṭi -mát (1.116.11), arci-mántā (10.61.15), avi-mā́n (4.2.5.), udani-mā́n (5.42.14), ṛṣṭi-mántaḥ (3.54.13), tviṣi-mat (3.31.12), tviṣi-matīm (5.63.6), tviṣi mate (1.55.5), tviṣi-mantaḥ (6.66.10), tviṣi-mān (2.22.2), dhúni-matīḥ (1.174.9), nidhi-mántam (2.39.1), nidhi-mát (10.59.2).

-ī -mat

taviṣi -mantam (5.58.1), vasī-mantam (10.20.6).

-u -mat

iṣu -mantaḥ (5.57.2), iṣu-mān (2.42.2), ṛbhu -mát (1.111.2), ṛbhu -mántam (3.52.6), ṛbhu -mántā (8.35.15), ṛbhu -mā́n (1.110.9), kratu-mát (6.47.31), kratu- mátā (10.59.1), krátu -mantā (1.183.2), krátu -mān (1.62.12), ketu -mantam (8.58.3), kṣu -mát (9.86.18), kṣu -mátaḥ (2.1.10), kṣu-máti (4.2.18), kṣu-mátī (10.11.3), kṣu-mátīḥ (10.2.6), kṣu-mántaḥ (1. 30.13), kṣu- mántam (2.4.8), gātu-mátyā (7.54.3), dā́nu- matyāḥ (5.68.5), dā́nu-mat (1.51.4), dyu -mát (1.74.9), dyu-mátaḥ (6.17.14), dyu- mátā (6.62.10), dyu-mátīm (6.38.1), dyu-máte (1.63.3), dyu-mántaḥ (5.12.4),dhenu-mátī (8.31.4), nadanu-mā́n (6.18.2), pitu-mát (1.101.1), bándhu-mantam (8.21.4), bhānu- mántam (5.1.11), harṣu -mántaḥ (8.16.4).

-ū -mat

vadhū -mataḥ (6.27.8)

-ṛ -mat

tváṣṭṛ -mān (6.52.11)

-o -mat

gó-mān (4.2.5), *gó-mantam* (1.83.4), *gó -mate* (9.77.3), *go-matī́m* (8.28.30), *gó -matīm* (8.6.23), *go-matīnām* (2.28.2), *go - matīḥ* (1.48.2) *gó -matī* (1.8.8), *gó-mat*i (1.92.14), *gó -matā* (7.72.1) *gó-mataḥ* (1.11.3), *gó-mat* (1.9.7),

-t/d -mat

kukút-mān (10.8.2)

DATA :- *mat* *B*

-ī - mat

hárīmān (10.105.7)

-c - mat

virúkmān (6.49.5)

-t - mat

divítmatā (1.26.2), *divıtmatī* (5.79.1), *vihútmatīnām* (1.134.6)

-s - mat

cákṣuṣmati (10.18.1), *jyótiṣmat* (1.136.3), *jyótiṣmatā* (7.78.1), *jyótiṣmatī* (1.46.6), *jyótiṣmatīm* (1.136.3) jyóiṣmantaḥ (9.113.9), *jyótiṣmantam* (3.23.3), *túviṣmantaḥ* (7.20.4), *túviṣmān* (1.55.1), barhıṣmatī (1.117.1), *barhıṣmān* (9.44.4), *barhıṣmate* (1.51.8), *mīhúṣmantaḥ* (6.50.12), *śociṣmān* (2.4.7), *havıṣmataḥ* (1.57.2), *havıṣmatā* (1.128.2).

II.1.2.b.6 *vat/vant*

The suffix *vat/vant* is an allomorph of *-mant/mat* which expresses possession. According to P *mat* and *vat*-forms are derived from fully inflected forms and the case-endings are dropped subsequently vide P2.4.71. This is implied by the *pada*-status of the stem. For instance, *pṛṣadvat*.

In the vedic language both *-mat* and *-vat* are in free variation. Both are found used after *a, i, u, ū,* and *ṛ*.. So, there is no fixed distribution of environments for these two suffixes, as it is so in the classical sanskrit, where *-mat* is found after voweis other than *a* and *ā*, and *-vat* after *a* and *ā*. In the *RV*, among consonats *ṇ, t, d, n, m, r,* and sibilant precede the suffix-vat. For example, *vṛṣaṇvantam* (1.100.16), *marútvān* (1.80.11), *śarádvān (1.181.6), ātmanvántam* (1.182.6), *samvátaḥ* (1.191.15), *svarvat* (1.173.1), *āśīrvān* (8.95.7), and *tápasvataḥ* (10.154.4).

So far as the analysis is concerned, the Pdk has separated this suffix after *a, ā, i, ī, u, ṛ,* and after stops other than *t* and *s*, e.g., *karṇa-vantaḥ* (10.71.7), *prajā́-vat* (1.113.17), *rayi- vataḥ* (6.68.5), *pátnī-vataḥ* (1.14.7), *viṣṇu- vantā* (8.35.14), *nṛ-vántaḥ* (7.41.3), *akṣaṇ-vān* (1.164.16), *pṛṣat- vat* (7.2.4) / Sp *pṛṣadvat* /, *pat-vat* (1.48.5) / Sp *padvat* /, *vanan-vataḥ* (8.1.31), *antáḥ-vatīḥ*, (3.55.5), *sam-vataḥ* (1.191.15) Sp *saṁvataḥ* /.

There are a few exceptional cases, where even though the above mentioned conditions are fulfilled, analysis is not shown. Such examples are *kakṣīvān* (1.126), *atṛṣṇuvantam* (4.19.3), *ṛghāvān* (1.152.2), *pavīravān* (10.60.3) etc. The reason behind this non-separation appears to be the non- availability of stems without *-vat*, which would have given a scope to the Pdk to think of stems like *kakṣī-, atṛṣṇu-, ṛghā-, pavīra-* and so on. In absence of any inflected forms of these stems, the Pdk leaves then unanalysed. Moreover, it is not an easy task to take any definite decision, because we come across forms like *pavīravān, pavīravi,* and *pavīravasya,* when it becomes difficult to take any decision whether the stem is *pavīra-*, or *pavi-* (plus two possessive suffixes, *-ra* and *-vat*). We have also two suffixes in *atṛṣṇuvantam*. It occurs only once in the *RV*. Naturally, the Pdk cannot take any decision about the stem and suffix. Similarly, in most of the other cases, simply because there is no way to come to a particular analysis, the Pdk leaves them unanalysed.

There arises a question : why are *n-stems-* when they do not drop their final *n-analysed* at all ? And secondly, even if they are analysed, how do they show *n* before a *pada*-forming suffix?

According to P *n* when it occurs at the end of *pada* is dropped. But when the actual forms are found with *n* in the *Samhitā* they are to be taken as exceptional cases. Probably the Pdk does not know that the dropping of *n* before a *pada* forming suffix is obligatory and therefore, he analysed these forms.

Here is another evidence to show how the Pdk represents a pre-pāṇian stage of grammar. According to him, it is not necessary that final ṇ or *n* should be dropped if they are followed by a *pada*-forming suffix. Whereas according to P VIII.2.7, a final *n* of a stem is elided before a *pada-* marking suffix. According to him *ṇ* or *n* of *vṛṣaṇvantam* (1.100.16), *ātmanvatībhiḥ* (1.116.3) etc. does not belong to the stem *vṛṣan-* or *ātman-*, but it belongs to the suffix *-vat*.[68]

The process in Pāṇinian system to get these forms is as follows :

vṛṣan + *matUP* (P V.2.94)

vṛṣan + *n* - *mat* (P VIII.2.16)

vṛṣa + *n* - *mat* (P VIII.2.7)

= *vṛṣa* + *n* + *vat* (P VIII.2.9)

= *vṛṣaṇvat* (P VIII.4.1-2)

P VIII.2.16 is not known to P VIII.2.9, so there is no difficulty in changing *m* to *v* by P VIII.2.9. We cannot get *n* to *ṇ* unless we adopt this process. The same ordering of rules will explain the derivation of the forms *ātmanvatībhiḥ* and so on. P also especially mentions *drumaṇvat* and *karmaṇvati, udanvat* and *rājanvat* which occur in the *Bhāṣya* also.

The Pdk thinks that this *n* belongs to the stem. In the case of *vṛṣaṇvatī* (8.68.18), etc., he does not restore the original dental nasal but puts the *avagraha* after the cerebral. But elsewhere the original sounds are restored, if they are cerebralised except in the case of suffixes. If a sound belonging to suffix is cerebralized, analysis is avoided. This is the reason why *-su* (the locative plural marker) is left unseparated when *s* has been retroflexed.

Why the Pdk has not restored the original sound in the *vṛṣaṇvat-etc.* is not clear. Moreover, if the stem *vṛṣan* is separated, its *n* should be dropped. This means that *vṛṣan* is not actually a *pada,* therefore the Pdk should have avoided the separation.

Moreover, the Pdk is aware of this particular grammatical rule that *n* coming at the end of a stem is elided when followed by a *pada*-marker. Because in the case of denominative suffix, we see that he has avoided analysis of *vṛṣaṇyati* (9.5.6), *ukṣaṇyantaḥ* (6.26.9), *dhiṣaṇyantaḥ* (4.21.6), and *brahmaṇyataḥ* (2.20.4) only because there has been no dropping of *ṇ* before *-ya*. Therefore, I see no reason why the Pdk attempted to give analysis of these forms. Otherwise, he is quite consistent in not separating *vat-* forms after *t* or *s* stems. Because in the Sp these two stops remain as they are without being changed to *d* or *u* or *r* which should have been done if these stems were *pada* s. Thus, the forms like *tapasvataḥ* (10.154.4), and *marutvān* (1.80.11) etc. are kept as they are. If *tapas- or marut-* had been *padas,* the forms should have been *tapovataḥ* and *marudvān* and so on as they are found in the case of *tapobhiḥ* (7.1.7), and *marudbhiḥ* (1.19.1). The analysis in that case would have definitely been like *tapaḥ- vataḥ* and *marut-vān* as it is so in *tapaḥ- bhiḥ* and *marut-bhiḥ*. It is interesting to note that P also does not consider stems ending in *t* and *s* as *padas* before the possessive suffix (P.1.4.19).

So the separation of *vṛṣan* and of *ātman* from *vat* is not justifiable. Or alternatively, just as P considers *ātman* and *vṛṣan* are *padas* so also the Pdk thinks they are *padas*. But here *n* is not dropped because they are exceptions. P also treats them as exceptional cases.[69]

Actually, if we check all the *data* it appears that there is no point in calling the stem *pada* before the suffix *mat* or *vat*. We have many counter examples. All these are counter examples where *n* before *vat* is retained. Moreover, *saṁ* is a *pada* before *vat* then we have *anusvāra* (see *mo'nusvāraḥ*) always. Since we have *anusvāra, saṁvataḥ* (1.191.15) is analysed as *sam-vataḥ*. Similarly *pṛṣadvat* is analysed as *prsat-vat* because *t* is changed to *d* by *pṛṣat* being a *pada*. Otherwise the *sandhi* (t to d) is not possible. These are the only cases where there is point in calling-*vat* a *pada*-forming suffix.

DATA : *-vat* A

-a - vat

áma - vatī (1.168.7), áma - vān (1.52.10), *áma - vantaḥ* (1.36.20), *ánna - vān* (10.117.2), *aśvá - vat* (1.48.12), *aśvá - vataḥ* (1.48.12) *áśva - vatā* (7.72.1), *áśva - vati* (1.83.1), *aśva - vatīḥ* (1.48.2) *aśva - vatīm* (10.97.7), *aśva - vate* (10.40.5), *aśva - vatyā* (1.30.17), *áśva - vantaḥ* (8.45.11), *áśva - vantam* (1.83.4), *ındra - vantā* (1.116.21), *iṣá - vān* (1.129.6), *ṛtá - vān* (2.24.7), ṛtvıya - vataḥ (8.8.13), *ṛtvıya - vatī* (8.12.10), *kárṇa - vantaḥ* (10.71.7), *kṛsaná - vataḥ* (1.126.4), *keśá - vantā* (10.105.5), *ghṛtá - vatī* (6.11.5), *ghṛtá - vantaḥ* (3.21.2), *ghṛtá - vantam* (1.34.10), *ghṛtá - vanti* (9.96.13) candrá - vatā (3.30.20), *caṣā́la - vantaḥ* (3.8.10), *dátra - vān* (6.50.8), *dā́na - vān* (8.32.12), *devá - vataḥ* (7.18.22), *devá - vantam* (6.47.10), *dyumná - vān* (5.28.4), *dhárma - vantā* (8.35.13), *dhitá - vānam* (3.27.2), *nī́la - van (8.19.31)*, *pastya - vān* (9.97.18), *bhága - vatī* (1.164.40), bhaṅgurá - vataḥ (7.104.7), *matsara - vān* (9.97.32), *mā́hina - vān* (3.39.4), *mitrāváruṇ - vantau* (8.35.13), *vāra - vantam* (1.27.1), *vayana - vat* (4.51.1), *śapha - vat* (3.39.6) *svá - vān* (1.35.10).,

-ā - vat

arvā - vátaḥ (3.37.11), *āmyā́ - vatīm* (1.112.20), *iḷiā - vān* (4.2.5), *iḷiā - vantaḥ* (10.94.10), *irā - vatīḥ* (5.69.2), *irā - vatīm* (5.63.6), *ilā - vatīm* (9.97.17), *omyā́ - vantam* (1.112.7), káśā - vatnā (8.25.24), *káśā́ - vatī* (8.68.18), *kṣapā́ - vān* (1.70.3), jā̃ - vataḥ (8.94.5), *tarṣyā́ - vān* (10.28.10), tvā̃ - vān (1.30.14), tvā̃ - vataḥ (1.91.8), *tṛṣyā - vataḥ* (7.103.3), *dákṣiṇā - vān* (10.107.5), *dákṣiṇā - vatī* (8.97.2), *dákṣiṇā - vate* (9.98.10), *dákṣiṇā - vantaḥ* (1.125.6), *daṁsanā - vān* (1.30.16), *dhānā - vantam* (3.43.4), *prahā́ - vān* (8.20.8), *prajā́ - vat* (1.113.17), *māyā - vān* (4.16.9), *mā́ - vataḥ* (1.17.2), *mehánā - vataḥ* (2.24.10), *vacanā́ sup back 30 - - vantaḥ* (9.68.1), *vapā́ - vantam* (6.2.5), *sīlamā - vatī* (10.75.8).

-i - vat

arci - vát (7.81.2), *ghṛ́ṇi - vān* (10.176.3), *jáni - vataḥ* (5.31.2), *jáni - vān* (5.44.7), *ni - vátaḥ* (3.20.10), *púrandhi - vān* (9.72.4), *rayi - vataḥ* (6.68.5).

-ī - vat

taviṣī - vān (10.105.3), *dhī́ - vataḥ - (8.92.11), dhī́ - vantaḥ* (7.83.8), *pátnī - vataḥ* (1.14.7), *vājinī - vān* (1.122.8), *vajinī - vati* (1.48.6), *śimī - vān* (1.100.13).

-u - vat

viṣṇu - vantā (8.35.14)

-ṛ - vat

nṛ - vántaḥ (7.41.3).

-ṇ (from n) - vat

akṣaṇ - vā́n (1.164.16), *akṣaṇ - vántaḥ* (10.71.7), *pūṣaṇ - vān* (1.82.6), *rómaṇ - vantu* (9.112.4), *vṛ́ṣaṇ - vantam* (1.100.16), *vṛ́ṣaṇ - vatī* (8.68.18).

-t - vat

pṛ́ṣat - vat (7.2.4)

-d (changed to *t*) *- vat*

ut - vátā (1.35.3), *ut - vátaḥ* (3.2.10), *dṛśát - vatyām* (3.23.4), *pat - vat* (1.48.5), *śarat - vān* (1.181.6).

-n - vat

aśman - vatī (10.53.8), *asthan - vantam* (1.164.4), *ātman - vántam* (1.182.5), *ātman - vátībhiḥ* (1.116.3), *udan - vátā* (5.83.7), *udan - vátīḥ* (7.50.4), *óman - vantam* (10.39.9), dā́man - vantaḥ (5.79.4), *dadhan - vataḥ* (6.48.18), *vánan - vataḥ* (8.1.31).

-m - vat

sam - vátaḥ (1.191.15).

r - vat

antáḥ - vatīḥ (3.55.5), *svaḥ - vat* (1.173.1).

-s - vat

āśī́ḥ - vān (8.95.7), *āśī́ḥ - vantaḥ* (1.23.1).

DATA : *-vat* B

-ā - vat

pávīravān (10.60.3).

-ā - vat

etā́vān (10.90.3), *etā́vatā* (10.132.4), *etā́vatī* (10.125.8), *etā́vataḥ* (8.7.15), *etā́vat* (5.79.10), *etā́vantam* (7.100.1), *ṛ́ghāvat* (10.27.3), *ṛghā - vān* (1.152.2), *tā́vān* (1.108.2), *tā́vat* (6.23.6), *gopā́vat* (7.60.8), *pā́rāvatam* (8.100.6).

-ī - vat

īvat (5.49.5), *kakṣī́vantam* (1.18.1), *kakṣī́vān* (1.126.2), *kakṣī́vantaḥ* (1.126.4), *kakṣī́vate* (1.51.13), *kakṣī́vatā* (1.117.6), *kakṣī́vataḥ* (10.25.10), *vṛcī́vataḥ* (6.27.5), *hṛṣī́vantaḥ* (2.31.1), *hṛṣī́vataḥ* (1.127.6).

-t - vat

niyútvatā (1.134.1), *datváte* (1.189.5), *niyútvān* (1.135.4), *niyútvataḥ* (2.41.3), *marútvate* (1.142.12), *marútvantam* (1.23.7), *marútvān* (1.80.11), *marútvatīḥ* (1.80.4), *marútvatī* (2.30.8), *marútvantaḥ* (9.109.25), *marútvantā* (8.35.13), *marútvataḥ* (5.42.6), *haritvatā* (10.112.3).

-s - vat

áṅgirasvantau (8.34.14), *aṅgirasvān* (2.11.20), *aṅgirasvat* (1.31.17), *ánasvantā* (5.27.1), *ánasvantaḥ* (1.126.5), *ápnasvatīm* (1.44.1), *ápnasvatīsu* (1.127.6), *indrasvantam* (4.37.5), *ū́rjasvatīḥ* (10.169.1), *ójasvantaḥ* (8.76.4), *ójastvantam* (8.76.5), *énasvantam* (8.18.12), *tápasvataḥ* (10.154.4), *tápasvān* (6.5.4), *távasvān* (9.97.46), *dāsvataḥ* (5.9.2), *dāsvān* (6.33.1), *dasvān* (4.2.7), *draviṇasvantaḥ* (9.85.1), *násvantaḥ* (7.88.6), *nábhasvatīḥ* (8.25.6), *námasvantā* (5.62.5), *namasvat* (1.185.3), *namasvantaḥ* (1.164.8), *namasvān* (1.171.2), *páyasvān* (1.23.23), *pīvasvatīḥ* (10.169.1), *prápasvatīḥ* (3.6.3), *bhā́svatī* (1.92.7), *bhāsvantam* (10.37.8), *mánasvān* (1.12.1), *máhasvān* (10.130.4), *mahisvantam* (7.68.5), *yasasvān* (10.20.9), *yáśasvati* (10.38.1), *yáśasvatī* (10.11.3), *yáśasvataḥ* (1.9.6), *yáśasvatīḥ* (1.79.1), *réknasvatī* (10.63.16), *rábhasvān* (10.3.7), *rodhasvatīh*

(1.38.11), *rabhasvataḥ* (1.9.6), *vyacasvantā* (6.25.6), *vyacasvatīḥ* (2.3.5), *vayasvataḥ* (2.24.15), *sarasvān* (10.66.5), *sarasvatī* (1.3.10), *sarasvati* (1.164.49), *hárasvatī* (2.23.6).

II.1.2.b.7 *-van*

Van is used in the *RV* as secondary suffix also. It is not as *frequently* used as other secondary suffixes. It is an allomorph of *vat/vant*. This suffix is found added to *a, ā, i, ī, d* and *r* stems in the *RV*.

Normally, the Pdk has separated this suffix from all stems excepting a few *a* - stems and *r* - stems.

As we would see in the case of the demoninative *ya* and as we have seen in the case of possessive *-vat*, long vowels have been shortened, e.g., *ṛtāyate* is analysed as *ṛta - yate, ṛtāvān* as *ṛta - vān* and so on. Similarly, before *-van* long vowels coming in the Sp are shortened in the Pp. For example.

ṛtāvā (1.77.1), as *ṛta - vā -*, *ṛṇāvānam* (1.169.7), as *ṛṇa - vānam, arātīvā* (1.147.4), as *arāti-vā*; but,

śruṣṭīvā́naḥ as *śruṣṭī - vā́naḥ* without shortening of *ī* to i.

śruṣṭī-is not made śruṣṭi-before *-vānaḥ* because the stem itself ends in a long vowel i.e., *ī*. Naturally, when a particular stem ends in a long vowel is not shortened in the Pp.

We have seen in the section dealing with *-vat* that although *ṛtāvan* is analysed as ṛta - vān, prajāvān is not analysed as *praja - vān*. The reason is that the stem is *prajā-* here and therefore, the analysis is offered like *prajā - vān*.

But why is such a method adopted at all?

It is very difficult to find any reason for this. The Pdk adopted some method and followed it through out.

Let us suppose that *prajāvān* is analysed as *praja - vān*. This would lead people to think that this lengthening is metrical or morphological and the stem is *praja-*. Similarly, let us suppose that *ṛtāvān* is analysed by the Pdk as *ṛtā - vān*. This, as well, would lead people to think that the stem here is ṛtā-. To avoid such confusions the Pdk might have adopted such a method and lengthening is removed.[70]

But still the question remains why has this suffix not been separated from *ā* - stem and *r* - stems?

So far the question of separation of this suffix after *ā* is concerned, it can be said that he does not consider the suffix as secondary suffix in these cases. In the compounds *somapā́vā* (5.40.4), *ṛṇayā́vā* (1.87.4), etc. the suffix - *van* is not added after the compounding of *soma-* and *-pā-* or, *ṛṇa-* with *yā-*; rather it is added with *pā-* and *yā-* first and after that *pāvan* and *yāvan* - are compounded with *soma-* and *ṛṇa-* respectively. Therefore, in these cases, because the suffix is directly added to the roots *pā* and *yā*, it is a primary suffix and that is why the Pdk does not separate it.

P also takes this suffix as a primary suffix and prescribes it after roots which end in *ā* (P III.2.74) : *āto manin-kvanib-vanipasca:* 'The affixes *manIN, KvanIP, vanIP* and VIC come in the Chandas, after verbs which end in long *ā* when a case-inflected word or an *upasarga* is in composition'[71]).

Svadhā - van (5.3.2), and *svadā - van* (8.50.5), are doubtful cases. But because, *svadhā* is found as independent stem with regular inflexion of *ā*-stem as *svadhā* (1.165.6), *svadhayā* (1.64.4). etc., the Pdk has separated it considering *-van* as the secondary suffix. Moreover, we come across forms like *svadhāvantaḥ* (7.37.2), *svadhāvān* (1.95.1), etc., formed out of secondary suffix - *vant,* together with its weak form *-vn* found in *svadhāvne* (5.32.10). All this clearly indicates that the form *svadhā-* was quite common in use as a noun after which *-vant* and *-van* are used as secondary suffixes.

The separation of *svadāvan* is done analogically after *svadhā - van*, as *svadā - van;* because, there is no stem like *svadā-* in the *RV* used independently which might give the Pdk a clue of separating *svadāvan* into *svadā-van*. It can be mentioned in this connection that no Say.-commentary of *RV* 8.50.5 is available. A commentary given in the foot-note of the VSM-edition of the *RV* paraphrases *svadāvan* as *āsvādanakuśala,* evidently from root *svad* 'to taste'.

In this case *svadā-* will be regular noun derived from/*svad-ā* if the above paraphrase is accepted. But, *sva - dā* like *sva - dhā* seems more probable. The accent is same as that of *svadhāvan.*

APrIV..17 and *VPr V*.8 take note of the analysis of this suffix, under the name of *taddhita* suffix with the meaning 'possessing'.

There is a *n* to *r* variation in the feminine forms. *Van* becomes *varī* in the feminine gender. We have, in the *RV*, forms like *ṛtā́varīm* (5.80.1), *vibhāvarī* (1.30.20), *sunṛtāvari* (4.52.4), *svadhā́varī* (7.31.7) and so on. In all these cases *-varī* has been separated and the long vowel has been shortened as usual.

Varī is found in the primary formation also. For example, *bhūridā́varīm* (8.2.21), *evayā́varī* (6.48.12), and so on. In none of these forms *-varī* is separated. They are analysed as *bhuri - dā́varīm, eva -yā́varī* and so on. This indicates that the Pdk does not consider *-varī* as a secondary suffix in these cases.

DATA : *-van*

-a - van

ṛtá - vā (1.77.1), *ṛtá - vānaḥ* (2.24.7), *ṛtá - vānam* (3.2.13), *ṛ́ta - vānā* (1.136.4), *ṛtá - vānā* (5.65.2), *ṛṇa - vā* (10.34.10), *ṛṇa - vā́nam*

(1.169.7), maghá - vā (1.32.3), maghá - vānaḥ (1.73.5), maghá - vānam (3.30.22), magha - vānā (1.184.5), mágha - van (1.82.1), saha - vā (3.49.3), saha - vānam (10.178.1),

-ā - van

savasā - van (1.62.11), *sahasā - van* (5.20.4), *svadā - van* (8.50.5), *svadhā - van* (5.3.2), *svadhā - vaḥ* (1.144.7).[72]

-i - van

amati - vā́ (8.19.26), *arāti - vā* (1.147.4), *dīdi - vaḥ* (1.12.5), *hari - vaḥ* (1.3.6).

-ī - van

śruṣṭī - vānaḥ (1.45.2), *śruṣṭī - vā́nam* (1.119.1), *taviṣī - vaḥ* (4.20.7), *śacī - vaḥ* (8.2.28).

-t (from *d*) *- van*

samat - vā (6.18.2).

DATA : *- vna (van) A*

ṛtá - vne (8.103.8), *svadhā́ - vne* (5.32.10).

DATA : *-varī A*

-a - varī

ṛtá - varīm (5.80.1), *ṛtá - varīḥ* (3.56.5), *ṛtá - varīḥ* (3.33.5), *ṛtá - varī* (3.61.6), *ṛta - vari* (2.41.18).

-ā - varī

vibhā - vari (1.30.20), *sunṛtā - vari* (4.52.4), *svadhā́varī iti svadhā - varī* (7.31.7).

DATA : *-van B*

-ā - van

dadhi - krā́vāṇam (7.44.3), agra - yā́vā (10.70.2), *ṛṇa - yā́vā* (1.87.4), *kratu - prā́vā* (10.100.11), *dadhi - krā́vā* (4.40.2), *pūrva - yā́vā* (3.34.2), *prataḥ - yā́vānam (10.40.1), prātaḥ - yā́vānaḥ* (1.144.13), *prātaḥ - yā́vānā* (2.39.2), *bhūri - dā́vā* (9.87.4), *vāja - dā́vā* (8.2.34), *vasu - dā́vā* (2.27.12), *śubham - yāvā* (5.61.13), *śubham - yā́vānaḥ* (1.89.7), *śubhra - yāvānā* (8.26.19), *suta - pāvan* (6.24.9), *soma - pāvan* (1.55.7), *soma - pā́vā* (5.40.4).

-t - van

sánitvaḥ (8.81.8), *sánitva - bhiḥ* (10.36.9).

-n - van

ındhanva - bhiḥ (2.34.5)[73]

-r - van

átharvaṇaḥ (6.16.14), *átharvaṇā* (10.21.5), *átharvaṇi* (8.9.7), *átharvāṇaḥ* (9.11.2).

DATA : *-vna* (from *van*) B

dadhi - krā́vnaḥ (4.39.2), *eva - yā́vnaḥ* (2.34.11), *prātaḥ - yā́vnaḥ* (1.45.9), *bhuri - dā́vnaḥ* (2.27.17), *vāja - dā́vnām* (1.17.4), *suta - pā́vne* (1.5.5), *suta - pā́vnaḥ* (8.2.7), *su - dā́vne* (1.76.3), *soma - pā́vnaḥ* (8.78.7), *soma - pā́vnām* (1.30.11), *soma - pā́v*ne (3.31.1), *sahasra - dā́vnām* (1.17.5).

DATA : *-varī B*

eva - yā́varī (6.48.12), *talpa - śī́varīḥ* (7.55.8), *bhuri - dā́varīm* (8.2.21), *sa - yā́varī* (7.31.8), *sa - yā́varīḥ* (1.84.10).

II.1.2.b.8 -*vin*

The adjectival forms made with -*vin* are not many. In the *RV* there are only ten such forms. The meaning of this suffix is the same as that of the suffix -*in*. It is always accented. The forms which are under discussion show that the suffix is used after *ā*, *t* and *s*- stems in the *RV*, though in later language it is found with other stems also (e.g., *ātmanvin*-, *vāgvin*- etc.). The Pdk has separated the suffix after *ā* (except a few) and *t* (<*d*), but not after *s*, like other secondary suffixes.[74]

The forms with -*ā*-stems are *māyā-vinam*,[75] *māyāvinā*,[76] *stukāvinām*,[77] *aṣṭrāvī*.[78] In all these cases -*vin* is separated in the Pp. We have only one form with a *t* - stem i.e., *dhṛṣadvinaḥ* (5.52.2), which has been analysed as *dhṛṣat* - *vinaḥ* dissolving the *sandhi* (*d to t*).

The *sandhi*, here, is peculiar in the sense that it is unlike *marutvān*. We seldom get this external *sandhi* of an unaspirated unvoiced stop plus a suffix with initial *v*-.[79] But since there has been a change like *t* to *d*, the Pdk has explained that by way of separating the stem and the suffix.[80]

There are a few forms of *ubhaya*-, *dvaya*-, and *advaya*-, which show lengthening to final *a* to *ā* before the suffix -*vin*, like *ubhayāvin* (10.87.3), *dvayāvinaḥ* (1.42.4), *advayāvī* (7.56.18) and so on. These forms are not analysed by the Pdk. I think this lengthening of the final syllables of the stems might be the cause of not separating -*vin* from the stems.[81]

The suffix -*vin* is not separated after *s*-stems, because *s*-stems are not pada before -*vin*. Had they been *pada*, the forms should have been *namovinaḥ* instead of what is actually found i.e., *namosvinaḥ* (1.36.7) etc. and in that case the Pdk would have analysed them as *namaḥ* - *vinaḥ* etc.[82]

DATA : -*vin* *A*

ā - vin

māyā - vinaḥ (9.83.3), *māyā - vinā* (10.24.4), *māyā - vinam* (2.11.9), *stuka - vinām* (8.74.13), *aṣṭrā - ví* (10.102.8).

-t - vin

dhṛṣat - vinaḥ (5.52.2).

DATA : *-vin* B

-a - (ā) - vin

advyāvinaḥ (1.159.3), *advayāvinam* (3.2.15), *advayāvī́* (7.56.18), *ubhayāvin* (10.87.3), *ubhayāvinam* (8.1.2), *dvayāvinaḥ* (1.42.4).

-s - vin

tarasvinaḥ (8.97.12), *tarasvinam* (8.97.10), *namasvinaḥ* (1.36.7), *namasvinam* (1.166.2), *rakṣasvinaḥ* (1.12.5), *rakṣasvinam* (7.94.12).

II.1.2.b.9 *va*

The suffix *-va* forms few adjectives, for instance, *arṇaváḥ* (1.55.2), 'billowy', *ajakāvám*[83] *'having the disease ajakā'*, *śraddhivám* (10.125.4), 'credible' etc.

The Pdk has analysed the forms *ajakāvá* and śraddhivá as *ajaka-vam*, and *śraddhi - vám* respectively. But nowhere he has separated *arṇavá-*. It is interesting to note that when the Pdk has recognised this suffix, P does not take notice of it. One more thing to be noted in this connecting that in the case of *arṇavá-* the Pdk has reason to separate *arṇa-*. because *arṇa-* occurs as an independent word in the *RV*. Still he does not separate. But *śraddhi-* does not occurs as an independent word in the *RV*. Still he separates. We can say that the Pdk must have realised that *śraddhi* is connected with *śraddhā*. Therefore, he separated.

Probably, he failed to see the connection between *arṇa-* and *arṇavá-*. So he left it unanalysed.

DATA : *-va* *A*

-ā - va

ajakā - vām̥ (7.50.1).

-i - va

sraddhi - vám (10.125.4).

DATA : *-va* *B*

-a - va

arṇaváḥ (1.55.2), *arṇavám* (1.19.7), *arṇavásya* (10.67.12).

II.1.2.c.1 -ka

Probably the suffix *-ka* was used to form adjectives expressive of connection. But very often it is added to substantives without affecting the meaning. On the other hand it is used as a diminutive suffix also. For its significant use we can cite *-antaka* -'meaning an end', from *anta* 'end', *asmāka-* 'our', from *asma-* 'us', *mamaka-* 'my', from *mama,* 'of me', *antika-* 'near' from *anti* 'before'.

In the following forms the suffix does not change the meaning of substantives:

dūraka- 'distant' from *dūra* 'far', *vamraka-* 'ant' from *vamra* 'ant', *avikā-* 'ewe' from *avi* 'sheep'.

The diminutive sense of the suffix can be seen in *arbhaka-* 'small', *kumāraka-* 'little boy', *pādaka-* 'little foot', *putraka-* 'little son'.

Sometimes a contemptuous meaning is expressed as in *anyaka*-'other' from *anya, alakam* 'in vain' from *alam* 'enough'.

The Pdk does not analyse any of these derivatives.

In fact, the Pdk knows many stems to which the suffix - *ka* is added as those stems have occurred several times independently in the *RV*. Therefore, he should have analysed at least those forms where he was sure about their stem part and suffix - parts. But most probably, he has avoided analysis since he does not find any evidence fo *pada-sandhi* to prove that *-ka* is a *pada*- forming suffix.

DATA : *-ka*

-a - ka

ántakam (1.112.6), *anyaké (8.21.18), arbhakā́ḥ* (8.30.1), *arbhakám* (1.114.7), *arbhakā́saḥ* (7.33.6), *armaké* (1.133.3), *iyattakā́ḥ* (1.191.15), *udakám* (1.161.8), *udakā́t* (10.166.5), *úlūkhalaka* (1.28.5), *kanī́nakā́ḥ* (10.40.9), *kumārakā́ḥ* (8.30.1), *Kuṣumbhakā́ḥ* (1.191.15), *tāvakébhyaḥ* (1.94.11), *tryambakam* (7.59.12), *dūrakám* (10.58.1), *dūraké* (1.22.4), *dévakam* (7.18.20), *putrakā́ḥ* (8.69.8), *pra-vartamānakā́ḥ* (1.191.16), *pādakau* (8.33.19), *mámaksya* (1.131.11), *mámakāya* (1.34.6), *maryakā́m* (5.2.5), *māmakā́ḥ* (10.159.1), *māmakám* (10.17.14), *māmakā́nām* (10.103.10), *viśvakaḥ* (8.86.1), *viśvakāya* (1.116.23), *viṣpuliṅgakā́ḥ* (1.191.12), *vīrakā́ḥ* (8.91.2), *syā́vakam* (8.3.12), *syā́vake* (8.4.2), *sā́yakam* (1.32.3), *somakā́ḥ* (4.15.9), *hárimanyu - sāyakaḥ* (10.96.3).

-ā - ka

nabhā̄ka - vát (8.40.4)

-i-ka

antikám (10.161.2), *avikā́* (1.126.7), *ciccikā́ḥ* (10.146.2), *tarikā́* (10.59.9).

-u - ka

úlūkaḥ (10.165.4), *tri - kadrukébhiḥ* (10.14.16), *niṣkám* (2.33.10), *niṣkā́m* (1.126.2), *peruké* (6.33.9), *su - niṣkā́ḥ* (4.37.4).

-ū - ka

jāgarūke iti (3.54.7), *maṇḍū́kaḥ* (7.103.4), *maṇḍū́kāḥ* (7.103.1).

II.1.2.c.2 *-ta*

A few forms like *tata-*, *-trita-*, *dvita-*, and *muhūrta-* show that there is a secondary value of the suffix *-ta* apart from the primary suffix *-ta*.

These forms are not analysed by the Pdk.

Either he does not know this suffix or since he does not find any evidence of *pada-sandhi* to prove that - *ta* is *pada-* forming suffix, he does not analyse these forms.

DATA : *-ta B*

-a - ta

tátaḥ (1.83.5), *tatáḥ* (9.112.3).

-i - ta

tritáḥ (1.52.5), *tritám* (2.34.10), *tritásya* (2.11.20), *tritā́ya* (2.11.19), *tritéṣu* (6.44.23), *dvitā́* (1.37.9).

-r - ta

muhūrtám (3.33.5).

II.1.2.c.3 *-tana/ - tna*

We find only two stems to which the suffix *-tana* and its syncopated form *-tna* are added. They are : *nū-* 'now' and *pra-* 'before'. About thirty forms derived with the help of these suffixes are found in the *RV*. Nowhere in the Pp this suffix is found separated form the stems.

Probably the Pdk does not know this secondary suffix. Moreover, to establish separation he does not find forms which show changes due to the *pada-* forming suffix.

DATA : *-tana B*

nū́tanaiḥ (1.1.2), *nū́tanam* (5.55.8), *nū́tanasya* (2.20.4), *nū́tanā* (2.11.6), *nū́tanāni* (3.1.20), *nū́tanābhiḥ* (6.44.13), *nū́tanāya* (3.47.5), *nū́tanāsaḥ* (6.21.5), *nū́tanena* (1.118.11), *nū́tanebhiḥ* (3.32.13).

DATA : *-tna B*

nūtnā́ḥ (7.18.20), *pratna* (6.39.5), *pratnáḥ* (1.117.1), *pratnám* (1.36.4), *pratnásya* (1.30.9), *pratnā́* (1.105.5), *pratnā́t* (9.73.6), *pratnā́ni* (1.108.5), *pratnā́bhiḥ* (8.13.24), *pratnā́m* (8.95.5), *pratnā́ya* (1.61.2), *pratnā́saḥ* (4.2.16), *pratnéna* (6.21.7), *pratnébhiḥ* (9.52.2), *pratnéṣu* (8.13.20).

II.1.2.c.4 *-tā*

In the *RV* there are about two dozen abstract nouns derived by suffixing *-tā* to nouns and adjectives. For example,

dīnátā (7.89.3), *nagnátā* (10.33.2), etc.

The accent is on the final syllable of the base.

The Pdk does not separate this suffix from any base. Probably, since he does not find any evidence of *pada- sandhi* to show that *tā* is a *pada-* forming suffix, he leaves the forms unanalysed.

DATA : *-tā*

-a - tā

avīrátā (7.1.11), *kavyátā* (1.96.2), *dīnátā* (7.89.3), *devátā* (1.22.5), *nagnátā* (10.33.2), *puruṣátā* (7.57.4), *mamátā* (6.10.2), *sarátā* (2.3.6).

-i - tā

su - sanitā (10.36.9).

u - tā

bandhútā (3.60.1), *vasútā* (6.1.13).

-o - tā

agótāyai (3.16.5).

II.1.2.c.5 *-tvatā*

The two abstract noun markers are pleonastically combined in the suffix *-tvatā*. We find two forms made of this suffix in the *RV*. They are *puruṣatvátā* (4.54.3), and *iṣitatvátā* (10.132.2). None of these is analysed by the Pdk.

Here the Pdk seems to be in the doubt the nature of the suffix. He knows *-tva*. But a combination of *-tva* and *-tā* puts him in confusion. He prefers not to analyse them.[84]

DATA : *-tvatā*

-a - tvatā

iṣitatvátā (10.132.2), *puruṣatvátā* (4.54.3).

II.1.2.c.6 *-tha*

The suffix *-tha* which denotes general numerical sense is found after two stems only in the *RV*. The stems are : *saptan* and *kati-*. The available forms are : *saptátham* (1.164.15), *saptáthasya* (10.99.2), *saptáthī* (7.36.6) and *katitháḥ* (10.61.18).

None of these forms is analysed in the Pp.

Probably this suffix is also not known to the Pdk. Moreover, we cannot say with certainty that the Pdk knows the numeral stems ending in *n* like *saptan*. This means that he may not know that the suffix *-tha* is a *pada-* forming suffix. Therefore, he prefers not to separate it.

DATA : *-tha*

saptátham (1.164.15), *saptáthasya* (10.99.2), *satáthī* (7.36.6), *katitháḥ* (10.61.18).

II.1.2.c.7 *-na*

The secondary suffix *-na* can be found in the forms *straiṇāni*, from *strī*, 'woman', *purāṇaḥ* from *purā* 'before', *viṣuṇaḥ* from *viṣu* 'apart', and *samānaḥ* from *sama* 'equal'. IN *straiṇa-* there is *vṛddhi* of *ī* of *strī-*, whereas in *samāna* there is lengthening of the final syllable. *Purāṇa-* and *viṣuṇa-* do not involve any change in the stem.

None of these forms is separated in the Pp. This indicates that the Pdk does not know this suffix. One can understand that the Pdk has some difficulties in analysing *straiṇa-* and *samāna-* but one fails to understand why he should not analyse *purāṇa-* and *viṣuṇa-* since both these forms are known to him. Probably, since there is no evidence of *-pada-sandhi* to prove that *-na* is a *pada-* forming suffix, he avoids analysis.

DATA : *-na B*

-a - na

samānáḥ (1.113.3).

-ā - na

purāṇáṇ (4.18.1), purāṇám (3.54.9).

-ī - na

straiṇāni (10.95.15).

-u - na

viṣuṇaḥ (5.34.6).

II.1.2.c.8 *-nī*

This suffix is used to form the feminine forms of *pati-* 'lord', *paruṣa-* 'knotty', and of many adjectives in *-ta* denoting colours.

For example, *patnī-*, and *rohinī-* from *pati-* and *rohita-*.

In none of these forms derived with the suffix *-nī*, the Pdk separates *-nī*.

Nī is not known as the secondary suffix to the Indian grammarians. P 4.1.33 adds *ṅīP* to *pati* and *i* of *pati* is replaced by *n*. In case of *rohiṇī* (4.1.39), *-ta* is changed to *-na* and *ṅīP* is added. Therefore, since *nī* is not a separate suffix, the question of separation does not arise.[85]

DATA : *-nī B*

pátnī (1.22.9), *páruṣṇī* (8.74.15), *páruṣṇīm* (4.22.2), *páruṣṇīṣu* (8.93.13), *páruṣṇyām* (5.52.9), *páliknīḥ* (5.2.4), *róhiṇyā* (8.101.13), *syénī* (1.140.9), *háriṇī* (9.70.7).

II.1.2.c.9 *-bha*

There are a few stems, mostly animal names, which are derived by this suffix. For instance, *vṛṣabha-* 'bull', *gardabha-* 'donkey', *rāsabha-* 'id', *sarabha-*[86] 'locust'.

It can be seen from the treatment of the Pdk that the Pdk is not aware of this suffix. He leaves all these cases unanalysed taking them to be single lexical items.

It is interesting to note that P· does not mention *-bha* as a secondary suffix in the forms listed below. However, P prescribes this suffix after *tundi, vali,* and *vati.*[87] *P* also records *kambha* and *sambha.*[88] But none of the Ṛgvedic forms derived with this suffix is recorded by P.

DATA : *-bha*

ṛṣabhám (10.166.1), *ṛṣabhásya* (6.28.6), *ṛṣabhā́saḥ* (6.16.47), *gardabhám* (1.29.5), *gardabhā́nām* (8.56.3), *vṛṣabháḥ* (1.31.5), *vṛṣabhám* (1.9.4), *vṛṣabhásya* (1.69.6), *vṛṣabhā* (5.63.3), *vṛṣabhā́ḥ* (10.94.3), *vṛṣabhā́nām* (8.53.1), *vṛṣabhā́ni* (2.16.6), *vṛṣabhā́ya* (1.51.15), *vṛṣabhā́saḥ* (1.177.2).

II.1.2.c.10 *-min*

In the *RV, ṛc-* is the only stem after which *-min* is added as a secondary suffix. However, inspite of the fact that the palatal has changed to velar before *-min,* which indicates that it is a *pada-* forming suffix, the Pdk has not separated it in the *Pada*-text for reason unknown.

Min is rarely used as a secondary suffix. For instance, *iṣminaḥ* (1.87.6), which may be derived by a adding the suffix *-min.* According to Sāy it is derived as follows :

/ *iṣA* -'to go' + *maK* + *inI.*

It means *gatimantaḥ* i.e., possessing *gati-* 'motion'. Therefore, according to *Sāy* there is no suffix like *-min* in *iṣminaḥ*.

But the form *ṛgmin* is a clear instance of the suffix *-min*. Still the Pdk does not separate it. In fact, the Pdk knows forms of the stem *ṛc-* like *ṛcā* (1.164.39), *ṛcaḥ* (1.36.11), etc. He also knows the change of *c* to *k* to *g* in *ṛgbhiḥ*. Therefore, it is not clear why he does not analyse *ṛgmin-* as *ṛk - min*.

P describes *-min* as a secondary suffix in connection with the stem *vāc-* only. Thus, the form *ṛgmin-* remains unaccounted for in the *Aṣṭā*. P 5.2.124 takes care of only vāgmin-, but not of *ṛgmin-*. The *ṚPr* remains silent in this matter. The other two *Prs, VPr* and *APr,* also do not record this form in the list of words which are left unanalysed in the *Pada*-text.

This suffix is never found as a primary suffix in the *RV*.

DATA : -min

ṛgmınaḥ (9.86.46), *ṛgmī́* (1.100.4), *ṛgmı- bhiḥ* (1.100.4), *ismınaḥ* (1.87.6).

II.1.2.c.11 *-mna*

Mna forms neuter nouns, for instance, *nṛmna* (9.70.3).[89] There are only four stems-out of which two are prefixes - after which this suffix is added. They are *ni, su, dyu-* and *nṛ-*. The available forms from *ni* are *nimnám* (1.30.2), *nimné* (9.69.7), etc.; from *su* are *sumnám* (1.43.4), *sumnā́* (1.38.3), etc.; from *dyu* are *dyumnám* (1.9.8), *ṛta - dyumna* (9.113.4), etc. and from *nṛ-* are *nṛmṇám* (1.80.3), *tveṣá - nṛmṇaḥ* (10.120.1).

None of the forms made of this suffix is analysed by the Pdk. All the four stems after which this suffix appears are known to him. Moreover, these stems are found used independently also. Therefore, it appears that this suffix is not known to the Pdk. This is not known to P either. According tc the Pdk these are single lexical items. That is why he does not offer any analysis.

DATA : *-mna*

-i - mna

nimnám (1.30.2), *nimné* (9.69.7), *nimnaiḥ* (10.78.5),

-u - mna

dyumnám (1.9.8), *dyumnásya* (5.7.6), *dyumnā́* (4.4.9), *dyumnā́ni* (1.122.12), *dyumnā́ya* (6.60.11), *dyumnī́* (1.36.8), *dyumné* (9.61.29), *dyumnéna* (1.48.1), *dyumnébhiḥ* (1.91.2), *dyumnéṣu* (3.37.7), *dyumnáiḥ* (1.78.1), *sumnám* (1.43.4), *sumnásya* (8.49.9), *sumnā́* (1.38.3), *sumnā́ni* (1.130.9), *sumnā́ya* (1.130.6), *sumné* (2.25.5), *sumnéna* (5.73.6), *sumnébhiḥ* (5.75.6), *sumnéṣu* (5.53.1).

-ṛ - mna

nṛmnám (1.80.3), *nṛmṇásya* (1.53.6), *nṛmṇā́* (1.67.2), *nṛmṇā́ni* (4.22.9), *nṛmnā́ya* (7.30.1), *nṛmṇáiḥ* (6.66.2).

II.1.2.c.12 *-yin*

It is a very rare secondary suffix. There is only one form in the *RV* which is derived with this suffix. For instance, *marāyī́* (10.60.4).

The Pdk has not analysed this form. Firstly, since the suffix *-yin* begins with *y* he may consider this suffix as a *non-pada*-marker. Secondly, and most probably, this suffix is not known to him and therefore, he might have left the form unanalysed. P also does not record this suffix.

II.1.2.c.13 *-ra*

In the *RV*, there are four prepositions and a dozen nominal stems to which this suffix is added. The prepositions are : *adha, apa, ava* and *upa*. The suffix -ra when added to these prepositions makes them adjectives of comparison. These adjectives mean 'lower', 'later', 'lower' and 'upper' respectively.

The secondary derivatives of this suffix with nouns are in most of the cases adjectival in sense. They have the sense 'belonging to' or connected with. For instance, *dhūmra-* 'gray' from *dhūma-*; *aśrīra-* 'ugly' from *'aśrī'* etc. In the case of *āgnīdhra-* 'belonging to the fire- kindler' from *agnīdh-*. It may be connected with *i* also, for instance, *medhira-* 'wise' from *medhā-* 'wisdom', and *rathira* 'riding in car' from *tatha* 'chariot'.

But, in the Pp nowhere *-ra* is separated from the base. Perhaps, for this reason that the bases preceding *-ra* i.e., *dhūm-, asrī, medhi-, rathi-* etc. are never used freely. So if the Pdk analyses *dhūmra* as *dhūm - ra, rathira* as *rathi - ra* and so on, there will be no confusion about the actual stems. That is why he does not attempt any analysis. Moreover, he has no evidence of *padasandhi* to prove that *-ra* is a *pada*-forming suffix.

DATA : *-ra*

-a - ra

ádharaḥ (1.32.9), *áparaḥ* (1.74.8), *ávaraḥ* (1.163.9), *úparaḥ* (10.27.20), *pataṅgaráḥ* (4.40.2), *purva - aparám* (10.85.18), *śámbaram* (1.51.6).

-i - ra

rathirá (3.1.17), *médhira* (1.32.2).

ī -ra

aśrīrám (6.28.6)

-u -ra

asuráḥ (1.35.7), *aṁhuráḥ* (10.5.6).

-d - ra

samudráḥ (1.30.3).

-dh - ra

ágnidhrāt (2.36.4).

II.1.2.c.14 *-la*

Few adjectives are formed with this suffix. It has the same sense as *-ra*. Sometimes in interchanges with *-ra*. The change of *r* to *l* is generally taken to be as a later development.

A few forms are of doubtful etymology. They are *mudgala-*, *pippala-*, *lāṅgala-*, *udumbala-* and *tilvila-*. In other cases derivation is clear. For example, *kapila-* 'brown', *bahula-* 'abundant', *madhula-* 'sweet', *śíśula-* 'little child', *vṛṣala-* 'little man' etc.

None of these forms is analysed. This gives the impression that the suffix is not known to the Pdk. Moreover, the Pdk has no evidence of *pada-sandhi* to prove that -la is a *paḏa*-forming suffix.

DATA : *-la*

-a - la

múdgalaḥ (10.102.5), *pippalam* (1.164.20).

-i - la

kapilám (10.27.16), *pipilaḥ* (10.16.6).

-u - la

madhulā́ (1.191.10), *bahuláḥ* (2.1.12)

-ū - la

śiśū́lāḥ (10.87.6).

II.1.2.c.15 *-vana*

This suffix occurs in the forms *pravaṇé* (1.52.5) and *nivanā́-iva* (10.40.9).[90] Neither of these forms is analysed by the Pdk. Most probably the Pdk does not know this suffix. It is not recorded by P even. The Pdk does not know the analysis of these words. So, probably, he treats them as single lexical items whose derivation is unknown. Similarly, he does not know the derivation of *vāgvana-*. Although the Pdk sees the *pada- sandhi* in *vāgvana-*, he does not want to commit himself with regard to *vana*.

II.1.2.c.16 *-śa*

There are nine stems in the *RV* to which this suffix is added. It forms adjectives.[91] While forming the substantives it does not change the original meaning. While forming adjectives it expresses possessive sense. The only substantive in the *RV* is *aṅkuśa-* 'hook'. The adjectives are : *etaśaḥ* 'variegated', *yuvaśa-* 'youthful', etc.

But none of these forms is analysed in the Pp. The Pdk may not know this suffix. Moreover, he does not find any evidence of *pada-sandhi* to prove that -śa is a *pada*-forming suffix.

DATA : *-śa*

-a - śa

árvaśaḥ (10.92.6), *etaśáḥ* (7.63.2), *kalaśaḥ* (3.32.15), *turváśaḥ* (7.18.6), *turváśam* (1.36.18), *turváśāya* (5.31.8), *turváśe* (1.47.7), *yuvaśā́* (1.161.3), *romaśám* (8.31.9), *lopāśáḥ* (10.28.4), *lomaśā́* (1.126.7).

-u - śa

aṅkuśaḥ (8.17.10), *aṅkuśam* (10.44.9).

II.1.3. ADVERBIAL SUFFIXES

There are several adverbial suffixes in the *RV* which form a number of advers. Out of these the following suffixes begin with a consonant:

-tas -tāt, -tra or *-trā, -thā, -dam, -dā, -dānīm, -dhā, -va* or *vam, -vat,* and *-śas.*

They are *pada*-markers.

The treatment of these suffixes by the Pdk is discussed here in three groups such as a., b., and c. Under a. comes the suffix *-śas* which is separated in the Pp without any exception; under b. come *-trā, -thā, -dānīm, -dhā,* and *-vat* which are separated with exceptions and under c. come *-tas, -tāt, -dam, dā,* and *va/vam* which are not separated in any case. It is observed that the Pdk avoids separation of these adverbial suffixes from a pronominal base. This seems to be a general principle. He adopted this principle probably because before a suffix is prominal base suffers a lot in morphophonemic change.

Let us discuss his treatment taking the suffixes group by group.

II.1.3.a.1 *-śas*

The suffix *śas* forms adverbs of measure or manner with a distributive sense. It is added to numerals or words implying number. For example, *sahasraśaḥ* (8.34.15) 'by thousands' etc. The stems to which this suffix is found added in the *RV* are :

sahasra- 'thousand', *śreṇi-* 'row', *ṛtu-* 'season', *deva-* 'god', *parva-* 'joint', and *manman-* 'desire'.

The Pdk has analysed all the forms with this suffix and has separated the suffix from the bases. This indicates that the Pdk takes this suffix to be a *pada-marker*. Moreover, he has ground to call it a *pada*-forming suffix. The word *parvaśaḥ* (1.57.6), is derived from *parvan-* and the *n* of *parvan-* is dropped because *parvan-* is a *pada* before the suffix *-śa*. Similarly, *manmaśaḥ* is derived from *manman-* and the *n* of *manaman-* is elided by virtue of *manman-* being a *pada* before *-śa*. The elision of *n* in both these cases is not possible unless the stems are termed as *padas* and this fact seems to be known to the Pdk.

II.1.3.b.1 *-trā*

The suffix *-tra or -trā* is mostly added to pronominal stems or stems allied to pronouns. It has a local sense. For instance, *atra* 'Here', *satrā* 'in one place', *devatrā* 'among the gods' etc.

All the forms with the suffix *trā* excepting *satrā́* (1.57.6), are analysed by the Pdk. But no form of *-tra* is analysed. Most probably, the reason is this that *-tra* is not added to a nominal stem. It is always added to a pronominal stem. Secondly, it is distinguished from *-trā* by the position of accent. In forms with *-trā* the accent is always on the suffix and in the forms with *-tra* the accent is on the stem.

Satrā́ is the only form with *-trā* which is not analysed by the Pdk. Since *sa-* of *satrā* is found only in compounds in the sense of 'together' and since it has got no independent usage, the Pdk leaves *satrā́* unanalysed.

Thus, it appears that this is the general principle of the Pdk to avoid separation of a suffix from a pronominal base and from a base which has not got an independent use.

DATA : *-trā A*

asma-trā́ (1.132.2), *dakṣiṇa - trā́* (6.18.9), *deva - trā́* (1.50.10), *pāka*

- *trā́* (8.18.15), *puru - trā́* (1.32.7), *puruṣa - trā́* (3.33.8), *bahu - trā́* (10.164.2).

DATA : *-tra/trā B*

anyátra (7.59.5), *ubhayátra* (3.53.5), *kútra* (5.7.2), *tátra* (1.9.6), *yátra* (1.13.5), *viśvatra* (10.61.25), *satrā́* (1.57.6).

II.1.3.b.2 *-thā*

This suffix forms quite a number of adverbs of manner. It is chiefly added to pronominal stems. It is also added to a nominal stem. For instance, *áthā* 'then', *ṛtuthā́* 'regularly' etc.

The Pdk separates this suffix only from a nominal and a pronominal adjectival stem and does not separate it from a purely pronominal stem, like *a-*, *ka-*, *ta-*, etc. Here too the reason for not separating *athā*, *kathā*, *tathā* and the like, seems to be the same i.e., non-availability of the free occurrence of these pronominal stems. Hence, the Pdk is not sure of the derivation of these forms and therefore, he does not commit himself to any particular etymology.

But this is not the case with *anyáthā* (4.32.8). The Pdk has separated other pronominal adjectives from *-thā*. For instance, *viśváthā* (1.141.9), is analysed as *viśvá - thā*. Similarly, *prūváthā* (1.80.16), is analysed as *pūrvá - thā*. Therefore, one finds no reason why *anyáthā* should not be analysed as *anyá - thā*. Here the Pdk is inconsistent.

DATA : *-thā A*

ūrdhvá - thā (10.23.1), *ṛtu - thā́* (1.162.19), *evá - thā* (8.24.15), *pūrvá - thā* (1.80.16), *pratná - thā* (1.96.1), *viśvá -thā* (1.141.9).

DATA : *-thā B*

áthā (2.3.9)[92], *anyáthā* (4.32.8), *itthā́* (1.2.6), *kathā́* (1.41.7),[93] *táthā* (1.30.12).

II.1.3.b.3 *-dānīm*

It is an extended form of the adverbial suffix *-dā*. There are three forms made with this suffix in the *RV*. They are *idā́nīm* (1.35.7), *tadā́nīm* (10.129.1), and *viśvadā́nīm* (1.164.40). Out of these, only *viśvadā́nīm* is analysed as *viśva - dā́nīm* in the Pp and the other two words are left as they are. Here too we find that Pdk separates this suffix only after a pronominal adjective and avoids separation after purely pronominal base.

II.1.3.b.4 *-dhā*

The suffix *-dhā* forms many adverbs in the *RV*. It is added to numerals or to a stem of cognate sense. It expresses the meaning 'so many times' or ways'. For instance, *dvidhā* 'two fold', *bahudhā́* 'in many ways' etc.

Curiously enough, the Pdk has analysed only the form *caturdhā́* (4.35.2), as *catuḥ - dhā́* and none of the forms made with suffix is analysed by him. When he has separated *-dhā* from *catur-* in *caturdhā́* there is no reason why he should not separate it from *dvi-*, *tri-*, *kati-*, *puru-*, *bahu-*, and *viśva-*. He may have some difficulty in separating *-dhā* in *tredhā́* (1.22.17) and in *śaśvadhā́* (3.33.7), because neither *tre-* nor *śaśva-* has any independent use in the *RV*. But in other cases cited above he has absolutely no such difficulty. All of those stems are used independently in the *RV* and hence the Pdk knows them very well. Moreover, we have seen under II.1.3.b.2 that *-thā* is separated from *viśva-*. Why not then *viśvádhā*?

In any case we cannot justify the non-separation of *-dhā* from the stems which are clearly known to the Pdk. Here again the Pdk is inconsistent in his treatment.

DATA : *-dhā A*

catuḥ - dhā́ (4.35.2)

DATA : *-dhā B*

katidhā́ (1.31.2), *trıdhā* (1.117.24), *tredhā́* (1.22.17), *dvıdhā* (10.56.6), *purudhā́* (1.122.2) *bahudhā́* (1.164.46), *viśvádhā* (1.141.6), *śaśvadhā́* (3.33.7).

II.1.3.b.5 *-vat*

This adverbical suffix[94] is added to substantives and adjectives. It means 'like'. For example, *'aṅgirasvát* 'like Angiras', *pratnavát* 'as of old', and so on. This suffix is added in the *RV* to the following stems :

angiras-, *manu-*, *manus-*, *purāṇa-* and *pratna-*.

The Pdk has separated this suffix from all the stems excepting *aṅgiras-* and *manus-*. In *aṅgirasvát* and *manuṣvát*, *-vat* is not separated because *aṅgiras-* and *manus-* are not *padas*. Had they been *padas* the forms would have been *ā́ngirovat* and **manurvat*. Since the *pada- sandhi* i.e., *s* to *r* to *u* has not taken place, *aṅgiras-* and *manus-* are not *padas*. Hence, they are not analysed by the Pdk. It is to be noted in this connection that Kātyāyana recorded these two forms and rightly wanted them to be included under the definition of *bha* in a *Vārttika* under P 1.4.18.

DATA : *-vat A*

purāṇa - vát (8.40.6), *pūrva - vát* (1.31.17), *pratna - vát* (1.124.9).

DATA : *-vat B*

aṅgirasvát (1.31.17), *manuṣvát* (1.31.17).

II.1.3.c.1 *-tas*

There are several adverbial forms made with this adverbial suffix in the *RV*. This suffix expresses the ablative sense 'from'. It is added to nominal, pronominal, adjectival and prepositional stems. For instance, *átaḥ*, 'hence', *hṛttáḥ* 'from the heart', *sarvátaḥ*, 'from all sides', *abhıtaḥ*, 'around', and so on.

None of the forms derived with this suffix is analysed by the Pdk. Why the Pdk should not analyse these forms is not clear. In fact, if we exclude pronominal stems, all other nominal, adjectival and prepositional stems after which *-tas* is added are known to the Pdk. All of them are used independently in the *RV*. Therefore, why should he not separate *-tas* from all these stems excepting pronominal stems? Moreover, the Pdk has evidence to show that the suffix *-tas* is a *pada*-marker. In the words *hṛttáḥ* and *pattáḥ* the *d* of *hṛd-* and *pad-* is changed to *t* before *t*. This change is a *pada* change. Therefore, *hṛd-* and *pad-* are *padas* and the *Pdk* should have separated them. This probably implies that the Pdk may not aware of this suffix as a *pada-* forming suffix.

DATA : *-tas*

agratáḥ (10.90.7), *átaḥ* (1.6.9), *anyátaḥ* (1.4.5), *ántitaḥ* (1.179.5), *abhıtaḥ* (1.53.3), *amútaḥ* (1.179.4), *itáḥ* (1.6.9), *ubhayátaḥ* (5.81.4), *kútaḥ* (1.136.1), *tátaḥ* (1.83.5), *dakṣiṇataḥ* (1.95.6), *pattáḥ* (10.27.1), *patsutáḥ* (8.43.6)[95], *sarvátaḥ* (2.43.2), *hṛttáḥ* (10.11.6),

II.1.3.c.2 *-tāt*

The suffix *-tāt*[96] expresses an ablative or a locative sense. It is added to adverbial case-forms and adverbial or adnominal prepositions. For example *ārā́ttāt* 'from near' *adhástāt* 'below', *purástāt* 'in or from the front' etc.

The Pdk does not analyse any of the forms made with this suffix. The reason seems to be this that either he has no idea about this suffix as a *pada-* forming suffix or he is not sure of the derivation of these words. He is likely to be confused about the derivation of the forms like - *uttarā́ttāt* where the part preceding *-tāt* is already an inflected from i.e., *uttarāt*. Therefore, he leaves them unanalysed.

DATA : *-tāt*

adhástāt (3.30.16), *avástāt* (3.22.3), *ārā́ttāt* (1.167.9), *uttarā́ttāt* (10.27.15), *údaktāt* (7.72.5), *parástāt* (3.22.3), *parākā́ttāt* (8.92.27), *paścā́ttāt* (7.72.5), *purástāt* (1.123.10).

II.1.3.c.3 *-dam*

There is only one word in the *RV* which shows this suffix. It is *sádam* (1.27.3), meaning 'always'.

The Pdk does not analyse this word. Most probably, the Pdk does not know this suffix and therefore he leaves it unanalysed considering it a single lexical item.

II.1.3.c.4 *-dā*

The suffix *-dā* forms adverb of time. It is added mostly to pronominal stem. In the *RV* we come across the following forms made with this suffix:

-idā́ (4.10.5), 'now'. *kadā́* (1.25.5) 'when', *yadā́* (1.82.1) 'at what time', *sadā́* (1.12.2) 'always'.

None of these forms is analysed by the Pdk because mostly the stems are pronominal stems. Moreover, the Pdk may not know the derivation of these forms.

II.1.3.c.5 *-va/vam*

These suffixes express similarity of manner. There are in all three forms in the *RV* which are derived with these suffix. Two are with *-va* and one with *-vam*. The forms are *-iva* 'like'[97], *evá* (1.1.3) and *evám* (10.151.3) 'thus'.

The Pdk might take these forms to be single lexical items and therefore he might have left them unanalysed.

II.1.4 *-ya* (Denominative)

There are 89 denominative forms in the *RV*. In all these forms except a few *-ya* is separated by *avagraha,* which means that this suffix is a *pada*-marker unlike P's concept of the term. According to P, *n*-stems only before the denominative suffix *y* are called *pada*[98], because the final *n* of n-stem is elided before this suffix[99]. *N* cannot be elided unless it occurs in the final position of a *pada*. For example, the denominative from *vṛṣan* will be *vṛṣāyáte*[99a] (5.55.2)/*vṛṣa - yáte* / and so on. The peculiarity of the Pp in analysing these forms lies in the shortening the long vowels of the Sp before - *ya,* e.g., *ṛtayaté* / *ṛta - yate* /; *vṛṣāyate* / *vṛṣa - yate* /; *devayaté* / *deva - yaté*/; *sakhīyaté* / *sakhi - yaté* /; *śatrūyatā́m* / *śatru - yatā́m* /; etc. Therefore, we find that the Pdk here violates his usual rule i.e. normally he does not separate forms which show lengthening. We must assume that the principles which the Pdk applies in the case of the case-terminations are not sometimes adapted in the case of analysing the integrated forms, *samāsa,* secondary suffixes etc. For instance, in *prajā́bhiḥ* - *bhiḥ* is not separated even though *-bhiḥ* is pada-forming suffix; not in *prajā́vān, vān* is separated from *prajā́-*. This is because the formation of *prajā́vān*[99b] is quite different from that of *prajā́bhiḥ*. In *prajā́vān, prajā* is a *pada* (P 1.4.14) whereas in *prajā́bhiḥ, prajā* is a *pada* (P 1.4.17). Before the formative suffixes he indicates the morpheme-boundary, but not so before the case-terminations and lengthening.

Similarly, in *nā́satyābhyām* (1.20.3) or in *devānām* (1.22.9) neither *-bhyām* nor *-nām* is separated, even though they are *pada*-forming suffixes. In the domain of case- suffixes when we have morphological lengthening etc. the Pdk avoids separation. Whereas, in the case of secondary suffixes i.e. denominatives in *ya* even when we have morphological lengthening separation is given by him and the stem form is shortened. For instance, *ṛtāyate* is analysed as *ṛta - yate, putrīyántaḥ* as *putri - yántaḥ*. In case of *putrīyanti,* the original stem i.e., *putra* is not restored although, the stem-form is shortened. This type of division in the case of *adhvarīyatā́m / adhvari - yatā́m /* has led K.P. Jog[100] to assuming a hypothetical stem **adhvari-*, in addition to already known stem *adhvara-* meaning sacrifice. His hypothesis demands rethinking. JOG has solely relied upon the mention of a form *adhvari* in the *RPr* 9.16. and this has led him to a rash conclusion. Similarly, in forms like *putrīyántaḥ / putri - yántaḥ/* he assumes a stem *putri- in addition to the stem *putra* in the same sense "even against Pāṇini's *Sutra 'na cchandasy aputrasya!"* *Putri-* is also mentioned in *RPr*9.16. But a close and comparative observation of *RPr* 7-9 reveals that the mentioning of a particular form and its not mentioning do not indicate the original form of the stem. The author of the *RPr* records the forms which occurs in the *Pada*-text and indicates certain changes which these forms undergo in certain environments. The author of the *RPr* simply records the forms which show lengthening either initially, medially, or finally in the Sp when the lengthening is not due to the combination of similar vowels. Moreover, he does not distinguish lengthening caused by morphological environment like *ṛtāyate* etc, from the metrical lengthening like *bhavā* (prs.Imp; 2nd sg. of *bhū* 'to be'). He puts all these cases in the same catagory. In both these cases there is *pluti,* according to the *RPr.*[100a] Moreover, it is a kind of *saṁdhi* in *ṛtāyate* or *bhavā* known as *sāmavaśa - saṁdhi*[100b]. It is a *sandhi-* as the author of the *RPr* says - because the Pdk has separated *putrīyántaḥ as purti- yantah* or *adhvarīyási* as *adhvari - yasi.* It is also called pluti of *i* to *ī*. His purpose is served by just recording these forms. He never takes into account the derivation of the forms. Neither thus he questions the treatment of the *Pdk,* nor does the justify these by way of a dialogue or reasoning. Therefore, so far the case of derivation is concerned, we cannot solely rely either upon the *RPr* or on the Pp. As far as the determination of stem is concerned we cannot take it for granted that whatever preceds the *avagraha*-sign is the original stem. Pdk's analysis is not a stem-suffix analysis. He simply provides us with oblique-stems. It can be seen in the analysis of *rā́jabhiḥ* (1.20.5), *rā́jabhyaḥ* (1.139.7), *kármabhiḥ* (3.36.1), *kármasu* (8.38.1) etc. that the stems preceding - *bhiḥ, -bhyām* and *-su* are *rāja-* and *karma-* and not *rājan-* and *karman-* which are original. Therefore, I see no reason in postulating stems like **adhvari-* or *putri-* simply because the Pdk has separated *adhvari* from *adhvarīyati* or *putri* from *purtīyati.*[101]

JOG remarks : "In the whole of the *Ṛgveda,* there is not a single instance - besides *putrīya-* (and *adhvarīya-* this is doubt) of a denominative derived from stems with a at the end that has changed to long *ī* according to *Pāṇini* 7.4.33." But the form *rathīyantīva* can be brought to this notice. This form belongs to the same type i.e., *rathīya- ratha-* denominative *-ya*. To my mind these forms i.e., *putrīyá-, adhvarīyá-,* and *rathīyá-* are obviously from *putra, adhvara* and ratha. I feel it is unnecessary to postulate the stems like *putri-* etc. as JOG does.

What I feel is the Pdk has analysed these three denominative forms after the analogy of *janīyá-* (where we have both *jani-* and *jana-*).[101a]

Now, following the pattern of analysing *janīyá-* as *jani - yá* or *kavī-ya* as *kavi - ya,* the Pdk applies the same analysis to *adhvarīyá-, rathīyá-* and *putrīyá*. In great majority of the cases, the Pdk analyses those stems which he finds to be used independently in the *RV*. But neither *putri-* nor *rathi-,* nor *adhvari-* is found used independently. Therefore, it is clear that the Pdk by his analysis like *adhvari -yá,* or *putri - yá* or *rathiya-* does not intend to say that *ahvari-, *putri- and *rathi- are the stems.

If at all there is any possibility, for considering that *adhvari, putri* and *rathi* are the stems, this can only be possible by assuming dropping of *n* in **avarin, *putrin* and **rathin*. N can be elided here because these are *pada*.[102] The lengthening if *i* to *ī* can be taken as metrical lengthening which is always made short in the Pp. But this analysis is not tenable for semantic reason. If we adapt this analysis the *putriyati* will mean 'he desires to have a person who has a son'.

Another explanation could be that the Pdk gives the middle stage in the derivation of these forms under discussion. In that case he thinks that the final *a* of the stem *putra* or *adhvara* or *ratha* is first changed to *i* and after that by usual process the short *i* becomes long *ī*. But we cannot say with certainty that the Pdk knows the middle stage. However, we may say that P's derivation makes use of such stage, (See P 7.4.33; 7.4.25).

There is still another point which attracts our attention. This denominative *-ya* is not separated after *ṇ, r* and *s*. the reason for not analysing *vṛṣaṇyati* and *namasyati* is quite clear. In these cases *-yati* cannot be considered as *pada*-marker. Because, had it been so, there should have been elision of *ṇ* from *vṛṣaṇyati* and substitution of *u* for in *namasyati*. But since these changes are not applied, *-yati* cannot be taken to be a *pada- marker*. So the Pdk cannot separated *vṛṣaṇyati* as *vṛṣaṇ - yati*. He avoids to analyse because he is not sure whether the form is derived from the stem *vṛṣan* or *vṛṣa*. Both these forms occurs in the *RV*. Similarly, if *-yati* in *namasyati* would have been a *pada*-marker, the form should have been *namoyati*. Therefore, since it retains *s* before *-yati, yati* cannot be considered here as the *pada*-forming suffix. This is why the Pdk keeps the forms of this type as they are.

Similarly, *r*-stems are not analysed because this analysis will change *r* to *visarga*. Therefore, here *ya* is not considered as a *pada-* forming suffix. It appears that *r* to *ḥ* change, according to the Pdk, requires *padāntatva* rather than *avasāna* 'pause'. The following are the cases of *r*- stems which are not analysed before *ya:*

ryántaḥ, adhvaryántā, ratharyataḥ, ratharyati, ratharyási, vithuryati, saparayátah, śratharyáti.

RPr does not say any thing about this except recording forms which show lengthening. APr IV.29 phrases a rule that 'a suffix commencing with *y* and preceded by a vowel in desideratives and denominatives and desiderative adjectives' is separated in the Pp. VPr V.10 presents the fact more briefly. It tells us that a suffix beginning with *y* which turns a nominal stem into a root when it is preceded by a vowel is liable to be separated by the Pdk.

DATA A

-a - ya

dama - yán (6.47.16), *maha - yaté* (7.32.19), *yuṣma - yantīḥ* (2.39.8), *vasna - yántā* (6.47.21), *deva - yán* (2.26.1), *devayántaḥ* (1.6.6), *ṛta - yántiḥ* (9.94.2), *sumn - yántaḥ* (8.7.11), *śarma - yántyā* (9.41.6), *vṛṣa - yate* (5.55.2), *vṛjina - yántam* (10.27.1), *vāja - yántam* (5.31.1), *deva - yaté* (1.15.12), *kṛpa - yátaḥ* (8.46.16), *ṛta - yaté* (1.90.6), *iṣa - yaté* (6.16.25), *aśva - yaté* (6.45.26), *agha - yáti* (1.131.7), *ajira - yate* (8.14.10), *ádeva - yantam* (2.26.1), *amitra - yántam* (1.131.7), *kanūka - yántiḥ* (1.132.7), *agha - yaté* (6.51.6), *agha - yatáḥ* (1.91.8), *deva - yántam* (1.40.7), *kṣema - yántaḥ* (4.33.10).

-ā - ya

dhiyā-yate (9.15.2), *tvā - yatā́* (6.40.3), *tvā - yantaḥ* (7.18.12), *sanā - yaté* (1.62.13), *bhandanā - yateḥ* (9.85.2), *pṛtanā - yántam* (1.169.7), *candanā - yatáḥ* (9.85.2).

-i - ya

putri - yántaḥ (7.96.4), *adhvari - yatā́m* (1.23.16), *kavi - yán* (9.94.1), *jani - yántaḥ* (4.17.16), *sakhi - yaté* (1.28.1), *sakhi - yataḥ*

(1.131.5), *śrudhi - yatáḥ* (6.67.3), *rayi - yán* (3.62.2), *anni - yate* (4.2.7), *arāti - yatáḥ* (1.91.1).

-ī - ya

taviṣī - yántaḥ (5.85.4).

-u - ya

pitu - yantáḥ (10.142.2), *aṅku - yántam* (6.15.17), *gātu - yán* (1.52.8), *kratu - yánti* (4.24.4), *ṛju - yátam* (1.89.2), *sukratu - yase* (10.122.6), *śatru - yántam* (7.20.3), *śatru - yatā́m* (1.33.15).

-ḥ - ya

vadhaḥ - yántīm (1.161.9).

DATA B

-ṇ - ya

ukṣaṇyántaḥ (6.26.9), *dhiṣaṇyántaḥ* (4.21.6), *brahmaṇyatáḥ* (2.20.4), *vṛṣaṇyati* (9.5.6), *vṛṣaṇyā́bhyaḥ* (9.19.5).

-r - ya

ajūryántaḥ (3.46.1), *adhvaryántā* (1.181.1), *ratharyataḥ* (8.101.2), *ratharyati* (9.3.5), *ratharyási* (10.37.3), *vithuryati* (10.77.4), *saparyátaḥ* (1.83.3), *śratharyáti* (10.77.4).

-s - ya

namasyáti (1.36.19), *makhasyáse* (9.61.27), *manasyasi* (8.45.31), *vanuṣyáti* (7.82.1), *vanuṣyán* (6.6.6), *vanuṣyā́t* (6.5.4).

DATA C

śámāye / śam - āye / 3.1.1

śamāyate / *śam* - *āyate* / 8.86.5[103]

II.1.5. PERFECT PARTICIPLE SUFFIX : *-vāṁs*

It can be seen from the classified data that the suffix *-vāṁs* is separated only after a short vowel i.e., after *a, i, u,* and *ṛ*. Nowhere it is separated after a long vowel or a consonant. Again, when this suffix is found with weak grade of ablaut i.e., as *-uṣ*, it is never separated except in one case by confusion and this is *susuvuṣaḥ* (10.94.14) where the separation is shown as *susu* - *vuṣaḥ*, as if, *-vusaḥ* is the suffix. Actually, the form is derived from republication of root *su* plus weak form of *-vas* i.e., *us*. The *v* between *u* of *susu* and *u* of *us* is a glide. According to P, *u* of *susu* is substituted by *uv*.[104]

Now, to what should this *v* belong, to the suffix *-us* to the stem *susu-*? According to P it belongs to *susu-*thus resulting into a stem-part *susuv-*. But I think, the Pdk takes this *v* to belong to the suffix. In that case *us* together with *v* is no longer a *svarādi* suffix i.e., a non-*pada*-marker. But, it becomes *vyañjanādi*.

Therefore, the Pdk following the general rule separated *susu* from *-vus*. Another reason why he may have given this analysis is that he has a form *susumān* (10.3.1) which is analysed as *susu* - *mān*. This gives him a base *susu-* on the analogy of which he might have separated *susuvuṣaḥ* as *susu* - *vuṣaḥ*.

Now, the question is how *-vāṁs* can be separated at all if it is a primary suffix. If this is the case, it is the only primary suffix which has been separated. There is no point in separating a primary suffix, because a primary suffix is not a *pada*- forming suffix.

It appears to me that the Pdk might have taken this suffix as a secondary suffix after the analogy of the possessive suffix *-vat*, because both the suffixes gives *-vān* in nominative singular and both begin with *-v*. There is probably stronger ground to assume that the Pdk considers *-vāṁs* to be a secondary suffix. We find a few forms derived from republicated verb-roots extended with short *i* in the *RV*. For instance,

papiḥ (6.23.4), *babhriḥ* (6.23.4), *dadiḥ* (6.23.4), *papriḥ* (1.52.3), *paprim* (1.91.21), *papriṇā* (2.23.10), *vayiḥ* (5.73.7), and *vavriḥ* (5.19.1). These forms are found used independently as action nouns. This might have given the idea to the Pdk that *-vāṁs* has been added to the stems *papi* and *yayi* in *papivān* and *yayivān.*

If we check the Pp of the other *Vedas*, we find that the Pp of the *TS* is the only Pp which presents an imporved picture. Since this Pp does not ananlyse this suffix, it indicates that by the time of this Pp, the idea of calling *-vāṁs* a primary suffix must have taken root. P also discribes it as a primary suffix.[105] But the Pp of the *AV* and *VS* treats this suffix in the same way as it is done by the Pdk of the *RV*. The *APr* IV.35-7 deals with the separation of this suffix.[106] So does *VPr* V.11. For the three rules of *APr*, the *VPr* gives only one, but covers all the aspects and conditions for the analysis of this suffix.[107]

Now, if the Pdk considers *-vāṁs* as a secondary suffix, why does he not separate it after a long vowel or a consonant? The reason so far the question of long vowel is concerned is that, generally, the Pdk avoids separation after a long vowel. Secondly, he does not find any independent use of these forms ending in long vowels, as he finds it in the case of forms ending in short *i*. In order to introduce separation after a short vowel it is not necessary that all forms should be attested and used independently. For example, he finds *papi-* used independently but not *tasthi*. So, what he has done is to build up a pattern and the examples are grouped according to that pattern. So, he assumes that *tasthi* belongs to the pattern of *papi* and separates it accordingly.

It can be seen in the treatment of case-endings that no *pada*-forming suffix is analysed or separated from a base ending in a long vowel. Because, according to the Pdk long vowel stems are not *prāti-padikas*. The same principle he applies here.

But what about non-separation after a consonant? What we find is that other secondary and case suffixes are separated after consonantal bases also. For instance, *marutsu* as *marut - su*, *marudbhiḥ* as *marut - bhiḥ* and so on. So, the Pdk should have separated here also.

The answer to this question is that with the exception of *cikit* there is no noun derived from reublicated roots ending in a consonant which has got independent occurrence in the *RV*. As far as cikitvas is concerned the Pdk refrains from separation because the separation would involve the question of changing *t* to *d*. In fact, nowhere *k*, or *t*, or *p* is changed to *g*, *d*, or *b* respectively before the suffix - *vāṁs* which is the essential test to call a suffix a *pada*-marker after a consonantal base. For this obvious reason the Pdk does not give any analysis of these forms. Since the *k* to *susukvāṁsaḥ* , *rurukvān* etc. remains as *k*, *t* o *cikitvāṁsaḥ* does not become *d*, and *p* of *susupvāṁsaḥ* does not change to *b*, and since neither *susuk* nor *ruruk*, nor *susup* is found used independently the Pdk cannot separate - *vāṁs* in all these forms. Therefore, he assumes that this suffix is not to be separated after consonants.

But all these speculations are made by just considering that the Pdk takes this suffix as a secondary suffix. In fact, it is a primary suffix, which was taken by him as a secondary suffix beginning with *v* like *-vat*, *-van* etc. There is no point in justifying the Pdk's treatment of this suffix by speculating the history of this suffix as NAWATHE[108] has done, when the character of this suffix in all the forms separated by the Pdk is primary and not secondary. This was realised by the Pdk of the *TS* and therefore, he did no separate this suffix in his Pp.

DATA : *vāṁs A*

-a - vāṁs

sasa - vā́ṁsaḥ (4.8.6), *sasa - vā́ṁsam* (3.34.8), *sasa - vā́n* (3.22.1),

-i - vāṁs

avatasthi - vā́ṁsam (8.96.4), *ātasthi - vā́ṁsam* (1.116.5), *ātasthi - vā́ṁsaḥ* (5.47.2),

āpapti - vā́n (1.73.8), *āpapri - vā́n* (1.73.8), *āpapri - vā́ṁsam* (1.186.1), *ā́proṣi - vān* (8.60.10), *ārari - vā́n* (1.147.4), *īyi - vā́ṁsam* (3.9.4), *upapapti - vā́ṁsam* (9.85.11), *oki - vā́ṁsā* (6.59.3), *tasthi - vā́n* (5.85.5), *tasthi - vā́ṁsam* (1.17.4), *tasthi - vā́ṁsā* (1.108.1), *tasthi - vā́ṁsaḥ* (1.33.15), *dīdi - vā́n* (2.9.1), *dīdi - vā́ṁsam* (2.2.11), *dīdi - vā́ṁsā* (10.106.3), *papi - vā́n* (1.61.7), *papi - vā́ṁsam* (3.43.5), *papi - vā́ṁsā* (1.108.13), *yayi - vā́n* (9.15.6), *papti - vā́ṁsaḥ* (1.107.20), *pareyi - vā́ṁsam* (10.14.1), *pīpi - vā́ṁsam* (5.76.1), *pepi - vā́n* (5.76.1), *prajajñi - vā́n* (3.2.11), *rari - vā́n* (1.138.4), *vavri - vā́ṁsam* (2.14.2),

-u - vāṁs

jūju - vā́n (4.11.4), *juju - vā́ṁsam* (5.31.11), *tastu - vā́ṁsaḥ* (1.89.8), *susu - vā́ṁsaḥ* (1.167.9), *sūsu - vā́ṁsam* (1.167.9), *susu - vā́ṁsā* (7.93.2), *suśru - vā́n* (10.71.5), *suśru - vāṁsā* (7.70.5), *susu - vā́ṁsam* (8.32.21).

-ṛ -vāṁs

cakṛ - vā́n (5.29.14), *cakṛ - vā́ṁsam* (6.17.13), *cakṛ - vā́ṁsaḥ* (1.161.4), *jāgṛ - vā́ṁsam* (8.5.36), *jāgṛ - vā́ṁsaḥ* (1.22.21), *jāgṛ - vā́ṁsā* (1.136.3), *dadṛ - vāṁsaḥ* (4.1.14), *pasṛ - vā́ṁsaḥ* (8.1.15), *mamṛ - vā́n* (1.116.3), *mamṛ - vā́ṁsam* (10.39.9).

DATA : *-vāṁs B*

-ī - vāṁs

jigīvā́n (2.12.4), *jigīvā́ṁsaḥ* (2.18.8), *bibhīvā́n* (10.105.3), *sam - jigīvā́n* (3.15.4).

-k - vāṁs

ririkvā́ṁsaḥ (1.72.5), *rurukvā́n* (1.149.3), *vivikvā́n* (7.67.3), *susukvā́n* (1.69.1), *susukvā́ṁsaḥ* (5.87.6),

-kh - vāṁs

cakhvā́ṁsam (2.14.4),

-ḍh - vāṁs

mīḍhvā́n (1.27.2), *mīḍhvā́ṁsaḥ* (8.25.14).

-t - vāṁs

acikitvā́n (1.164.6), *cikitvā́n* (1.25.11), *cikitvā́ṁsam* (4.7.5), *cikitvā́ṁsaḥ* (7.60.7), *sam - cikitvā́n* (4.7.8),

-d - vāṁs

ávidvāṁsaḥ (6.15.10), *vividvā́n* (3.31.15),

sú - vidvāṁsam (8.24.23)

-dh -vāṁs

vavṛdhvā́ṁsam (8.95.7),

-n - vāṁs

ā - jaganvā́n (7.7.5), *jaganvā́n* (1.117.15), *jaganvā́ṁsā* (5.65.1), *jaganvā́ṁsaḥ* (8.45.19), *jaghanvā́n* (1.32.11), *tatanvā́n* (7.61.1), *dadhanvā́n* (9.67.2), *niḥ - jaganvā́n* (10.1.1), *vavanvā́n* (10.27.9), *vavanvā́ṁsā* (10.61.4).

-p - vāṁs

susupvā́ṁsaḥ (1.161.13)

-bh - vāṁs

jagṛbhvā́n (4.23.4), *tastabhvā́ṁsam* (2.11.5).

-r - vā́ṁs

jujurvā́n (1.158.6), *titirvā́ṁsaḥ* (1.36.7),

-s - vāṁs

dadaśvā́n (4.38.6), *dāśvā́n* (1.40.7), *dāśvā́ṁsaḥ* (1.47.3), *dāśvā́ṁsaḥ* (7.37.4).

-ṣ vāṁs

jujuṣvā́n (2.20.5),

-h - vāṁs

ririhvā́ṁsam (10.79.3), *sasahvā́n* (1.100.5), *sasahvā́ṁsam* (8.16.10), *sasahvā́ṁsaḥ* (7.92.4).

DATA : *-vāṁs (us) B*

ájaghnuṣī (8.67.15), *apa - tastúṣaḥ* (9.19.6), *abibhyúṣā* (1.6.7), *abibhyúṣaḥ* (1.11.5), *upa - sedúṣe* (8.47.16), *cikitúṣe* (6.61.13), *cikitúṣaḥ* (1.73.1), *cikitúṣi* (10.125.3), *jaghnúṣaḥ* (1.32.14), *dāśúṣeḥ* (1.3.7), *pari - prúṣaḥ* (10.27.12), *bibhyúṣā* (9.77.2), *vidúṣī* (10.95.11), *vividúṣaḥ* (8.19.12).

DATA : *-vāṁs C*

susu - vúṣaḥ (10.94.14).

II.2.1 COMPOUNDS

In the *RV* no compounds of more than three independent members occur; and those which consist of three members are very rare, such as *ádabdha- vratapramatiḥ* (2.9.1), 'superior - minded owing to unbroken observances' and *hári- manyu - sāyakaḥ* (10.96.3) 'stimulating the mettle of the bays'.[109]

The basic formal features of a compound are (1) single accent and (2) uninflected first member(s). There are, however, exceptions to these rules. For example, in *sádaspáti* (1.21.5) we have two accents and in *bṛ́haspátiḥ* (1.62.3) we have the first member inflected.

The Pdk has generally adhereed to the basic features of a compound while offering the analysis of compounds. His *avagraha-* sign generally follows uninflected member of a compound, such as *vásu - patiḥ* (4.17.6), *nṛ - patiḥ* (4.20.1), and so on. Ofcourse, the Pdk analyses repeatative compounds also and in that case his *avagraha-* sign comes after an inflected member. For instance, *agnim - agnim* (1.12.3), *dáme - dame* (1.128.4), *rathena - rathéna* (2.17.3), *sā́mnaḥ - sāmnaḥ* (2.23.17), and so on. But, it can be observed that in all these repeatative forms there is only one accent even though their first components are inflected. If a compound word shows double accent, the Pdk does not analyse it.

It is not only the accent that makes the Pdk analyse a compound form. His main purpose is to dissolve the *sandhis* in compounds if they are there. Again, since there is *sandhi* there is *padatva*. Unless the components are termed *padas* no *sandhi* is possible. Therefore, his *avagraha* indicates *padatva* of the constituents after which it comes. For example, *aghā́svāya aghá - asvāya* (1.116.6), *vayovṛ́dhaḥ - vayaḥ - vṛ́dhaḥ* (5.54.2), *sādádyonim / sādát - yonim /* (5.43.12), etc. In all these cases *sandhi* has taken place in the Sp because, the stems preceding the *avagraha* are *padas*[110].

Similarly, in forms like *sádmabarhiṣaḥ* (1.52.4), *dhāmasā́cam* (3.51.2), *dharmakṛ́te* (8.98.1) the *n* of *sadman-*, *dhāman-*, and *dharman-* is dropped because these stems are *padas.*[110] Had these not been *padas* the dropping of *n* was not possible.

If this phenomenon is looked from the linguistic point of view, it can be said that the *avagraha*-sign indicates morphemic boudary which allows *pada-sandhis*. In other words, it indicates junctures. That is why the analysis is extended to all the forms with or without *pada-sandhis* and it is not restricted to those forms only which show a *śandhi*. For instance, both *vásupatiḥ* (4.17.6), and *rohıdasvaḥ* (4.1.8) are analysed. Though there is no *sandhi* alternation in *vásupatiḥ* , there is junction between *vasu* and *pati* and therefore, the Pdk shows it as *vásu - patiḥ* Similarly, *rohıdasvaḥ* is analysed as *rohıt - asvaḥ*.

The symbol *avagraha* further indicates the immediate constituents of a compound. Here the Pdk takes into account the meaning - integration of the constituents involved in compounding. For example, *prajā́patiḥ* (4.43.2), is analysed as *prajā́ - patiḥ* . Here there are three components in this compound namely, *pra, jā* and *pati.* From the semantic point of view it is only the first two i.e., *pra* and *jā* which have the meaning-integration and the last only i.e., *pati* is added after *prajā* is formed. There the Pdk shows the immediate components of the *samāsa, prajāpati* as *prajā - pati.* Of course, when the compound form is simply *prajā́* (10.95.18) it is analysed as *pra - jā́*. Here *pra* and *jā* are the immediate constituents of *prajā.*

Similarly, the form *ádabdhavratapramatiḥ* consists of five constituents, *a, dabdha, vrata, pra* and *mati.* Here the first integrated group is formed with *dabdha* and *vrata* like *dabdhavrata.* Then *dabdhavrata* is related to a forming *adabdhavrata.* The second group is formed with *pra* and *mati* as *pramati* and finally these two groups namely, *adabdhavrata* and *pramati* are joined to the highest node. This is the hierarchy in the formation of the coumpound *adabdhavratapramati.* Now, when the process of dissolution startes, the first step in this direction will be *adabdhavrata* and *pramati*. This is what the Pdk has done. This means that *adabdhavrata* and *pramati* are the immediate constituents. Similarly, when the Pdk divides the compound *hárimanysāyakaḥ* as *hárimanyu - sāyakaḥ* , it means that *harimanyu* and *sāyaka* are the immediate constituents of this compound.

That the analysis of compound forms is based on the principle of ICA is further confirmed by the fact that the Pdk has not analysed the form *niṣaṅgiṇaḥ* (3.30.15). Here the hierarchy of formation is *(ni + saṅga) + in)*- and not like *(ni - (sanga + in)*. Had the position been like *(ni + (saṅga + in)-*, the Pdk would have analysed the form under discussion as *ni - saṅginaḥ* . Since he has not analysed this form we can take it for granted that the Pdk does not take *ni* and *sanginaḥ* to be the immediate constituents of the compound *niṣaṅgiṇaḥ* . This also tells that the analysis of compounds has resemblance with the idea of ICA. It is reflected in ninety per cent cases of compounds in the Pp.

But, if *niṣaṅgiṇaḥ* is not analysed on the ground that the secondary suffix *-in* is added to the whole of *niṣaṅga* and as such the immediate constituents of the form are *niṣaṅga* and *in* and not *ni-* and *saṅgin,* one does not get any clue why the Pdk should analyse *śatagvindam* (1.159.5), as *śata - gvinam*. Similarly, when *saúkṛtyāya* (10.136.4) is unanalysable because the immediate constituents of this form are *sukṛta* and the suffix *-ya* and not *su-kṛtya,* one get puzzled why the author of the Pp should analyse *gā́rhapatyāni* (6.15.19) as *gā́rha - patyāni*. There are some more cases of deviation of this type on the part of the Pdk. They are *kṣáitra - patyeṣu* (1.112.13), *gā́rha - patyāya* (10.85.27), *gā́rha - patyena* (1.15.12), *gairi - kṣitásya* (5.33.8), *naicā - śākhám* (3.53.14), *páuru - kutsim* (7.19.3), *pauta - kratáḥ* (8.56.2), *sām - rājyásya* (8.25.7), *sā́m - varṇau* (3.51.1), etc.

But these examples are very few as compared to the examples of regular cases. Therefore, we can treat these examples as exceptions to the general rule.

This is another point in the Pp which is worth-noticing from the point of view of linguistics. We come across a few cases in the Sp as *dyā́va ha kṣā́mā* (10.12.1), *nárā ca śáṁsam* (9.86.42), *nárā vā śáṁsam* (10.64.3), *śúnascicchépam* (5.2.7), *saptá me saptá* (5.52.17), and the like. This phenomenon is known as tmesis of compounds. The Pdk offers *nárāśáṁsam ca* / and *nárāśáṁsam* / *vā* / for *nárā ca śáṁsam* and *nárā vā śáṁsam* respectively, and *śúnaḥśépam* / *cit* for *sunascicchepam*. When the components of a compound are intervened by a word or words in the Sp, it is known as *anānupūrvya - saṁhitā* in the *RPr.*[111]

It can be observed that the restored compounds are not further analysed by *avagraha,* probably, because their components are already known from the Sp, or because they are proper names. Moreover, *śúnaśśépam* is shown as *śúnaḥśépam* but without *avagraha.*

It can be further observed that the restoration of compounds is done by the Pdk only when they are proper names. In other cases he does not restore. Why so?

The reason seems to be like this : in compounds expressing proper names their constituents loose their meanings and semantic focus is given to the person having that name, but unless their components are together such focus is also not possible. Therefore, the Pdk restores those names in their proper forms. But it is not the case with other compounds, namely, the *dvandva-* compounds, and specially, the *dvandva-* compounds wherein both the constituents are in dual number. In such compounds both the components have direct semantic relationship in a sentence. This is the reason why the Pdk does not think it necessary to restore this type of compounds when they are intervened by a word or words. Therefore, neither *dyā́va ha kṣā́mā* is restored as *dyā́vākṣā́mā*, nor *saptá me saptá* as *saptáspatá* although in the *RV* there are occurrences of *dyā́vākṣā́mā* (1.96.5) and *saptásaptá* (10.55.3).

Similarly, *dyā́vā cidasmai pṛithivī namete* (2.12.13) is also a case of a compound whose components are intervened by other words. The Pdk uses *iti* after *pṛthivī* and *dyāyā* is kept as it is, which indicates that the Pdk is aware of the fact that *dyāvāpṛ thivī* is a compound.[112] Likewiese, *Indrā* and *Varuṇā* are intervened by *no atra* in 4.41.1; *náktā uṣasā́* by *barhiḥ sadatām* in 7.42.5; *Indrā* and *Puṣaṇā* by *nu* in 6.57.1; *Indrā* and *Agnī* by *nu* and *yo* in 5.59.3 and 6.60.1 respectively, *mitrayor* and *varunayoḥ* by *ām eti priyam* in 6.51.1. Nowhere the Pdk thinks it necessary to restore the compounds.

In certain cases in the Sp we come across such pairs of *dvandva-* compound the first component of which shows dual number whereas the second one does not. For instance, *mitrā --- varuṇaḥ* (8.25.2), and *ındrā ... varuna* (6.68.5). The Pdk makes *varuṇa* of 6.68.5 as *varuṇā* in his Pp.

Again in *mitra rājānā varuṇā* (5.62.3)[113] only the second member shows duel and not the initial one.

None of these cases is resotred in the Pp for the same reason discussed above.

Another point to be noted in this connection in the Pp is the dropping of some sounds of Sp in the Pp. The Pdk considers some of the sounds in the Sp as inorganic which are introduced in the Sp at the time of *sandhi*. Therefore, he removes these inorganic sounds in the Pp anticipating that these dropped sounds will automatically come at the time of reciting the Sp. The forms of *pari* plus root *kṛ* take *s* in between the prefix and the root. Thus, we have *pariṣkṛṇvan* (9.39.2), *pariṣkṛṇvanti* (9.14.2), *pariṣkṛtaḥ* (3.38.2), *pariṣkṛtam* (9.61.13), *pariṣkṛtasya* (8.1.26), and *pariṣkṛtāsaḥ* (9.46.2). These are analysed by the Pdk as *pari* -

kṛṇvan, pari - kṛṇvanti, pari - kṛtaḥ, pari - kṛtam, pari - kṛtasya, and *pari - kṛtāsaḥ* respectively. In all these forms the Pdk has dropped the *s* which means that the Pdk takes this s to be non-organic.

But he does not analyse *sáṁṣkṛtaḥ* (8.33.9) and *saṁskṛtám* (5.76.2). According to P these forms are derived from *sam* plus the root *kṛ* and the *s* in between the prefix and the root is an *āgama.*[114] Probably, the Pdk is not sure of the derivation of these forms and therefore, he leaves them unanalysed. We are not sure whether the Pdk takes the *s* in these forms as organic either.

Similarly, *vanarṣádaḥ* (2.31.1), *vanarṣádam* (10.132.7), *sváśeandram* (1.52.9), and *háriścandraḥ* (9.66.26) are analysed by the Pdk as *vana - sádaḥ , vana - sádam, svá - candram* and *hári - candraḥ* respectively. In *vanarṣádaḥ* and *vanarṣádam* he takes *r* as inorganic and therefore, removes it in the Pp. It appears that the Pdk has no idea of a stem like *vanar* and what he knows is the stem *vana,* and accordingly he has analysed these forms.

In *sváścandram, háriścandraḥ , súścandra* (5.6.5), and *súścandram* (2.34.13) the *s* is inorganic according to the Pdk and therefore, he puts them without *s* in the Pp. P also describes the derivation of these forms and thinks that the *s* in these forms is inorganic. According to P 6.1.151, '*in a mantra,* the *SUṬ* is added to *candra* when it is the second member in a compound and is preceded by a short vowel'. [115] Naturally, this rule of P refers to the above cases, and it is worth-nothing that the Pdk removes *s* from these very cases.

Another aspect of the treatment of compounds by the Pdk is the not-putting of the *avagraha*-sign in between the constituents of a few compounds, but changing the sibilant at the juncture into a *visarjanīya*. The forms are *añjaspáiva* (10.94.13). *gnáspátiḥ* (2.38.10), *gnāspátnībhiḥ* (4.34.7), *jáspatiḥ* (7.38.6), *jáspátim* (1.185.8), *jāspatyám* (5.28.3), *diváspṛthivyóḥ* (2.2.3), *ráthaspátiḥ* (5.50.5), etc. The Pdk has analysed them as *añjaḥpāḥ-iva, gnā́ḥpátiḥ, gnāḥpátnībhiḥ, jā́hapátiḥ, jā́ḥpátim, jāḥpatyám, dıvaḥpṛthīvóḥ* , and *ráthaḥpátiḥ* respectively. No *avagraha* is put in any of these forms. Moreover, the sibilant in each form is changed to *ḥ* . We have already seen above that in *śúnaḥśépaḥ* and *śúnaḥśépam* although no *avagraha* is put the *sandhi* is dissolved into *ḥ*.

These are the aspects of the treatment of compounds by the Pdk. We will be discussing now those compound-forms which are not analysed by him.

While analysing compound-forms the Pdk has left many of the unanalysed. It can be seen from the list of unanalysed compounds given at the end of the discussion that in almost all these the Pdk has some doubt about the derivation of those forms. There are various reasons on the part of the Pdk to have a doubt. These reasons can be classified as follows.

Some compounds are proper names, such as *evayā́marut* (5.87.1), *viśvā́mitra* (3.53.9), etc. Here, as we have seen already in the case of *nárāśaṁsa*, the components of these names do not play any semantic role in the sentence. It is only the integrated meaning i.e., the person having such names that takes part in understanding the meaning of a sentence where it occurs. Therefore, the Pdk is justified in not showing the components of these proper names. But, there are exceptions to this principle. The names *jamádagninā* (3.62.18), *jātávedāḥ* (1.77.5) and *bharádvājaḥ* (10.181.2), have been split into their constituents. They are shown as *jamát - agninā, jātá - vedāḥ* , and *bharát - vājaḥ* respectively. Excepting these three cases, the Pdk is consistent in dealing with the compounds expressing proper names.

Some are *devatā-dvandva-* compounds, such as, *ángīparjanyau* (6.52.16), *ındrāsómā* (7.35.1), *uṣasānáktā* (1.122.2), *maitrāvaruṇáḥ* (7.33.1), *sómārudrā* (6.74.1), *mitrā́ váruṇā* (1.2.9), etc. The most common type of *dvandvas* is the *devatā-dvandva* in the *RV*. Here, each member is generally separately accented. Historically each member is put in a dual.

The Pdk does not show separation probably because he thinks that the components are clear by accentuation and inflection themselves. Or, non-separation by the Pdk might be due to what he thinks lengthening of the final vowel of the first member.[116]

Some show two accents and first members inflected, e.g., *vánaspátiḥ* (1.90.8), *bṛ́haspátiḥ* (1.62.3), etc. In these compounds also the components become *gauṇa* so far as their semantic relation with the other parts of the sentence is concerned. Moreover, there is ample scope for doubt about the derivation of these words. In the case of *vánaspátiḥ* whether the stem is *van-* or the normal one *vana-* or *vanar-* or *vanas-* is the puzzle.[117] Similarly, in the case of *bṛhaspátiḥ* whether the stem is *bṛh-* or *bṛhat-* or *bṛhas-* is the doubt. In this way if we take account of all the forms of this type, we find that the Pdk has some doubt regarding the derivation of these forms, and therefore he does not analyse them.

Some compounds have derivatives of root *añc* as the second member and as such a lot of morphophonemic change is introduced within the compound. The Pdk finds it difficult to separate the components of these compounds because in that case he may have to go far away from the Sp. The forms are

údañcaḥ (10.86.22), *údīvaḥ* (10.131.1), *ghṛtā́cīḥ* (7.5.5), *nī́cīḥ* (1.66.5), *párācaḥ* (1.164.9), *párāncaḥ* (1.164.19), *pratyáncam* (2.10.5), *madryañcam* (7.24.3), *visvā́cī* (7.43.3), *sadhryancaḥ* (4.4.12), and *samyáñcaḥ* (9.73.2).

As we have observed above that every rule of the Pdk has some exception generally, here as well we come across some exceptions. The forms *samīcīnāḥ* (9.39.6), *samīcīḥ* (3.29.13) have been analysed as *sam - īcīnā́ḥ* , and *sam - īcī́ḥ* respectively. Mostly, the compounds with the root *añc* have prefixes as their first members. We will be discussing them in details in the section dealing with the separation of prefixes.

Some compounds show unusual lengthening e.g. *adhīvāsám* (1.140.9), *sūnṛ́tāḥ* (1.48.2), etc. Here the Pdk gets doubt because of the lengthening of the final syllables of the first members. It is neither a metrical lengthening nor a lengthening caused by *sandhi*. Therefore, he avoids separation. It can be mentioned in this connection, that the Pp of the *TS* offers the analysis of *adhīvāsa* as *adhi - vāsa*.

On the contrary, some compounds do not show lengthening which is expected. For instance, *abhiṣṭiḥ* (1.9.1), *páriṣṭiḥ* (1.65.2), and so on. Here, the expected forms were *abhīṣṭiḥ, parīṣṭiḥ* and so on. Therefore, the Pdk leaves them as they are. We will be discussing these forms in the section dealing with the treatment of prefixes.

Some compounds are of very obscure derivation, such as *ádbhutaḥ* (1.94.12), *ánatidbhutā* (8.90.3), *puroḷā́śam* (1.162.3) etc. Indian grammarians derive *adbhuta* as *at* + *bhū* + *Uṇādi DutaC.*[118] Some of the modern scholars derive it from the root *dabh.*[119] Some derive it from *atibhūta.*[120] In this way we can see that the compounds falling in this group are obscure so far their derivation is concerned. And for this very reason the Pdk leaves them unanalysed.

Similarly, if the first member of a compound has no independent use in the *RV*, the Pdk avoids the analysis of such compound. This seems to be his general principle. Thus, *vanarguḥ* (1.145.5), is not analysed. Here, neither *vanar-* nor *gu* has any independent use in the *RV*. Therefore, the Pdk is doubtful about the constituents of this compound. Such doubts lead the Pdk for non-separation.

The forms of the type of *úttambhitā* (10.85.1), etc. also create difficulty for the Pp. Here; the form is a combination of *ut* plus *stambhitā*. The *s* is dropped in the *sandhi*. Whether the Pdk of the *RV* is aware of this fact cannot be ascertained so easily. Because all the forms showing *sandhi* of this type have been left unanalysed by him. Or, since he has to consider one more point that he should not insert any sound in his *Pada-text* which is not there in the *Saṁhitā-text,* he has avoided the analysis of *uttambhitā, útthitam* (10.149.2), and the like. It can be mentioned in this connection that the Pp of the *TS* analyses these forms as *ut-stambhita* and *ut- sthita* respectively. Thus the Pdk of the *TS* improves upon the Pp of the *RV.*

There are a few forms in the Sp, of the *RV* the initial sounds of which are missing. Naturally the Pdk is puzzled about the derivation of these forms and finally he decides to leave these forms as they are in the Pp. The forms *ıṣkartā* (8.1.12), *ıṣkartāram* (8.99.8), *ıṣkṛtiḥ* (10.97.9), *ıṣkarta* (8.20.26), and *ıṣkṛṇudhvam* (10.53.7) can be cited as examples of this group. In all these forms the first component is *ni,* the *n* of which is dropped. Therefore, how to show simply *iḥ* in the Pp which is meaning-less is the actual problem before the Pdk. *ıṣkarta* and *ıṣkṛṇudhvam* are verbal forms having semantic relation with *nis* which is reduced to *is*. In both the forms *i* of *is* is accented which gives the clue to assume that the whole expression is not a single verbal form, since there is no reason there to support the accent on the verb. Sāy.[121] also gives the same reason for not separating *iṣ* from these forms. *Patañjali,* while commenting on the derivation of the form *iyakṣamāṇa* which is derived from the root *aś* according to the *Vārttikakāra*[122], offers a few examples of *varṇalopa*. The form *iṣkartāram* is given there as one of the examples. Naturally, he also takes it to be *niṣkartāram.*[123]

Now, we are left with a few forms where although there is none of the difficulties mentioned above, the Pdk does not analyse them. Such forms are *gopāḥ* (1.22.18), *pravāsaḥ* (10.77.5), and the like.

When the Pdk analyses *somapā́* (1.21.3), as *soma - pā́,* or *tanūpā́ḥ* (4.16.20), as *tanū-pā́ḥ* or *gópatiḥ* (1.101.4) as *gó - patiḥ,* it is not clear why he should not separate *gopā́ḥ* as *go - pā́ḥ* and all other in the same manner. If one argues that when *gopā-* means *'guardian'* it is a secondary integrated meaning and as such the Pdk does not show separation,; the counter argument would be : Why should the Pdk then analyse *prajá* as *pra - já*? Because, here too the meaning realised is secondary i.e. 'subject'. Therefore, we do not have satisfactory unswer for this exception.

Similarly, the form *viśpátiḥ* (1.26.7) is not analysed whereas *dámpatim* (1.127.8) is analysed as *dam - patim*. The Pdk knows both the components of *viśpati*; there is only one accent in this compound; it is not a proper name; there is no lengthening either. Therefore, there is no reason to form any doubt for the Pdk. Still he does not analyse it.

To me it appears that the reason for not separating this compound is of a different kind. In Sanskrit, *ś* is not a permitted final. In other words, *ś* cannot remain as it is at the terminal position of a word before a pause. Now, if the Pdk wants to introduce a pause in between *viś* and *pati*, he must change this *ś* to *ṭ* before the *avagraha*-sign in which case there is bound to be a confusion regarding the Sp. This will go against the very purpose of the Pp i.e., to preserve the *Saṁhitā*-text in correct form. Therefore, the Pdk might have avoided the analysis.

In the case of *sádaspátī* (1.21.5) of course, the Pdk finds it difficult to account for the two accents it bears. Otherwise, the constituents of this compound are known to the Pdk. Moreover, he does not find the first member inflected which would have explained the existence of two accents in this compound. Most probably, it is a case of *haplology*. The compound *sádaspátī* with two accents stands for **sádasapátī*. Being unable, thus, to account for the two accents, the Pdk avoids separation.

Thus, from the above discussion it can be assumed that the guiding factor for not analysing a compound-form is some kind of doubt in the mind of the Pdk regarding several aspects of a normal compound-formation. He has further delimitted the scope of his *avagraha* by putting certain other conditions such as the *devatā-dvandva* s should not analysed, neither the proper names and so on.

As the Pdk has not analysed a few compound-forms, he has analysed a few wrongly. One of the such wrongly analysed form is *prayógam* (10.7.5) which is analysed as *pra - yogam*. But, as it is an adjective to *agnim*, the separation should have been like *prayaḥ - gam*. The word *prayaḥ* occurs many times in the *RV*. Sāy. paraphrases it as prayoktavyam.

It means that Sāy. also takes it a adjective to *agni*. But he paraphrases it keeping in mind the division of the Pdk i.e., *pra* plus *yoga* which is from root *yuj*. This division is wrong. Actually the word *prayogam* stands for *prayas* plus *ga* (from the root *gā* 'to go') and means 'going for the meals'.[124]

On the other hand, the Pdk has takes a few forms as compound-forms which are not so. Thus, he separates *ásvapnajaḥ* (2.27.9) as *ásvapna - jaḥ*; and *átṛṣṇajaḥ* (10.94.11) as *átṛṣṇa - jaḥ* thinking that *svapnajaḥ* and *tṛṣṇajaḥ* are compounds of *svapna* plus the root *jan* and *tṛṣṇā* plus the root *jan* respectively. Similarly, *tṛṣṇájaḥ* (7.33.5), *tṛṣṇájam* (1.105.7), and *tṛṣṇáje* (1.85.11) are analysed by the Pdk as *tṛṣṇá - jaḥ*, *tṛṣṇá - jam* and *tṛṣṇá - je* respectively. Now, so far as the form *tṛṣṇajaḥ* and *-svapnajaḥ* are concerned they are in nominative plural and as such cannot be the forms from *tṛṣṇaja-* and *svapnaja-* unless otherwise explained as irregular singular ending for the plural as is explained by Sāy.[125] The form *tṛṣṇájam* is in accusative singular and as such does not create any problem because we can have regular *tṛṣṇajam* from a stem *tṛṣṇaja-*. But the actual problem is with *tṛṣṇaje* which is dative singular qualifying *gotamāya*. Unless we have stem like *tṛṣṇaj-* this difficulty cannot overcome. In this case of *tṛṣṇaje* also Sāy. explains the mind of the Pdk regarding the division of this form as follows :

"------*padakārasya Śākalyasya tv ayam abhiprāyaḥ / 'anyeṣvapi dṛśyate' iti dṛśi-grahaṇāt kevalad api janer Ḍa-pratyayaḥ / tṛṣṇā jātā yasya sa tathoktaḥ / ṄyāPoḥ sajñ ācchandsor bahulam iti hrasvatvam / bahuvrīhau pūrvapadaprakṛtisvaratvam /*" (on RV 1.85.11).

Now, if this is the case the stem with the suffix *Ḍa* will be *tṛṣṇaja*-and the dative singular form from this stem will be *tṛṣṇajāya* and not *tṛṣṇáje* which is the form used in the Sp. Therefore, it is difficult to know the mind of the Pdk and still more difficult to correlate the form and the explanation given by Sāy. In order to get the form *tṛṣṇáje* in dative singular we must get a stem *tṛṣṇaj*- and this is what is done by P[126] and following him by *Sāy*. and the modern scholars. Though *Sāy*, tries to justify the division of these forms by Pdk putting as *Śākalyasya tv evam abhiprāyaḥ*, or sometimes as *tadetat padakārasyāṇabhipretam*[127], he has not ignored the actual position described by P. Sāy quotes his rule and derives this form accordingly, P 3-2-172 takes care of the formation of these forms under discussion. The *sūtra* runs as follows

svapitṛṣor najīṄ which means "the affix najīṄ comes in the sense of the agents having such a habit & c after the verbs *svap* 'to sleep' and *tṛṣ* 'to be thirsty".[128]

The modern scholars[129] also take *tṛṣṇaj*- and *svapnaj*- as the stems in the forms discussed above and derive them from the roots *tṛṣ* and *svap* with the primary suffix *naj*. Most probably, the Pdk is guided by the usual forms of those roots namely, *tṛṣṇā́* (7.89.4), and *svápnaḥ* (7.86.6).

To sum up. we can say that the main aim of the Pdk is to show the ICs of a compound-form and the *pada*-status of the constituents preceding the *avagraha*-sign. Naturally, he shows the morphemic boundaries in compounds. In other words, he points out the juncture-features existing in a word. In linguistics these junctures shown by the Pdk are known as *sharp transitions.*[130] Since these junctures can be found only at the morphemic boundaries in sanskrit and since the Pdk was not sure of the morphemic boundaries, he left a few forms unanalysed. Some are wrongly analysed out of confusion. But, it can be seen that nowhere the Pdk has made any attempt to indicate any particular variety of compounding.

DATA : *Compounds* *A*

agni - jihvā́ḥ (1.44.14), *agni - tápaḥ* (5.61.4), *agni - dūtaḥ* (10.14.13), *agni -rūpāḥ* (10.84.1), *aghá - aśvāya* (1.116.6), *ádri - dugdhāḥ* (1.54.9), *ádri - mātaram* (9.86.3), *adhvara - śriyam* (1.44.3), *ánna - kāmāya* (10.177.3), *anyá - vratam* (8.70.11), *anyá - rūpāḥ* (10.22.8), *indra - patnī* (10.86.9), *indra - śatruḥ* (1.32.6), *indra - sakhā* (7.34.24), *indra - sārathiḥ* (4.46.2), *indra - senā́* (10.102.2), *iṣu - balāḥ* (6.75.9), *iṣu - hastaiḥ* (10.103.3), *ukthá - śuṣmaḥ* (6.36.3), *ukṣá - annāya* (8.43.11), *ugrá - dhanvā* (10.103.3), *úgra - patre* (8.67.11), *ugrá - bāhavaḥ* (8.20.12), *úgra - bahuḥ* (8.61.10), *ahi - hā́* (2.19.3), *asura - ghnáḥ* (6.22.4), *ṛk - sāmā́bhyām* (10.85.11), *ṛju - krátuḥ* (1.81.7), *ṛ́ṣi - manāḥ* (9.96.18), *kárṇa - yonayaḥ* (2.24.8), *kévala - aghaḥ* (10.117.16), *kéta - vedāḥ* (1.104.3), *kṛṣṇá - garbhāḥ* (1.101.1), *kṣīra - pākám* (8.77.10), *gṛhá - patnī* (10.85.26),

gó - sakhā (8.14.1), *gó - mātaraḥ* (1.85.3), *ghṛtá - yonim* (3.4.2), *ghṛtá - pṛṣṭhaḥ* (1.164.1), *dhṛṣṇú - senaḥ* (3.54.15), *dhṛṣát - varṇam* (10.87.22), *dhṛṣṇú - ojasaḥ* (2.34.1), *dhṛṣat - manaḥ* (1.52.12), *dhūmá - gandhi* (1.162.15), *dhūmá - ketuḥ* (1.27.11), *dhūmá - ketavaḥ* (8.43.4), *dhruvá - kṣemā* (5.72.2), *nava - padī* (1.164.41), *nitya - hotā* (10.7.4), *nī́la - lohitam* (10.85.28), *nṛ - pátiḥ* (4.20.1), *nṛ - cakṣaḥ* (10.87.9), *nṛ - pátnīḥ* (1.22.11), *nṛ - manaḥ* (1.51.5), *nṛ - meghaḥ* (10.132.7), *pañca - daśám* (1.164.12), *páñca - raśmim* (2.40.3), *páñca - pañca* (3.55.18), *páñca - pādam* (1.164.12), *pati - lokám* (10.85.43), *palasti - jamadagnáyaḥ* (3.53.16), *pāvaká - varṇāḥ* (8.3.3), *pāvaká - sociṣaḥ* (3.11.7), *pā́śa - dyumnasya* (7.33.2), *pāvaká - varcāḥ* (10.140.2), *pā́ñca - janyaḥ* (1.100.12), *pī́vaḥ - aśvaḥ* (4.37.4), *púṇya - gandhaḥ* (7.55.8), *puru - médhaḥ* (9.97.52), *puru - rū́paḥ* (2.33.9), *pitṛ - yā́nam* (10.2.7), *pitṛ - vittáḥ* (1.73.1), *pitṛ - yajnāya* (10.16.10), *pitṛ -śrávaṇam* (1.91.20), agnım - agnim (1.12.2), ágram - agram (1.123.4), adhvare - ṣṭhāḥ (10.77.7), asmā́n - asmān (4.32.4), asmai - asmai (6.42.4), aham - pūrváḥ (1.181.3), idám - idam (7.59.1), ékam - ekam (1.20.7), gā́tre - gātre (8.48.9), girā́ - girā (6.48.1), gṛhám - gṛham (1.123.4), gṛhé - gṛhe (1.28.5), goṣu - yúdhaḥ (6.6.5), jánam - janam (5.15.4), dáme - dame (1.128.4), dure - ante (1.185.7), dyavi - dyávi (1.4.1), dháne - dhane (5.35.7), dhī́vataḥ - dhīvataḥ (6.55.3), návyāḥ -navyāḥ (3.55.16), patháḥ - pathaḥ (6.49.8), padé - pade (5.41.15), párvaṇā - párvaṇā (1.94.4), parvaṇi - parvaṇi (10.163.6), bhadram - bhadram (1.123.13), yajñā́ - yajñā (1.168.1), yátra - yatra (6.75.6), yáthā - yathā (4.19.10), rathe - sthéna (2.17.3), rucā́ - rucā (9.65.2), vayám - vayam (10.22.12), vásyasā - vasyasā (10.37.9), śátroḥ - satroḥ (6.19.3), sā́mnaḥ - samnaḥ (2.23.17),

kṣáitra - patyeṣu (1.112.13), gā́rha - patyāni (6.15.9), gā́rha - patyāya (10.85.27), gā́rha - patyena (1.15.12), gairi - kṣitásya (5.33.8), naicī́ - śākhám (3.53.14), paúru - kutsim (7.19.3), pauta - kratáḥ (8.56.2), sām - rājyásya (8.25.17), sā́m - varṇam (8.51.1),

dám - patim (1.127.8), dám - supatnīḥ (4.19.7), nṛ - pátiḥ (4.20.1), vásu - patiḥ (4.17.6), vā́ja - patiḥ (4.15.3), śácī $\frac{1}{3}$ - patiḥ (4.30.17), sát - patiḥ (1.54.7), svadhā - pate (6.44.1), svá - patiḥ (10.31.4),

girā - vṛ́dham (9.26.6), krátvā - maghāsaḥ (5.33.9), jātū́ - bharmā (1.103.3), jātū́ - sthirasya (2.13.11), tanū - pā́ḥ (4.16.20), doṣā - vastaḥ (1.1.7) , dvā - dva (8.68.14), dhiyā́ - vasuḥ (1.3.10), yuṣmā́ - dattasya (5.54.13)

aghaśaṁsa - hā́ (9.24.7), ánabhimlāta - varṇaḥ (2.35.13), abhimati - hā (9.65.15), jamádagni - dattā (3.53.15), prátijūti - varpasaḥ (3.60.1), bṛ́haspáti - prasūtāḥ (10.97.15).

DATA : *compounds B*

ánatidbhutā (8.90.3), anabhīśúḥ (1.152.5), antárikṣam (1.52.13), abhiṣṭıḥ (1.9.1), abhī́kam (9.92.5), abhīddhā́t (10.190.1), abhīṣā́t (7.4.8), arcanā́nasam (5.64.7), asmatrā́ñcaḥ (6.44.19), asmadryā́k (3.54.22), asmadryañcaḥ (7.19.10), ahīśúvaḥ (10.144.3), ahīśúvam

(8.32.2), *ahorātrā́ṇi* (10.190.2), *ā́gnīdhrāt* (2.36.4), *ārṣṭiṣeṇā́ḥ* (10.98.5), *ārṭiṣeṇéna* (10.98.6), *ilībiśasya* (1.33.12),[132] *úttabhitā* (10.85.1), *útthitam* (10.149.2), *udumbalaú* (10.14.12), *úddhitam* (8.51.2), *uśīnárāṇyāh* (10.59.10), *ṛciṣama* (6.46.4), *ṛcīṣamāya* (1.61.1), *ṛjiśvanā* (1.53.8), *ṛṣiṣā́ṭ* (9.76.4), *evayā́marut* (5.87.1), *kikidīvınā* (10.97.3), *kimīdınā* (7.104.23), *kimīdıne* (7.104.2), *kṛkadāśvam* (1.29.7), *gāthānyah* (1.190.1), *gırvāhaḥ* (1.30.5), *gırvāhasam* (4.44.1), *gopávanaḥ* (8.74.11), *catvārimśát* (1.126.4), *catvāriśyām* (2.12.11), *calācalāsaḥ* (1.164.48), *jā́mātā* (8.2.20), *táskaraḥ* (6.28.3), *trasádasyu* (4.38.1),

páḍbīśam (10.97.16), *patatrıṇaḥ* (1.49.3), *parivatsarī́ṇam* (7.103.8), *parivatsaré* (10.62.2), *páriṣṭiḥ* (1.65.2), *páriṣṭiṣu* (10.147.3), *purāṣā́ṭ* (10.74.6), *puroḷā́sam* (1.162.3), *pṛtanā́jaḥ* (9.87.5), *pṛtanāṣā́ṭ* (1.175.2), *bṛ́haspátiḥ* (1.62.3), *madyáṁdinam* (10.151.5), *madhyáṁdināt* (4.28.3), *madhyáṁdine* (5.69.3), *maśarśārasya* (1.122.15), *māṁspácanyāḥ* (1.162.13), *mātarıbhvarīḥ* (10.120.9), *mātariśvā* (1.60.1), *mā́dhyaṁdiṇe* (4.28.3), *rayisā́t* (1.58.3), *lópāmudrā* (1.179.4), *vaneṣā́ṭ* (10.61.20), *varṣāgirā́ḥ* (1.100.17), *viṁśatıḥ* (1.80.9), *viśváha* (2.15.15), *viśváhā* (1.111.3), *viśvā́naraḥ* (1.186.1), *viśvā́mitra* (3.53.9), *viśvā́hā* (1.25.12), *vispuliṅgakā́ḥ* (1.191.12), *vṛthāṣā́ṭ* (1.63.4), *vṛṣā́kapiḥ* (10.86.1), *vaiśvānarāḥ* (8.30.4), *śirımbiṭhasya* (10.155.1), *śúnāsīrā* (4.57.8), *satrāṣā́ṭ* (7.20.3), *sālāvṛkā́ṇām* (10.90.15), *sālāvṛkā́n* (10.73.3), *sāśanāśané* (10.90.4),

ágniparjanyau (6.52.16), *ágnīṣomē* (1.93.2), *ágnīṣomau* (1.93.8), *ındravāyū iti* (1.2.4), *ındrākutsā* (5.31.9), *ındrāparvatā* (3.53.1), *ındrāṣómā* (7.35.1), *uṣasānáktā* (1.122.2), *dyā́vākṣā́mā* (1.96.5), *dyāvāpṛthivī* (1.35.9), *náktoṣásā* (1.13.7), *parjanyavā́tā* (6.50.12), *pṛthivī́dyā́va* (3.46.5), *mitrā́váruṇā* (1.2.9), *maitrāvaruṇā́ḥ* (7.33.11), *vātāparjanyā́* (10.66.10), *śamīnahuṣī* (10.92.12), *sūryācandramásā* (1.102.2), *sómāpūṣaṇā* (2.40.1), *sómārudrā* (6.74.1) ráthaḥpátiḥ (5.50.5), rādhaḥpate (8.61.14), vánaspátiḥ (1.90.8), viśpátiḥ (1.26.7),

sádaspátī (1.21.5)

údañcaḥ (10.86.22), údīcaḥ (10.131.1), ghṛtā́cīḥ (7.5.5), nī́cīḥ (1.66.5), párācaḥ (1.164.19), párāncaḥ (1.164.19), pratyáncam (2.10.5), madryañcam (7.24.3), viśvā́cī (7.43.3), sadhryañcaḥ (4.4.12), samyáñcaḥ (9.73.2),

ıṣkaram (10.48.6), ıṣkarta (8.20.26), ıṣkartā (8.1.12), ıṣkṛṇudhvam (10.53.7), ıṣkartāram (8.99.8), ıṣkṛtāsaḥ (7.76.2), ıṣkṛtiḥ (10.97.9)

árṇācitrárathā (4.30.18), ubhayāhastı (5.39.1), ubhayāhastyā (1.81.7), ékādśa (1.139.11), ekādaśám (10.85.45), ekādaśā́n (8.39.9), ekādásā́ḥ (8.57.2), ekādaśaıḥ (1.34.11), gopā́jihvasya (3.38.9), tādṛ́kk (5.44.6), turāṣā́ṭ (3.48.4), dvā́daśa (1.25.8), nīhāréṇa (10.82.7), mātárāpitárā (4.6.7),

gopā́ (7.91.2), gopā́ḥ (1.22.18), pravā́saḥ (10.77.5), mıtrarājānā (5.62.3), śraddhā́ (7.32.14)[132].

DATA : Compounds C

pra - yógam (10.7.5)

ásvapna - jaḥ (2.27.9), tṛṣṇá - jaḥ (7.33.5), tṛṣṇá - jam (1.105.7), tṛṣṇá - je (1.85.11),

II.2.2 *iva* - compounds

Through out the *Pada*-text, the lixical item *iva* 'like' is separated by *avagraha*. There is only one case of violation of this rule. In the case of *gartārúgiva* (1.124.7) the analysis offered is *garta - ārugiva* where as per the rule of the Pdk the separation should have been as *gartāruk-iva*.[133] The only reason for doing so is, the Pdk wants to explain the sandhi of *gartāruk* so that one may not form a notion that *gartā* plus *ruk* is the division.[134]

The transgression of general rules for the explanation of *sandhi* can be seen else where also. For instance, we have a general rule that in the sequence : prefix plus prefix plus nominal form, the analysis should be given as (prefix) + (prefix plus nominal form). But this is violated in the case of *duṣprāvyaḥ* (4.25.6), *suprāyanátamam* (6.63.3), *suprāyanā́ḥ* (2.3.5), *suprāvī́ḥ* (1.83.1), *suprāvyaḥ* (2.13.9), *suprāvyam* (1.60.1), and *suprāvye* (1.34.4). These words are analysed as *duḥpa - avyaḥ, supra - ayanatamam, supra - ayanāḥ, supra - avīḥ, supra - avyaḥ, supra - avyam, supra - avye* respectively. But, the expected analysis is *duḥ prāvyaḥ, su - prāyanatamam, su - prāyanaḥ, su - prāvīḥ, su - prāvyaḥ* and so on.

In the case of *suprāyanatamam,* two rules are violated. First, the principle of ICA according to which we expect the cut *suprāyana - tamam, tama* being the immediate constituent and at the same time a *pada-* forming suffix. But this is not what we find here. The next possibility is to separate *su* from *prāyanatamam*. But, this is not adopted either. This clearly shows how much importance the Pdk has given to analysing the *sandhi* in order to avoid confusion regarding the components of a compound.[135]

RPr has nothing to say in this matter. *APr* IV.41 and *VPr.*V.18 prescribe separation of *iva.*[136]

P does not prescribe a compounding with *iva*. It is interesting to note in this connection that the Pdk of the *TS* also does not treat these cases of *iva* as compounds. He puts *iva* separately within two *daṇḍas* as an independent item. So, P and the Pdk of the *TS* agree on this point. But, Kātyāyana specially prescribes compounding with *iva* and calls it a *nitya-samāsa*. Thus, the Pdk and *Kātyāyana* appear to be of the same opinion.

Another argument in favour of treating *iva* as compound-member is the accent. The compounds with *iva* have one accent just as any other normal compound-form. This must be the reason for treating the forms with *iva* as compound-forms.[137]

DATA : *iva*-compounds A

-a - iva

adhvarásya - iva (6.60.10), *anyásya - iva* (2.35.13), *abhriyasya - iva* (10.68.1), *áha - iva* (7.34.5), *ákṣeṇa - iva* (10.89.4), *áśvasya - iva* (10.34.3), *iha - iva* (1.37.3), *upa - iva* (8.3.21), *kū́cakreṇa - iva* (10.102.11), *kāmapréṇa - iva* (1.158.2), *kṣádma - iva* (1.30.4), *kṣṇótreṇa - iva* (2.39.7), *dā́ma - iva* (2.28.6), *dhánva - iva* (3.45.1), *dhánva - iva* (3.45.1), *dhárma - iva* (8.6.20), *nimnéna - iva* (9.17.1), *parjányasya - iva* (9.22.2), *párvatasya - iva* (3.57.6), *pā́trasya - iva* (1.175.1), *pitryasya - iva* (8.48.7), *na - iva* (1.161.8), *putrā́ya - iva* (10.39.6), *praticákṣya - iva* (2.24.6).

-ā - iva

ātmā́ - iva (1.34.7), *āṇḍā́ - iva* (10.68.7), *áhā - iva* (4.33.6), *astā́ - iva* (1.70.6), *asúryā - iva* (1.68.7), *āraṅgarā́ - iva* (10.106.10), *iryā́ - iva* (10.106.4), *iṣukṛtā - iva* (1.184.3), *iṣudhyā́ - iva* (1.122.1), *ukṣā́ - iva* (9.71.9), *ugrā́ - iva* (10.106.4), *udanyajā́ - iva* (10.106.6), *pakṣā́ - iva* (8.34.9), *pādā́ - iva* (2.39.5), *paśvā́ - iva* (10.106.3), *dhī́rā - iva* (5.50.4), *nadyā - iva* (2.39.5).

-i - iva

abhrā́ni - iva (6.44.12), *ádhi - iva* (8.7.14), *ápi - iva* (3.38.8), *gātuyáni - iva* (1.169.5), *áhā ni - iva* (8.48.7), *ā́yudhāni - iva* (1.92.1), *ghṛ́ṇi - iva* (2.33.6), *divi - iva* (1.22.20), *dhuri - iva* (7.24.5), *puri - iva* (6.2.7),

ī - iva

aśvī́ - iva (2.27.16), *aṅkī́ - iva* (1.162.13), *aśvā́janī - iva* (5.62.7), *udrī́ - iva* (8.49.6), *uśatī́ - iva* (10.61.25), *kā́radhunī - iva* (1.180.8), *pátnī - iva* (1.122.2), *paripanthī́ - iva* (1.103.6), *pitumáti - iva* (4.1.8), *pūrvī́ - iva* (10.61.25), *prajānatī́ - iva* (1.124.3), *pragardhinī - iva* (10.142.4),

-u - iva

urú - iva (9.96.15)

-au - iva

agnaú - iva (2.16.1), *adhvagaú - iva* (8.35.8), *karṇau - iva* (2.39.6), *gauraú - iva* (5.78.2), *dvaú - iva* (1.28.2), *pā́dau - iva* (6.45.15).

-t - iva

abhrā́t - iva (10.75.3), *amṛ́tāt - iva* (10.176.4), *udakā́t - iva* (10.166.5), *kū́lāt - iva* (8.47.11).

-n - iva

agnīvā́n - iva (7.104.2), *átyān - iva* (2.34.3), *abhīśún - iva* (6.57.6), *arā́n* ¾ *- iva* (5.13.6), *árvān - iva* (9.97.25), *avatā́n - iva* (8.62.6), *aśánimān - iva* (4.17.13), *āśū́n - iva* (10.68.2), *udadhī́n - iva* (3.45.3), *paraśumān - iva* (8.73.17), *paridhī́n - iva* (1.52.5) *pitumā́n - iva* (1.144.7), *pū́rvān - iva* (5.53.16), *pradhī́n - iva* (4.30.15).

-m - iva

avī́rām - iva (10.86.9), *áśvām -iva* (2.34.6), *áśvam - iva* (10.149.1), *avadyám - iva* (4.18.5), *árvatām - iva* (9.47.5), *ártham - iva* (10.113.6), *abhrám - iva* (10.68.5), *ányām - iva* (8.27.11), *atyam - iva* (1.130.6), *baddhám - iva* (8.67.14), *ghṛtám - iva* (4.57.2), *gā́m - iva*, (8.65.3)

-ḥ - iva

dúdhāḥ - iva (8.50.3), *diváḥ - iva* (2.2.2), *deváḥ - iva* (10.34.8), *kanyāḥ - iva* (4.58.9), *kapótaḥ - iva* (1.30.4), *nābhiḥ - iva* (8.41.6),[138]

DATA : *iva*-compounds B

garta - ārúgiva (1.124.7)

II.2.3 *sa* **from** *saha*

It is a substitute morpheme of *saha* in the *Bahuvrīhi*, the *Upapattatpuruṣa* and *Avyayībhāva* compounds. In most of the cases of *Bahuvrīhi*, the accent is on *sa*, whereas the *Avyayībhāva*-forms carry the general *samāsa*- accent.[139]

The Pdk has separated *sa* in all forms without any exception. There are a few forms derived with *saha*. also. These forms are also analysed by the Pdk. There are only two instances of the *Upapattatpuruṣa* in the *RV*, one with *saha* e.g., *saha - jā́ḥ* (10.88.6), and the other with *sa* namely, *sa - jū́ḥ* (1.23.7). Both the forms have compound accent and both are analysed properly.

DATA : *sa* from *saha* *A*

sá - ketāḥ (6.9.5), *sá - krtavaḥ* (2.27.2), *sá - kratuḥ* (10.148.4), *sa - kṣıtaḥ* (6.44.6), *sa -kṣıtau* (1.140.3), *sá - gaṇaḥ* (1.101.9), *sá - citaḥ* (10.64.7), *sá - cetasaḥ* (8.58.1), *sá - cetasam* (10.44.4), *sá - catasā* (10.113.1), *sá - cetāḥ* (1.61.10), *sá - janyā* (4.50.9), *sá - jātāḥ* (10.103.6), *sá - jātān* (1.109.1), *sá - jātyam* (2.1.5), *sá -jātyasay* (10.64.13), *sá - jātyānām* (8.83.7), *sá -jātye* (8.18.19), *sá - jātyena* (8.20.21), *sa - jıtvarīḥ* (10.97.3), *sa - jıtvānam* (1.8.1), *sa - jıtvanā* (3.12.4), *sa - jū́ḥ* (1.23.7), *sa - jóṣaḥ* (6.2.3), *sa - jóṣasaḥ* (1.43.3), *sa - jóṣasam* (10.153.4), *sa - jóṣasā* (3.58.7), *sa - jósasau* (8.35.1), *sa - jóṣāḥ* (1.65.1), *sa - dıvaḥ* (2.19.6), *sa - dṛ́n* (1.94.7), *sá - niḷāḥ* (1.34.9), *sá - nilābhiḥ* (9.72.2), *sa - niḷebhiḥ* (1.100.5), *sa - pátnāḥ* (10.128.9) *sa - pátnān* (10.174.2), *sa - pátnānām* (10.166.1), *sa - pátnī* (10.145.3), *sa - pátnīḥ* (10.159.6), *sa - pátnīm* (10.145.1), *sa - pitvám* (1.109.7), *sá - balaḥ* (8.93.9), *sa - bā́dhaḥ* (1.64.8), *sa - bā́dhasah* (5.10.6), *sa - bhavasaḥ* (5.54.10), *sá - bharāḥ* (10.101.3), *sa - mádam* (10.125.6), *sa - mádām* (6.75.1), *sá - manasaḥ* (1.186.8), *sá - manasā* (1.92.16), *sá - manyávaḥ* (7.25.1), *sa -maryatā́* (5.44.7), *sa - maryám* (4.24.8), *sa - maryé* (1.63.6), *sa - yā́varī* (7.31.8), *sa - yā́varīḥ* (1.84.10), *sa - yā́vānam* (5.35.7), *sa - yúk* (10.168.2), *sa - yúgvā* (10.130.4), *sa - yújaḥ* (3.30.11), *sa - yújam* (10.124.9), *sa - yújā* (1.164.20), *sá - yoniḥ* (1.164.30), *sá - yonīḥ* (3.1.6), *sa - rátham* (1.171.6), *sa - ráthā* (5.43.8), *sá - rūpā* (4.16.10), *sá - rásmīḥ* (1.135.3), *sá - rātayaḥ* (8.27.14), *sá - rūpeṇa* (10.55.3), *sá - rūpaiḥ* (8.34.12), *sá - lakṣmā* (10.10.2).

DATA : *saha*

sahá - gopāḥ (10.27.8), *sahá - chandasaḥ* (10.130.7), *saha - jā́ḥ* (10.88.6), *sahá - jānuṣāṇi* (1.104.8), *sahá - dānum* (3.30.8), *sahá - devaḥ* (1.100.17), *sahá -pramāḥ* (10.130.7), *sahá - mūrāh* (10.87.19), *sahá - mūlam* (3.30.17), *sahá - vatsā* (1.32.9), *sahá - vasum* (2.13.8), *saha - vā́haḥ* (7.97.6), *sahá - vīram* (3.54.13), *saha - śéyyāya* (10.10.7), *sahá - stomāḥ* (10.130.7),[140]

II.2.4 NEGATIVE PARTICLE *a/an*

Nowhere in the Pp of the *RV* this particle is separated. It means that the Pdk does not consider this negative particle as a *pada*, probably because *na* in its form *a / an* is not independently used.

According to P, unless *na* is *pada*, it cannot form compounding with another inflected words. We also find that *na* occurs independently in a sentence. According to P 6.3.73 *n* of *na* is elided when it becomes member of a compound. A of *na* takes a *nUṬ - āgama* when the following member begins with a vowel.[141] In other words, *a* and *an* are in allomorphic distribution having stop and vowel as their distributive context respectively.

But, the actual difficulty with the Pdk is even though this *a* or *an-* has the same meaning as that of *na*, it does not occur independently in a sentence. So, how to give a *pada-* status to this? In other words, because the Pdk is not getting *a/an* as *na* in the compounds, he leaves the forms compounded with *a/an* unanalysed.

It is very difficult to come to any particular conclusion from the above discussion. But, what appears, the Pdk is aware of the fact that *a/an* has got the grammatical *pada*-status, but simply because it is derived from *na* and thereby because it has lost its phonetic shape, he avoides the analysis. This is quite usual with him. In the case of derivatives of root *añc* very often suffers considerable change in its shape when compounded with prefixes.[142] In all these cases no separation is shown. Similarly, we can come to the above tentative conclusion.

Apart from the reason for not separating this privative particle from the following member of a compound, we find a few cases of inconsistency in the treatment of these forms themselves. For example, it is always seen that if any prefix comes immediately after this negative particle, and if it is a separable[143] prefix, the *avagraha*- sign is put after the prefix; that is to say, the cut is shown just after the prefix, e.g.,

áni - baddhaḥ (4.13.5), *áni - bhṛṣṭaḥ* (10.116.6), *áduḥ - kṛtám* (3.33.13), *ananu - kṛtyám* (10.68.10), *ánapi - naddham* (6.72.4), *anabhi - druhā* (2.41.5), and so on.

But *aniṣaṅgáya* (1.31.13), *anabhīśúḥ* (1.152.2), *ánādhṛṣṭaḥ* (7.15.4), *ánānataḥ* (8.64.7), *anāyudhā́saḥ* (4.5.14), *anārambhaṇé* (1.116.5), *ánāviddhāya* (6.75.1), *ánāvṛt* (10.95.14), *ánāśavaḥ* (1.135.9), *anāsthāné* (1.116.5), *ánāhutim* (10.37.4), etc. are left unanalysed even though these are in the sequence :

prefix + prefix + noun.

So far the cases of *aniṣaṅgáya*, *anabhīśúḥ*, *anāyudhā́saḥ* and *ánāśavaḥ*, are concerned, it can be observed that the prefixes are never separated from these forms.[144] Now, when these forms even without negative paticle are not separated, the question of separating them with negative particle can be avoided.

Again forms like *ānata-*, *āviddha-* and *āsthāna-* do not occur independently in the *RV*. Naturally, we do not know the treatment of these words in the Pp. In addition, we have the following counter examples :

ánādhṛṣṭaḥ, anārambhaṇé, ánāvṛt (10.95.4), and *ánāhutim* (10.37.4).

Here the Pdk does not analyse these forms although he analyses *ā - dhṛ́ṣaḥ* (2.1.9), *ā - dhṛ́ṣe* (1.39.4), *ā - rámbhaṇam* (10.81.2), *ā - vṛ́taḥ* (10.130.7), and *ā́ - hutiḥ* (1.105.5).

Therefore, one more point to be noted is in the sequence : negative particle + prefix + noun, if the prefix is *ā*, it is never separated. This holds good only for the prefix *ā*.

DATA : Negative particle *a* / *an* *B*

ákava - arim (3.47.5), *ákaviṣṇu* (7.4.4), *ákāma - karśanaḥ* (1.53.2), *akútra* (1.20.8), *ákumāraḥ* (1.155.6), *ákṛtam* (6.18.15), *ákṛṣi - valām* (10.146.6), *ákravi - hastā* (5.62.6) , *ákṣetra - vit* (5.40.5), *ákhidrayāma - bhiḥ* (1.38.11), *ágṛbhīta - śociṣaḥ* (5.54.5), *ácaramāḥ* (5.58.5), *ácchidyamānayā* (2.32.4), *ácchina - patrāḥ* (1.22.11), *ájātān* (5.15.2), *ájāta - śatruḥ* (8.93.15), *ájñata - ketāḥ* (5.3.11), *ajñāta - yakṣmā́t* (10.161.1), *ádabdhavrata - pramatiḥ* (2.9.1), *áduḥ - krtau* (3.33.13), *áduḥ - makasya* (8.75.14), *áduḥ - maṅgalīḥ* (10.85.43), *aducchunā́ḥ* (9.61.17), *ádvayāvinam* (3.2.15), *ániḥ - kṛtam* (8.99.8), *ániḥ - śastāḥ* (4.34.11), *áni - padyamānam* (1.164.31), *áni - bhṛṣṭaḥ* (4.13.5), *anibhṛṣṭa - taviṣiḥ* (2.25.4), *ani - mānā́ḥ* (1.27.11), *áni - miṣā* (3.59.1), *ánimiṣat - bhiḥ* (1.143.8), *áni - meṣam* (1.31.12), *áni - viśamānāḥ* (7.49.1), *áni - śitam* (2.38.8), *ániśita - sargāḥ* (10.89.4).

aniṣaṅgā́ya (1.31.13), *aniṣvyā́ḥ* (10.108.6), *ániḥ - stṛtaḥ* (8.33.9), *ápari - itam* (8.24.9), *áparā - jitam* (1.11.2), *ápra - āyu* (50.80.3), *apra - ketám* (10.129.3), *ápra - jāḥ* (1.21.5), *áprati - mānam* (8.96.17), *ápratidhṛṣta - śavasam* (1.84.2), *ápra - bhuḥ* (9.73.9), *ábadhiram* (8.45.17), *amıtram* (6.73.3), *amṛ́tam* (1.23.19), *ávasānāḥ* (3.1.6), *ásu-nıtam* (10.12.4).

ánagni - trāḥ (1.189.3), *ánagni - dagdhāḥ* (10.15.14), *ananu - kṛtyám* (10.68.10), *ananu - dáḥ* (1.53.8), *ánanu - diṣṭaḥ* (10.160.4), *ánau - bhūtiḥ* (6.47.17), *anantáḥ* (1.113.3), *ánapa - cyutaḥ* (4.31.14), *anapatyā́ni* (3.54.18), *ánapi - naddham* (6.72.4), *ánabhi - druhā* (2.41.5), *anabhimlāta - varṇaḥ* (2.35.13), *anabhīśúḥ* (1.152.5), *anavadya - rū́pāḥ* (10.68.3),

ánādhṛṣṭaḥ (7.15.14), *ánānataḥ* (8.64.7),, *ánāpiḥ* (8.21.13), *anāyudhā́saḥ* (4.5.14), *anārambhaṇé* (1.116.5), *ánāviddhāya* (6.75.1), *ánāvṛt* (10.95.14), *ánāśīh - dām* (10.27.1), *anāśávaḥ* (1.135.9), *anāsthāné* (1.116.5), *ánahutim* (10.37.4), *ánṛtam* (1.23.22).

II.3. PREFIXES

II.3.0. Introductory Remarks

Prefixes may be considered as fossilized adjectival stems without inflection which have acquired the function of preposition and verbal prefixes. At the primitive state of Indo-European they were independent words.[145] They could govern nouns as well as verbs. In the *RV* itself there are fifteen (if *sam* is included) such prefixes which govern cases.[146] Their place in a sentence was as free as that of any other word in that sentence. They could occur either immediately before verbs, or after verbs, or even if intervened by other words.[147] Even the classical Sanskrit retains *anu, ā* and *prati* as relics of the old character of the prefixes. They are known as *karma- pravacanīya.*[148]

So far as the meaning and function of the prefixes are concerned, there is a great deal of controversy among traditional scholars. According to *Śākaṭāyana* as quoted in the *Nir* 1.3, the prefixes have no independent meaning.[149] They simply modify the meaning of verbs and nouns. But, *Gārgya* and *Yāska* do not think so.[150] According to them prefixes do have independent meaning, because, -they say-, unless prefixes have a meaning of their own, they cannot modify the meaning of words to which they are prefixed. *RPr* xii.22, 25 holds the same view as that of *śākaṭāyana* and enforses thereby the meaningfulness of the prefixes only when they are attached to verbs or nouns.[151] This type of controversy was also carried over to other schools of grammar.[152]

śāk, who in his Pp separates prefixes from verbs and nouns by keeping them between two vertical strokes when they are accented, seems to belong to that school which favours the meaningfulness of prefixes. However, *śāk's* main purpose in separating is to indicate the word-boundary which involves some phonological changes applicable to a *pada*. Still, wherever the word-boundary occurs we have meaningful units.

The total of prefixes, according to *RPr* 12.20,[153], *VPr* 6.24,[154] *Nir* 1.3,[155] and the *Gaṇapāṭha* on P 1.4.58[156] comes to twenty. *śākaṭāyana* adds three more : *accha, śrat* and *antar.*[157] But, *TPr* 1.15[158] records only ten. Whitney, in his note on *TPr* 6.4[159] which prescribes that *s* is converted into *ṣ* before prefixes or *niṣ,* discovers at least one reason why the *TPr* 1.15 enumerates only ten prefixes. In the sequence *anu - sthāna* (TS 5.6.1.3), *s* is not changed to *ṣ,* because it is preceded by *anu* which is not mentioned in the *TPr* 1.15, whereas in *pratiṣṭhā - payati* (*TS* 6.1.4.2) *s* has become *ṣ* since it is preceded by *prati* which is listed in the *TPr* 1.15. So, it means that those are considered to be prefixes which involve *ṣatva* etc. in the verbal stem. This is the only purpose, one can think of, which lies behind the listing ten prefixes in the *TPr* 1.15.[160]

But, there are many other examples which undergo *ṣatva* etc. in connection with the prefixes which are not mentioned in the *TPr* 1.15.[161] Thus, the problem still remains.

The subject which concerns us here is the treatment of prefixes in the Pp of the *RV*. It can be easily observed that the Pdk has taken the prefixes to be *pada* since he separates them. It is to be further noted, in this connection, that P, also has granted *padatva* i.e., *subantatva* in Pāṇinian terminology, to the prefixes. According to P case-suffixes are added after the prefixes and these are dropped by P 2.4.81.[162]

From the fact that *śāk* separates prefixes we, therefore, conclude that he treates prefixes as *padas*. However, we do not know whether according to *śāk* every *pada* put between two vertical strokes is to be viewed as *subanta*. The sofisticated theory may belong to the later period.

The distribution of these prefixes in the *RV* is as follows:

(1) Prefix + Nominal stem + Case suffix

(b) Prefix + Nominal stem + Nominal Stem + Case - Suffix[163]

(c) Prefix + Prefix + Nominal stem + Case - Suffix[163]

(d) Prefix + Verb

(e) Prefix + Prefix + Verb[164]

(f) Prefix + Suffix

(g) Prefix + Suffix + Suffix

(h) Prefix + Indiclinable

(i) Prefix + Prefix

(j) Prefix (free)

Now, we will take up each group separately and see the treatment of the Pdk.

II.3.1.a

A B C

{(Prefix) + (Nominal Stem)} + (*pada*-forming suffix)

Examples :

ati

ativrájat - bhiḥ (1.116.4)

api

apidhā́na - vantam (5.29.12)

abhi

abhidyu - bhiḥ (1.6.8)

abhivrájat - bhiḥ (1.144.5)

abhīśú - bhih (5.44.4)

ava

avatasthi - vā́ṁsaḥ (8.96.14)[165]

ā

ātasthi - vā́msaḥ (5.47.2), *ātasthi - vā́ṁsam* (1.116.5), *ātasthi - vā́ṁsā* (2.12.8), *āpapri - vā́ṁsam* (1.146.1), *āpapri - vā́n* (1.73.8), *āmiśla - tamaḥ* (6.29.4), *ārujatnu - bhiḥ* (1.6.5)

upa :

upapati - vā́ṁsam (9.85.11), *upamāti - vániḥ* (5.41.16)

ni :

nikāma - bhiḥ (10.92.9), *nidhi - bhiḥ* (10.179.2), *niyút - bhiḥ* (1.135.3), *niṣaṅgi - bhiḥ* (10.103.3)

parā :

parāyát - bhyaḥ (10.34.5), *pareyi - vā́ṁsam* (10.14.1)

pari :

páribhūti - bhiḥ (7.66.10)

pra :

prajā́ - vat (1.113.17), *prajā́ - vatī* (8.31.4), *prapathin - tamam* (1.173.7)[166] *práyakṣa - tamam* (1.62.6), *prayat - bhyaḥ* (5.54.9)

vi :

vigā́ma - bhiḥ (1.155.4), *vidyúnmat - bhiḥ* (1.88.1)[167], *vibhú - bhiḥ* (7.48.2),

sam :

samit - bhih (3.1.2)

su :

sukárma - bhiḥ (9.70.4), *sukṛ́t -taraḥ* (1.31.4), *sukṛ́t - tarāya* (8.46.27), *sukṛ́t - su* (7.9.1), *sukratu - yā́* (1.31.3), *sugātu - yā́* (1.97.2), *sudā́nu - bhiḥ* (10.172.2), *sudīti - bhiḥ* (5.8.4), *sunīti - bhiḥ* (2.23.4), *suprayā́va - bhiḥ* (5.44.12), *sumati - bhiḥ* (2.16.8), *sumántu - bhiḥ* (1.129.7), *sumánma - bhiḥ* (3.2.12), *suśasti - bhiḥ* (1.20.7), *sustuti - bhiḥ* (6.24.6)

II.3.1.b

A B C

[{(Prefix) + (Nomina stem)} - (Nominal stem)] + (Non-pada-forming suffix)

Examples :

anu :
anukāma - kṛ́t (9.11.7),[168]
abhi :

abhibhūti - ojasam (1.52.7), *abhibhūti - ojāḥ* (3.34.6), *abhimāti - sáhaḥ* (1.91.18)[169], *abhimāti - saháḥ* (10.83.4),[170] *abhimāti - sáham* (10.47.3), *abhimāti - sáhye* (3.37.3), *abhimāti - hánam* (3.51.3), *abhimāti - hā́* (7.95.15), *abhiśasti - cā́tanaḥ* (3.3.6), *abhiśasti - pā́ḥ* (9.23.5), *abhiśasti - pā́m* (6.52.3), *abhisasti - pā́vā* (1.76.3)

ava :

ávayāta - heḷāḥ (1.171.6)

ā :

ā́pānta - manyuḥ (10.89.5), *ābharát - vasuḥ* (5.79.3), *āhuti - vṛ́dham* (9.67.29)

upa :

upāká - cakṣasam (8.6.25)

dur :

duroka - sóciḥ (1.66.3), *duroṇa - śat* (4.40.5)[171]

ni :

niṣikta - pā́m (7.36.9),

pra :

prajā́ - patiḥ (4.53.2), *prájā - pate* (10.121.10), *praśasti - kṛ́t* (1.113.9), *prācína - raśmim* (10.36.6), *práyata - dakṣiṇam* (1.31.15), *prakala - vit* (7.18.15), *pravāte - jáh* (10.34.1)

vi :

vijeṣa - kṛ́t (0.84.5), *vidyút - mahasaḥ* (5.54.3), *vidyút - rathaḥ* (3.14.1), *vidyút - rathāḥ* (3.54.13), *vidyút - hastāḥ* (8.7.25), *vibhā́ - vasuḥ* (3.2.2), *vibhā́ - vasum* (5.25.2), *vibhā - vaso* (1.44.10), *vibhu*

- *krátum* (8.69.15), *vıbhūta - dyumnaḥ* (1.156.1), *vıbhūta - rātim* (8.19.2), *vısṛṣṭa - rātiḥ* (1.122.10)

sam :

sámiddha - agniḥ (5.37.2),

su :

suparṇá - yātum (7.104.22), *supārá - kṣatra* (7.87.6), *sumántu - nāmā* (6.18.8), *suyavasa - át* (1.164.40), *surūpa - kṛtnúm* (1.4.1) *suhávītu - nāmne* (9.85.6), *sūkta-vākám* (10.88.8), *sūkta - vākéca* (10.88.7), *sūktá - vācaḥ* (5.49.5).

II.3.1.c

A B C D

[(Prefix) - {(Prefix) + (Nominal stem)}] + (Non-pada-forming suffix)

Examples :

adhi :

ádhi - nirnijaḥ (8.41.10), *adhi - vikártanam* (10.85.35)

apa :

apa : ắkṛtim (8.47.2), *apa - āvṛtaḥ* (8.80.8)

abhi :

abhi -āyaṁsényā (1.34.1), *abhi - āvartıne* (6.27.5), *abhi - āvartī́* (6.27.8), *abhi - prabhaṅgınaḥ* (8.45.35), *abhi - pramúrā* (10.115.2)

ā :

ā́nu - stubhasya (10.181.1)

upa :

upa - ā́bhṛti (1.128.2), *upa - nipádyamānam* (1.152.4), *upa - prayántaḥ* (1.74.1), *upa - prayám* (1.103.4)

dur :

duḥ - ādharsam (6.49.7), *duḥ - ādhyaḥ* (7.18.8), *duḥ - āpanā* (10.95.2), *duḥ - niyantavaḥ* (1.135.9), *duḥ - niyántuḥ* (1.190.6),

pari :

pari -āvivṛtsan (7.63.2)

vi :

vi - ānaśiḥ (3.49.3), *vi - anasé* (8.86.15)

sam :

sam - ā́śirām (1.30.2)

su :

su - abhiṣṭáyaḥ (1.173.9), *su - abhiṣṭi* (7.102.2),[172] *su - abhiṣṭiḥ* (6.33.1), *su - abhiṣṭim* (1.51.2), *su - abhīśúḥ* (8.68.18), *su - abhīśū́a* (8.68.16), *su - ābhúvaḥ* (1.151.2), *su - ābhúvam* (5.6.3), *su - ābhúvā* (10.122.3), *su - āyasám* (10.53.9), *su - āyujaḥ* (1.92.2), *su - āyudha* (9.4.7), *su -āyudhásya* (9.3.6), *su - āyudhaḥ* (9.86.12), *su - āyudhám* (6.17.13), *su - āyudhā́ḥ* (5.57.2), *su - āyudhā́saḥ* (5.87.5), *su - āveśaḥ* (7.54.1), *su - āvésā́* (10.63.16), *sú - āśitaḥ* (10.27.1), *su - āhuta* (7.16.7), *sú - āhutaḥ* (1.44.6), *sú - āhutam* (1.44.4), *su - upavancanā́* (10.18.11), *su - upasthābhiḥ* (9.61.21), *su - upāyanáḥ* (1.1.9), *su - upāyanā́* (10.18.11), *su - nidhā́* (3.29.12), *su - saṁsádam* (1.112.7), *sú - saṁskṛtā* (8.77.1), *sú - saṁskṛtāḥ* (1.38.12), *su - saṁkāśā́* (1.123.11). *sú - sammṛṣṭāsaḥ* (3.43.6)

su - práketaḥ (9.108.2), *su - praketám* (4.50.2), *su - praketébhiḥ* (1.171.6), *su - praketáiḥ* (10.3.3), *su - prácetasaḥ* (1.159.4), *su - prajā́ḥ* (4.50.6), *su - prajā́m* (4.53.7), *su - prajā́vatim* (1.111.2),[173] *su - praticákṣam* (7.1.2), *su - prátīkaḥ* (1.94.7), *su - prátīkam* (3.29.5), *su - prátīkasya* (1.143.3), *su - prátikā* (1.92.6), *su - prátīke* (1.185.6)[174], *su - pratū́ḥ* (8.23.29), *su - pratūrtim* (1.40.4), *su - prarītayaḥ* (8.27.12), *su - prátītiḥ* (1.73.1), *su - pránītam* (10.63.10), *su - pránītī* (5.42.18), *su - pranīte* (3.1.16), *su - prapānám* (5.83.8), *su - prapāné* (6.28.7), *su - pravācanám* (1.105.12), *sú - prāṅ* (1.162.2), *su - pravargám* (8.22.18).

But,

duḥpra - avyaḥ (4.25.6), *suniḥ - ájam* (1.10.7), *suniḥ - máthā* (3.29.12), supra - ayanátamam (6.63.3), *supra - ayanā́ḥ* (2.3.5), *supra - avī́ḥ* (1.83.1), *supra - avyaḥ* (2.13.9), *supra - avyam* (1.60.1), *supra - avye* (1.34.4).

II.3.1.d

A B C

[(Prefix) - (Nominal stem)] + (Non-*pada*-forming suffix)

Examples :

ati :

áti - avih (9.13.1), *áti - ūrmiḥ* (9.17.3), *ati - divyaḥ* (10.42.9), *áti - matim* (1.129.4), *ati -yājásya* (6.52.1), *áti - viddhā* (8.96.2), *ati - viddhe* (.562.9).

adhi :

ádhi - akṣaḥ (10.129.7), *adhi - kṣitáḥ* (8.40.3), *ádhi - gartasya* (5.62.7), *adhi - nīyámānaḥ* (10.89.6), *ádhi - patyam* (10.124.5), *adhi - pā́ḥ* (7.88.2), *ádhi - bhojanā* (6.47.23), *adhi - mánthanam* (3.29.1), *ádhi - rathā* (10.98.10), *adhi - rājám* (10.128.9), *adhi - vaktā́* (1.100.19), *adhi - sthānam* (10.81.2).

anu :

anu - attitā́ (10.109.2), *anu - kāmám* (1.17.3), *anu - gāyasam* (8.5.34), *anu - dhūpitāsaḥ* (2.30.10), *ánu - pathāḥ* (5.52.10), *ánu - bhṛtam* (10.61.5), *ánu -mate* (10.59.6), *anu - madyamānaḥ* (7.63.3), *anu - mā́dyasya* (7.6.1), *ánu - yatam* (5.41.13),

apa :

ápa - udakābhiḥ (1.116.3), *apa - kāmám* (6.75.2), *apa - goham* (2.15.7), *ápa - citim* (4.28.4), *apa - tasthúṣaḥ* (9.19.6), *apa - próthantaḥ* (9.98.11), *apa - bhartā́* (2.23.7), *ápa - mluktam* (10.52.4),

api :

ápi - iteḥ (1.21.10), *api - kakṣe* (4.40.4), *api - karṇé* (6.48.16), *api - dhā́nā* (1.51.4), *api - naddham* (10.68.8), *api - yántam* (1.162.20), *ápi - riptāya* (1.118.7), *api - vātáyantaḥ* (1.165.13)

abhi :

abhi - áñjanam (8.3.24), *abhi - ā́ram* (8.72.11), *abhi - kṣatā́raḥ* (2.29.2), *abhi - khyātā* (4.17.17), *abhı - gītaḥ* (9.96.23), *abhi - dipsúḥ* (2.23.10).

ava :

ava - ásṛjaḥ (6.43.3), *ava - krakṣ'ıṇam* (8.1.2), *ava - khādaḥ* (1.41.4), *ava - tsārásya* (5.44.10), *ava - dhūṇuṣe* (1.74.4), *áva - naddham* (1.116.4)

ā :

ā - áñjanena (10.18.7), ā́ - iṣṭau (6.28.8), ā́ - uktā (1.63.9), a - karáḥ (5.34.4), ā́ - gatāḥ (10.85.31), ā - cakrıḥ (6.24.5), ā - jániṣṭhāḥ (5.30.5),

ut :

ut - áñcanaḥ (5.44.13), út - ojasaḥ (5.54.3), ut - bhıt (8.79.1), ut - yát (7.81.2), ut - savé (1.102.1), út - nītaḥ (9.81.1), ut - pátan (2.43.3)

upa :

upa - aṁśú (10.83.7), upa - kákṣāsaḥ (10.71.7), upa - kṣı́taḥ (8.19.33), upa - jıhvikā (8.102.21), upa - tıṣṭhamānam (8.101.16), úpa - nītam (1.121.9), upa - prútam (9.71.2), upa - bárhaṇam (10.85.7)

dur[175] :

duḥ - uktáiḥ (1.147.4), duḥ - évām (10.42.10), duḥ - ókam (7.4.3), duḥ - kŕ̥ttam (6.16.32), duḥ - gáhasya (8.65.12), duḥ - gā́ni (1.99.1), duḥ - géṣu (6.21.22), duḥ - dábhaḥ (3.2.2), duḥ - matıḥ (1.131.7)

ni :

ni - áñcanam (5.27.18), ni - ikṣaṇam (1.162.13), nı -uptāḥ (10.27.17), nı - okase (1.9.10), nı - kāmam (6.17.10), nı - khātam (1.117.5), nı - gūḷham (6.44.23), nı - cetārā (1.184.2), nı júraḥ (2.29.6), ni - todınaḥ (10.34.7), ni - dhātúḥ (5.30.2), nı - naddhaḥ (6.75.5)

nir[176] :

niḥ - áje (3.30.10), nıḥ - ṛtam (1.119.7), nıḥ - kṛtiḥ (10.97.9), nıḥ - taptā (2.23.11), niḥ - nık (5.62.4), niḥ - yuvānáḥ (4.48.2), niḥ - śásā (10.164.3), niḥ - sáhamānaḥ (1.127.3),

parā :

parā - áyanam (10.19.4), *párā - gatāḥ* (10.97.21), *párā - jitāsaḥ* (10.84.7), *parā - dadıḥ* (1.81.2), *parā - núde* (1.39.2), *párā - bhṛtam* (8.45.41),

pari :

pári - kṛtasya (8.1.26), *pári - gadhitā* (1.126.6), *pári - chinnāḥ* (7.33.6), *pari - járbhurānaḥ* (1.140.10), *pári - takmyā* (5.30.14), *pári - taptam* (1.119.6), *pari - dhıḥ* (1.125.7), *pári - patim* (6.49.8)

pra :

pra - adhvané (4.58.7), *pra - kāśaḥ* (10.124.6), *pra - khādáḥ* (1.178.4), *pra - gardhınaḥ* (4.40.3), *pra - jā́* (10.95.18), *prá - tatāḥ* (3.31.20),, *pra - divā* (5.60.8), *prá - nītīḥ* (6.48.20).

prati :

práti -ardhiḥ (10.26.5), *prati - kāmám* (3.48.1), *prati - doṣám* (1.35.10), *prati - dháyaḥ* (10.85.8), *práti - buddhaḥ* (1.191.5), *práti - bhṛtā* (7.68.1), *prati - mānāni* (10.89.5), *prati - lobháyanti* (10.103.12)

vi :

vı - aṁsaḥ (4.18.9), *vi - ānáḥ* (10.85.12), *vı - enasā* (3.33.13), *vi - ódane* (8.63.9), *vı - kaṭe* (10.155.1), *vi - gadéṣu* (10.116.5), *vi - cakṣaṇáḥ* (1.101.7), *vı - jāmātuḥ* (1.109.2), *vı - tatā* (1.152.2), *vi - dyútaḥ* (1.105.1),

sam :

sám - aktam (2.3.10), *sam - anikéṣu* (10.107.11), *sám - iddhaḥ* (1.94.14), *sám - okasaḥ* (1.64.10), *sam - krándanaḥ* (10.103.1), *sám - gatim* (4.41.1), *sam - cárṇīḥ* (6.24.4), *sam - jıtaḥ* (5.42.5), *sam - tanıḥ* (5.73.7), *sam - dadıḥ* (9.99.7)-, *sám - dhātā* (8.1.12).

su :

su - áṅgaḥ (10.1.1), *su - ādhyam* (1.71.8), *su - iṣúḥ* (5.42.11)_, *su - uktám* (7.58.6), *su - ūtáyaḥ* (8.47.1), *su - ojaḥ* (6.22.6), *su - kármā* (4.33.9), *su - gávaḥ* (1.116.25),

II.3.1.e

A B C D

[(Stem) - {(Prefix) + (Stem)} + (Non-*pada*-forming suffix)]

Examples :

uru - vyácasam (6.36.3), *uru - vyácasā* (1.160.2), *uru - vyácase* (7.31.11), *ghṛtá - āsutiḥ* (1.156.1), *ghṛtá - āhavanam* (8.74.5), *ghṛ́tta - āhavana* (1.12.5), *ghṛtá - nirnijaḥ* (4.37.2), *ghṛtá - pratīkaḥ* (3.1.18), *ṛta - prajātaḥ* (1.65.5), *hıraṇya - abhīśuḥ* (8.22.5), *hıraṇya - praügam* (1.35.5),

But,

karmaniḥ - sthā́m (10.80.1), *puruniḥ - sıdhe* (1.10.5), *puruniḥ - sıdhvanam* (4.38.2), *puruniḥ - sthāḥ* (5.1.6), *puruniḥ - sthāḥ* (8.2.9).

II.3.1.f

A B C D E

[(Stem) - {(Prefix) + (Prefix) + (Stem)} + (Suffix)]

Example :

pṛṣṇi - nipreṣitāsaḥ (7.18.10)

II.3.2.a

A B

(Prefix) - (Verb)

Examples :

ati :

ati - éṣi (9.97.31), *ati - tasthaú* (10.60.3), *ati - rócate* (10.187.2), *ati - rohati* (10.90.2)

adhi :

adhi - átiṣṭhat (1.163.9), *adhi - ásthāt* (5.31.1)

anu :

anu - āvindat (2.12.11), *anu - dádāti* (2.12.10)

apa :

apa - ávapat (2.14.6), *ava - ávṛṇoḥ* (8.100.6)

api :

api - éti (10.115.1)

abhi :

abhi - gácchati (10.146.5), *abhi - dā́sati* (1.79.11)

ava :

ava - ákhyat (1.161.4), *ava - ábhinat* (2.11.18)

ā :

a - kárāmahe (10.156.2), *ā - jıgāti* (1.117.2), *ā - juhóti* (7.1.23), *ā - dadhársati* (8.27.9)

ut :

ut - ájāyanta (4.18.1), *ut - ắcarat* (7.55.7)

upa :

upa - ávati (10.146.2), *upa - ắgahi* (1.91.10)

dur :

duḥ - gṛbhīyase (5.9.4)

nir :

niḥ - áhan (1.101.1), *niḥ - éhi* (10.124.6)

ni :

ni - pắti (1.73.2), *ni - sī́dati* (7.16.8)

parā :

parā - dádāti (1.81.6)

pari :

pari - ákṣarat (9.64.11), *pari - átiṣṭhat* (1.32.8)

pra :

pra - codáyāt (3.62.10), *pra - dádātu* (7.104.9)

prati :

prati - ghnánti (8.25.15), *prati - bhū́ṣataḥ* (8.62.5), *prati - bhū́ṣati* (6.52.8), *prati - śikṣanti* (10.29.5),

vi :

vi - ucchánti (1.113.18), *vi - undánti* (1.38.9), *vi - cáranti* (1.51.1), *vi - cinóti* (10.42.9), *vi - jā́yante* (2.12.9),

sam :

sam - ákṛṇvan (10.82.4), *sam - ákṣaran* (10.43.7), *sam - ájagṛbhīt* (8.6.17), *sam - ájāsi* (7.32.7), *sam - añjánti* (10.52.3)

II.3.2.b

A B C

(Prefix) - (Prefix) + (Verb)

Examples :

ati :

ati - ā́yāhi (3.35.5), *ati - prasardháyat* (8.31.6)

abhi :

abhi - praghnánti (6.46.10)

ud :

ut - ā́carat (7.55.7)

upa :

upa - ā́gahi (1.91.10), *upa - ā́carat* (1.46.14), *upa - ā́caret* (10.159.2)

duḥ :

duḥ - parihántu (2.27.6)

pari :

pari - prayāthá (4.51.5), *pari - prasyandate* (9.101.2),

prati :

prati - ā́vartaya (6.47.31)

sam :

sam - avartati (2.38.6)

II.3.3.a

A B

(Prefix) - (Suffix)

Examples :

ud :

ut - tamā́ḥ (3.5.10), *út - taram* (1.50.10), *út - tarāt* (4.26.6)

ni :

ni - vataḥ (3.2.10), *ni - vatā* (8.45.38)

parā :

parā - vát (4.50.3), *parā - vátaḥ* (1.34.7)

pra :

pra-taram (1.53.11), *pra - vátaḥ* (1.144.5)

But,

pravátvati (5.54.9), *pravatvati* (5.84.1), *pravátvantaḥ* (5.54.9).

vi :

vi - tarám (1.123.11)

sam :

sam - tarā́m (8.33.19), *sam - vátaḥ* (1.191.15)

su

su - tárā (7.97.8)

II.3.3.b

A B C

{(Prefix) + (Suffix)} - (Suffix)

Examples :

pra :

pravát -bhiḥ (1.33.6), *pravát - su* (6.47.4)

II.3.3.c

A B C D

{(Prefix) + (Suffix) + (Suffix)} + (Suffix)

Example :

pra :

pravátvatībhiḥ (8.13.17)

II.3.4.a

A B

(Prefix) - (*iva*)

Examples :

adhi :

ádhi - iva (8.7.14)

api :

ápi - iva (3.38.8)

upa -

úpa - iva (8.3.21)

pra :

prá - iva (1.103.7)

vi :

vi - iva (7.55.2)

II.3.5.a

A B

(Prefix) - (Prefix)

Examples :

ápa - apa (5.34.3), *abhi - abhi* (9.110.5), *út - ut* (4.21.9), *úpa - upa* (1.126.7), *párā - parā* (1.38.6), *prá -pra* (1.40.7), *sám - sam* (10.191.1).

II.3.5.b

A

(Prefix) : *Free*[177]

Examples:

mano ruhanā / áti / yanty āpaḥ (1.32.8), divo vā rocanād / ádhi / (1.6.9), āt aha svadhām / ánu / (1.6.4), / ápa / vṛdhi (1.7.6), indram / abhí / (1.5.1), tvam viṣṇum / áva / atiraḥ (1.11.7), saḥ devān /ā́/ vakṣati (1.1.2),

Similarly, 1.9.4; 1.1.7; 1.5.1; 1.4.5; 1.4.4; 1.6.1; 1.3.12; 1.1.4; 1.3.12; 1.6.3; and 1.9.6 can be referred to for the examples of other remaining prefixes.

II. 3.6 COMMENTS ON II.3.1a to II.3.5.b

II. 3.1.a

In the sequence of ABC, the analysis is given like (AB)-C, because (AB) is P_2[178]. Again, A and B are also independently P_1[179]; but they are not indicated as such because in the system of Pdk, the division is shown only once based on the ICA. Moreover, the Pdk wants to show the *aikārthibhāva* i.e., single integrated meaning of A and B. Therefore, if the Pdk would analyse as A-(BC), he would indicate the *aikārthibhāva* of (BC) which is not desired.

II.3.1.b.

Suppose, the sequence is ABCD, and the analysis offered is like AB - CD. Here, D is not separated from ABC because it is not a *pada* - marker. Again, A -BCD can not be done because A is not taken as an immediate constituent. Therefore, the remaining possibility is AB-CD in which case meaning-integration of AB is indicated and that of BC is denied.

II. 3.I.c.

The sequence is ABCD. The analysis offered is A - BCD. Evidently, D cannot be separated from ABC because it is not a *pada-* forming suffix and thereby ABC-is not a *pada* before D. The possibility of separating CD from A B can also be denied because AB cannot be an immediate constituent since A has no relation to B, but it has relation to the whole of BCD. Naturally, the analysis A -BCD is supported by the principles of ICA. But sometimes this principle of ICA is violated by the Pdk. It appears that in the cases like *kavāribhyaḥ, gartārugiva,* etc. he prefered to solve the *sandhis* rather than to follow the principle of ICA. Therefore, he offered the analysis as *kava - aribhyaḥ and garta - ārugiva* where the separation would have been *kavāri - bhyaḥ* and *gartāruk -iva* if ICA is adopted. Similarly, in the analysis of forms like *duṣprāvyaḥ sunirajam, suprāyanaḥ, suprāvīḥ, suprāvyah, suprāvyam, supravye etc.,* the principle of *ICA* is violated and *sandhi* has been explained by offering an analysis like *duḥpra* $\frac{3}{4}$ *avyaḥ suniḥ - ajam, suniḥ - mathā, supra - āyanatamam, supra - ayanāḥ, supra - avīḥ, supra - avyaḥ, supra - avyam,* and *supra - avye..*

In the form *suprāyanatamam,* there were two possibilities : either- *tamam* should have been separated because it is an immediate constituent, or, otherwise *su* could have been separated, because it was the next immediate constituent. But none of these ways has been adopted by the Pdk because importance has been given to the explation of the *sandhi*. It is to be noted in this connection that the Pp of the *TS* has analysed *suprāyanāḥ* (5.1.11.2) as *su - prāyanaḥ* which follows the method of ICA.

II. 3.1.d.

In the sequence of ABC here, C cannot be separated because it is not a *pada-* forming suffix. Therefore, the only possible separation is A-BC which is offered by the Pdk.

II. 3.1.e.

In this sequence of ABCD, D cannot be separated, because it is not a *pada*-forming suffix. CD cannot be separated either because BC gives single integrated meaning. Obviously, the only possible division is A-BCD. It is in line with ICA. That is, A is added after BC is formed and so A is separated. But this rule is violated if there is *sandhi* between B and C. And in that case the division is AB-CD, e.g., *karmaniḥ - sathām* for *karmaniṣṭhām* (10.80.1, etc.

Then, why *uruvyacasam* (6.36.6),*uruvyacasā* (1.160.2), *uruvyacāḥ* (1.104.9), *uruvyañcam* (5.1.12) and *gonyoghāh* (9.97. 10) have not been analysed as *uruvi -acasam, uruvi - acasā, uruvi -acah, uruvi -ancam, and goni - oghāḥ*, but as *uru -vyocasam,*[180] , *uru -vyacasā*[180] , *uru - vyācā*[180] , *uru - vyañcam*[180], *and go - nyoghāḥ*?

The reason is neither of these words, namely, vyacas etc. is found analysed in the Pp. Nowhere a form consisting of a prefix and the root *añc* is analysed in the Pp. This may be because the Pdk does not know the derivation of *vyac* as *vi - añc*. The forms with *vi-añc* used frequently are *vyacaḥ* (1.30.3), *vyacasvatīḥ* (2.3.3), *vyacasvantā* (6.25.6), *vyaciṣṭham* (2.10.4) and *vyaciṣṭhe* (5.66.6). None of these is analysed by the Pdk. Therefore, whenever, a *sandhi* between B and C is analysable according to him, the priciple of ICA is violated, otherwise, if that is non-separable in his system, the principle of ICA is consistently followed. This is further supported by the fact that the form *gartārugiva* is analysed as *garta ārugiva*. But according to ICA, *iva* should have been separated. But as the Pdk wants to analyse *sandhi* he violated his normal process. The same is the case with *kavāribhyaḥ* where - *bhyaḥ* should have been separated because it is a *pada*-forming suffix as well as an immediate constituent. But, had he adopted an analysis like *kavāri - bhyaḥ* the *sandhi* in *kavāri* - would have remained unexplained. Therefore, for the sake of *sandhi*-analysis he sometimes violates his usual method.

II. 3.1.f.

Here the separation is found as A - BCDE. Evidently, E cannot be separated as it is not a *pada-* forming suffx. Again, DE cannot be separated because it does not have an independent meaning, but, when DE occurs together with the preceding prefixes (BC) it has some meaning in this particular sequence. Similarly, CDE also cannot be separated because in that case AB would carry no meaning. Moreover, there is no *sandhi* between B and C.So the question of a separation like AB - CDE does not arrise. Therefore, the remaining possibility is A- BCDE which has been adopted by the Pdk.

But, when *preṣitaḥ* (7.73.3) and *preṣitāḥ* (10.98. 6) are analysed as *pra* - *iṣitaḥ* and *pra* - *iṣitaḥ* why, then, ABC - DE is not done?

This shows that the Pdk tries to give ICA as far as possible. Here, before DE there are two prefixes. B and C. But, we do not get any other example to examine what his usual treatment to this type of sequence is.

11. 3.2.a

The question of separation of verbal suffixes does not arise at all as they are not *pada* forming suffixes.Naturally, in the sequence of (Prefix +Verb), we can only separate the prefix if the sequence is taken to be a compound. The treatment of the Pdk indicates that he considers the sequence to be a compound. P does not consider (prefix+Verb) a compound, although the *Vārttikakāra* considers it to be a *samāsa*. But, what is the reason of terming it as a *samāsa*? In other words, what is the gain obtained by the designation *samāsa* to a sequence (prefix+Verb)?

The same question has been raised and answered variously by different commentators of the MBhā on P 2.1.2. But, it appears to me that since the *prātipadika-saṁjnā* is the main result of the application of the term *samāsa* to a particular sequence and since the sequence (Prefix +Verb) cannot be taken as *prātipadika*, the application of the grammatical precept *samāsa* to the sequence under discussion stands unjustified. The *Vārttikakāra* seems to be guided by the single-integrated meaning which we see in the forms *prabhavati*. Therefore, he calls them *samāsa*. Moreover, such compounds show single accent.

Some say that case-ending can be added to this type of compound. But,others refute this view on the ground that when in a verbal form there is already a suffix denoting number etc. What is the point in adding a case-ending and then eliding it ? The *Pūrvapakṣin,* again says that this is possible because in *prātipadikārtha-liṅgaparimāna-vacana-mātre prathamā* (P2.3.46), *vacana* is taken separately. Therefore, in the case like anuvyacalat, a case-ending can be added. The other argument in favour of this sequence being a *samāsa* is the accent. According to this argument, *anu-vyacalat* will be accented on the final syllable only if we consider it as a compound. But, P.8.1.28 prescribes that a verbal form preceded by non-verbal form remains unaccented. So the compound accent is not derived. But in the Vedic language, we do come across such sequencial forms with accent on the verbal ending where P's rule *tiṅi codāttavati* (8.1.71) becomes applicable. When an accented verb follows preverbs lose their accent. This means that the preverb and a verb has a single accent. This indicates that preverb plus verb is treated as a compound. This is the only plausible reason for calling the sequence (Prefix-Verb) a *samāsa.* And perhaps, this is the reason why the Pdk analyses this sequence in the same way as he does in the case of nominal compounds.

But, P does not follow the Pdk's school because he does not find any structural reason to call these sequences as compound. Nevertheless, P has observed that sometimes these sequences have single accent.

To put it more particularly, in this particular sequence, veral endings cannot be separated because they are not *pada*-forming suffixes. Naturally, the next possibility is to separate the prefix i.e., A, because A is the immediate constituent. It is observed that if the prefix is accented both the prefix and the verbal form are considered to be two independent words and are kept within two *daṇḍas*. However, if the accent lies on the verbal form, the sequence is treated as a compound and the constituents of the compound are separated by *avagraha*. Here, A is P2 and B also is P2 and the *avagraha* shows that they are compounded with each other.

II. 3.2.b.

Here also ABC is P1 jointly and again separately A, B, and C are P2 in this particular sequence. Now, which one should be separated from which one ? Obviously, A is the immediate constituent because, BC conveys one single integrated meaning and that is why an analysis like A - BC is offered in this case.

II.3.3.a

The sequence Preverb + Suffix is one of the proofs that prefixes are somewhat independent words. This also agrees with the fact that they received inflexion in an earlier period of the IE language. *Tare, tama* and *vat* are the secondary suffixes which are added with the prefixes. The Pdk has analysed all these forms by separating the suffixes from the prefixes. The following is the treatment :

AB is P1. A is P2. B is a *pada*-forming suffix. Therefore, B is separated from A.

II. 3.3.b

Obviously, C is here an immediate constituent and that is why it is separated from AB.

II. 3.3.c

Here, D is the immediate constituent. But, this cannot be separated because the final syllable of the stem (ABC-) is lengthened and the lengthening is not phonologically conditioned. The lengthening is conditioned morphologically conditioned. The lengthening is conditioned morphologically which is out of the scope of the Pp. CD also cannot be separated because the stems ending in *t* before the possessive suffix *vat* or *mat* are not considered to be *pada*. The remaining possibility is A-BCD. But, this cannot be taken into consideration because A is semantically connected with B and not with BCD. If an analysis like A-BCD is adopted it would indicate the relation of A with BCD which is neither desired nor ture.

Pravat-has been analysed as *pra - vat*. Here, the analysis is perfectly all right because *pra* is P2, But *-vatvatībhiḥ*, here, will carry no meaning. So, the analysis is avoided.

II. 3.4.a

Iva is found to be compounded with the prefixes *adhi, api, upa, pra,* and *vi* only. It should be noted in this connection that P does not consider these sequences as compounds. In fact there is no provision for *iva*- compound in the *Aṣtā*. But, the Pdk has treated them as compounds. That is to say, he has separated *iva* i.e., B from the prefix A. Following the Pdk, Kātyāyana[181] has prescribed compounding of *iva* with any nominal stem which indicates preverbs also. This sequence must be a compound, because we have single accent and a fixed order of the constituents.

II. 3.5.a

This set of data proves that the prefixes were free forms. Prefixes could enter into a compound like nominal stems. These sequences have single accent which is the main reason to consider them as compounds. We come accorss only seven such compound forms. The another peculiarity is all these examples show a combination of phonetically similar prefixes. No example of a compound consisting of dissimilar prefixes is met with throughout the *RV*. Similarly, there is no example to show that such a compound of prefixes consists of more than two similar or dissimilar prefixes.

The analysis offered here is A-B.

II.3.5.b

Under this catagory come the prefixes which are freely used as independent words as well as those which are attached to the verbal forms, but are accented. In both these cases, they are put between two *daṇḍas*. This method is consistantly followed.

II.3.7 PREFIXES NOT SEPARATED

adhīvāsám (1.140.9)[182], *anuṣṭhú* (1.95.3)[183], *anūcáḥ* (3.30.6)[184], *anūpé* (9.107.9).[185], *anūrút* (3.55.5)[186], *apadran* (6.20.4)[187], *apamásya* (10.39.3)[188], *áparam* (1.31.4)[189], *ápāk* (3.53.11)[190], *ápāktāt* (7.104.19)[191], *apīcyena*, (7.60.10)[192], *abhiıṣṭayaḥ* (1.52.4)[193], *abhikam* (9.92.5)[194] *abhiddhāt* (10.10.1)[195], *abhīpatáḥ* (1.164.52)[196], *abhī́śvaḥ* (1.38.12)[197], *abhī́śūnām* (6.75.9)[198], *abhīṣā́t* (7.4.8)[199] *avamáḥ* (4.1.5)[200], *ávaraḥ* (1.163.9)[201], *ā́kim* (1.14.9)[202] *āké* (2.1.10)[203] *akhaṇḍala* (8.17.12)[204], *ākhúm* (7.69.30)[205], *ā́ghṛṇiḥ* (1.23.14)[206], *ā́dam* (1.126.2)[207], *ādhráḥ* (7.41.2)[208], *āpéḥ* (2.27.17)[209], *āprásya* (1.132.2)[210], *ābhúvaḥ* (1.64.1)[211], *ābhā́ṣu* (1.56.3)[212], *ā́yudham* (2.15.4)[213], *āritáḥ* (1.101.4)[214], *ārī́ḥ* (1.77.3)[215], *ārúṣī* (10.155.2)[216], *āvī́ḥ* (1.31.3)[217], *āśuśukṣáṇáṇiḥ* (2.1.1)[218], *āśuṣāṇáḥ* (5.36.4)[219], *āskrāḥ* (1.186.2)[220], *āhanaḥ* (10.10.6)[221], *uttamā́yyam* (9.22.6)[222], *uttarā́t* (6.19.9)[223], *uttarā́ttāt* (10.27.15)[224], *uttānáḥ* (4.13.5)[225], útthitam (10.149.2)[226], *údīcaḥ* (10.131.1)[227], *udārathıḥ* (1.187.10)[228], *udumbaláu* (10.14.12)[229], *uddháran* (10.68.4)[230], *údaktāt* (7.72.5)[231], *úddhitam* (8.51.2)[232], *úttabhitā* (10.85.1)[233], *upabdıḥ* (1.74.7)[234], *upabdaıḥ* (7.104.17)[235], *úparaḥ* (10.27.20)[236], *úpastiḥ* (10.97.23)[237], *upākáyoḥ* (1.81.4)[238], *upānasáḥ* (10.105.4)[239], *ducchúnāḥ* (1.116.21)[240], *duronám* (1.117.2)[241], *duróṣam* (9.101.3)[242], *durya* (7.1.11)[243], *duryoṇé* (1.174.7)[244], *dustáraḥ* (3.24.1)[245], *dustárītave* (2.21.2)[246], *dustárītu* (6.1.1)[247], *niṇık*

(4.5.8)[248], *niṇyáḥ* (1.164.37)[249], *nıtyaḥ* (1.66.1)[250], *nimnám* (1.30.2)[251], *niyutvaḥ* (1.101.9)[252], *nirāmınaḥ* (2.23.16)[253], *nirekám* (8.24.4)[254], *niṣaṅgınaḥ* (3.30.15)[255], *niṣkám* (2.33.10)[256], *niṣṭigryaḥ*, (10.101.12)[257], *niṣṭyaḥ* (6.75.19)[258], *niṣṣapī* (1.104.5)[259], *niṣṣā́t* (1.181.6)[260], *nīcā́* (2.13.12)[261], *nīlám* (10.5.2)[262], *nivyābhiḥ* (6.32.4)[263], *nyak* (8.4.1)[264], *niravásya* (1.122.11)[265], *parākā́t* (1.30.21)[266], *parimśa* (1.187.8)[267], *parivatsarī́ṇam* (7.103.8)[268], *páriṣṭiḥ* (1.65.2)[269], *pratna* (6.39.5)[270], *prathamáḥ* (1.31.1)[271], *pravaṇé* (1.52.5)[272], *pravatvati* (5.84.1)[273], *práṣṭiḥ* (1.39.6)2[74], *práskaṇvam* (8.3.9)[275], *prā́ktāt* (7.104.19)[276], *prāṇáḥ*, (1.66.1)[277], *prātáḥ* (1.16.3)[278], *prātā́* (7.16.8)[279], *prāvargám* (8.4.6)[280], *prā́vṛtasya* (1.162.2)[281], *prāvṛ́ṣi* (7.103.3)[282], *prāvepā́ḥ* (10.34.1)[283], *prā́śavyān* (8.31.6)[284], *prāśuṣā́ṭ* (4.25.6)[285], *prā́śūnām* (8.32.6)[286], *préṣat* (1.180.6)[287], *prátīkam* (6.50.8)[288], *pratī́tyam* (7.68.6)[289], *pratīvyam* (8.23.1)[290], *pratyák* (10.87.15)[291], *vipanyáyā* (1.119.7)[292], *vipanyā́mahe* (1.180.7)[293], *vipanyúvaḥ* (9.86.17)[294], *vipṛ́kvat* (5.2.3)[295], *virúkmataḥ* (1.85.3)[296], *vıvasvat* (1.44.1)[297], *viviktáḥ* (8.12.24)[298], *vivicim* (5.8.3)[299], *viṣṭápaḥ* (8.34.13)[300], *viṣṭambháḥ* (9.2.5)[301], *vispáṭ* (1.18.6)[302], *vispitásya* (7.60.7)[303], *viṣpuliṅgakā́ḥ* (1.191.12)[304], *vī́cyā* (10.10.6)[305], *vitantasā́yyaḥ* (6.18.6)[306], *sámanam* (1.48.6)[307], *samudráḥ* (1.30.3)[308] *samyák* (4.58.6)[309], *saṁvatsaráḥ* (10.190.2)[310], *sáṁskṛtaḥ* (8.33.9)[311], *súgmyah* (1.173.4)[312], *sumnám* (1.43.4)[313], *surabhı* (4.39.6)[314], *suṣṭhú* (8.22.18)[315], *sūnṛta* (8.46.20)[316], *sūnáraḥ* (8.29.1)[317], *sā́bharvam* (10.102.5)[318], *sūrmyam* (8.69.12)[319].

II.3.7.a CONCLUSION

The study of the list given in II.3.7 shows that there are a good many compound words, the first member of which is a prefix, and which the Pdk has not analysed. They can be put under two groups

A. Cases of non-separation although the derivation is not obscure; and

B. Cases of non-separation where the derivation is obscure.

Under A. will come from like *ākhaṇḍala, āghṛṇiḥ, ābhuvaḥ āyudham, āhanaḥ, etc.*

B. can be further divided under following heads

B1. Cases of non-separation where the derivation of stems is unknown to the Pdk.

B2. Cases of non-separation where there is loss of a phoneme or of a syllable.

B3. Cases of non-separation where the final syllable of the prefix is lengthened.

B4. Cases of non-separation where the secondary suffixes are not known to the Pdk.

Under B1. come forms like *udārathiḥ, udumbalau upabdaiḥ, āskrāḥ āruṣi, etc.*

Under B2. will come forms like *anūcaḥ, apāk, apicyaḥ, abhiṣṭiḥ, abhīkam, abhīpataḥ, upastiḥ, nīcā, pratīkam, vīcvā* etc.

Under B3. will come forms like *adhīvāsam abhīṣau-ṭ, prāvṛtaḥ, sunṛtaḥ, sūnaraḥ, sūkaram* etc.

And, under B4 come forms like *aparaḥ, avaraḥ, uparaḥ, pratnaḥ prathamaḥ* and *pravaṇe.* Here, the suffixes *-ra, -tra, -thama* (from tama) and *-vaṇa* are most probably not known to the Pdk and therefore, he does not analyse them.

II.4 ITI-KARAṆA

To add iti after certain words or word-groups is a phenomenon employed by the Pdk. This device of *iti- karaṇa* is known as *anārṣa -itikaraṇa* both in the *RPr* 1.58 as well as in P.1.1.16. Since this *iti* is added by the Pdk in Pp in addition to the vocables of the Sp, it might have come to be known as *anārṣa iti* i.e. an iti which is not used by the *ṛṣi*

The purpose of the iti - *karaṇa* in the Pp is as follows:

(A) It indicates the *pragṛhya* vowels which do not undergo any change even when they are followed by some other combinable vowels.

(B) It specifies mainly a *visarjaīya* which comes from *r* in order to distinguish it from those which are derived from *s*.

(C) It restores the word *īm* whenever it is found as simply *ī* in the Sp.

(A) After *pragṛhya* - vowels iti is put in the following situations

a. o. vocative[320] e.g., *viṣṇo ıti* (1.156.1)

b. *o* particle[321] e.g., *ó ıti* (10.117.5)

c. *o* terminal[322] e.g., *eṣó ıti* (1.46.1)

d. *ī, u, e* dual[323] e.g., *ındrābṛhaspátī ıti* (4.49.5); *ındravayū ıti* (1.2.4); *dvé ıti* (1.95.1).

e. *ī, u* locative[324] e.g., *camū́ ıti* (8.76.10); *sarasī́ ıti* (7.103.2)

f. *asme, yuṣme, tve, ami*[325] e.g., *asmé ıti* (8.5.15); *yaṣme iti* (8.68.19); *tve iti* (1.26.6); *amī́ ıti* (1.105.10).

ū̄ (from *u*, a particle)[326] e.g., *ū̄ ıti* (1.24.8).

It is to be noted in this connection that in *iva-* compounds if the vowel preceding *iva* is a *pragṛhya*-vowel, the *iti* is added after *iva* and not after the *pragṛhya*-vowel. Then the whole compound is repeated after *iti* and *iva* is separated by an *avagraha*. For instance, *nṛpátı ivéti nṛpátī - iva* (7.104.6).

(B) After a *ḥ* coming from *r*, *iti* is added in the following situations:

i) *ḥ* resulting from *r* of a nominal, e.g.,

duhitarıti (6.65.6)

netarıti (5.50.5)

pitarıti (6.51.57)

prātarıti (1.125.1)

savitarıti (1.35.11)

hótarıti (1.13.1)

ii) *ḥ* resulting from *r* of a verbal, e.g.,

akarıty akaḥ (1.33.15)

adardarıty adardaḥ (10.67.7)

ástarıtyástaḥ (7.18.11)

asparıty aspaḥ (5.15.5)

āvarıty āvaḥ (1.92.4)

karıty kaḥ (1.61.11)

In all these cases of (A) and (B), *iti* is added to a *pragṛhya* vowel and to a *riphita-visarjanīya*[327]

The other notable point is that a word or a word-group after which *iti* is added, is sometimes, repeated after *iti*. Now, why after some words or word-groups only? The reason is as follows:

If *iti* comes after a compound which, again, is separable in its component parts, the whole compound is repeated and division is shown, e.g., *kavikrato ıti kavi -krato* (3.14.7). Here, *iti*, first of all indicates that *o* of *kavikrato* is a non-combinable vowel i.e., a *pragṛhya*-vowel. Secondly, repetition of *kavikrato* after *iti* is meant for showing the diviable components of the compound. But if the compound is not dividable in the opinion of the Pdk, repetition is not done, e.g., *Indrābrahmaṇspatī* ıti (2.24.12) *symbolndrāvıṣṇū ıti* (4.2.4), etc. In this case, the Pdk is quite consistent in indicating a *pragṛhya*-vowel by adding *iti* and showing the division of the compound wherever it is divisible to his opinion, excepting one case where he has not indicated the *paragṛhya*-vowel. It is in the case of *Índrāgnī* (7.94.8) which is analysed as simply *Índrāgnī* when it should have been analysed as *Índrāgnī ıti,* in the Pp.

But, the procedure is not the same in the case of *iti* following a *r.* Sometimes, the word, even though it is not a compound, is repeated (See Bii above) again sometimes not (See B i) above). The word *akaḥ* at *RV* 2.12.4 is repeated after *iti* as *ạkrity akaḥ* whereas, at *RV* 5.83.10 it is not. Both the forms are derived from root *kṛ.* Both show accent on the same syllable. Similar is the case of unanccented *akaḥ*. It is repeated after *iti* at *RV* 1.33.15; but, not so at *RV* 1.24.8. What is the purpose behind this treatment of the Pdk?

A close comparative study of these forms both repeated and unrepeated, reveals that the main purpose of the Pdk behind this treatment lies in this that he wants to indicate that the *visarjanīya* there is derived from *r*. If *r* is already there in the Sp by way of *sandhi,* the Pdk does not feel it necessary to indicate it again in the Pp. For example, in *akranchatrūyatām dharā vedanā kaḥ* (1.33.15), it is not clear that the *visarjanīya* of *akaḥ* is derived from *r,* because it comes at the end of the *pāda*. So the Pdk has added *iti* to it. Not only that, the *akaḥ* is repeated after *iti* giving an explanatory paraphrase, as it were. The statement *akarity akaḥ* thus means 'the form *akaḥ* as found in the Sp *(iti)* is to taken from *akar*. This procedure is quite consistently followed.

However, in *apáde pā́dā prátighātave' karutā́pavaktā́ hṛdayā vıdhascit* (1.24.8), the form *akaḥ* is kept as it is, because, here, that the form akaḥ is derived from akar is quite clear from the Sp itself. Had it been from *akas* the *sandhi* would have been like......*pratighātave'ka uta*.... and not with *r* as is actually found in the Sp. Therefore, the Pdk does not add *iti* to it, which will be superfluous. Thus, he cannot write *akariti*. He cannot write *akarity akaḥ* also, because the Sp shows *akar* and *akaḥ*. Naturally, when he cannot write *akariti*, the question of repetition does not arise.

So far we have taken cases of *ḥ* that comes at the end of a *pāda*. Now let us turn to the cases of ḥ occurring within a *pāda*. Thus, if a ḥ resulting from *ṛ* remains as ḥ inside a *pada* what method should the Pdk adopt to indicate it? Here too, the Pdk has added *iti* to indicate the origin of ḥ. The following *ṛk* can be taken in order to make this point clear:

prātā́r agnım prātár ındram havāmahe

prātā́r mitrā́váruṇā prātáravınā /

prātár bhágam pūsáṇam bṛáhmaṇaspátim

prātáḥ sómam utá rudrám huvema // 7.41.1.

Now, here, form *prātar* occurs as *prātaḥ* once, and as *prātar* in the remaining places. *Prātaḥ* occurs in the middle of the fourth *pāda*. It is followed by *somam*. The result is that the *r* of *prātar* has become ḥ before *s* of *somam*. Therefore, the Pdk adds *iti* to show that the original form is *prātar*. The Pp runs as follows:

prātáḥ / agnım/ pratáḥ / ındram / havāmahe/ prātáḥ/ mitrā́vā́ruṇā / prātáḥ/ aśvınā/ prātáḥ / bhágam/ pūṣáṇam / bráhmaṇaḥ/ pátiḥ / prātárıti / sómam / utá / rudrám / huvema//

Thus, wherever the Sp shows r in *prātar*, the Pp is consistently *prātaḥ i.e.,* without *iti*. Here too the reason is that one can know from the Sp itself that *prātar* ends in *r*. and the ḥ results from *r*. But, one cannot know just from prataḥ somam that the ḥ here comes from *r* unless it is indicated in the Pp and that is why the Pdk indicates it by adding *iti* to it.

Now, one can question, why is *prātaḥ* not repeated after *iti* i.e., as *prātariti, prataḥ*, as is done so in the case of *akaḥ* discussed earlier?

The answer to this question is that the Pdk wants to distinguish ḥ resulting from *r* of a nominal from ḥ resulting from *r* of a verbal. Through this device, the Pdk, I think, makes clear distinction between ḥ resulting from *r* which comes from ṛ of a root and ḥ resulting from *r* of a nominal stem. Thus, ḥ in *akaḥ* is derived from *r* of the root *kṛ* which becomes *kar* by gunation, whereas, ḥ in *prātaḥ* is directly from *r* of *prātar*. This is shown by repeating *akaḥ* after *iti* and not repeating *prataḥ* after *iti*. But, that ḥ comes from *r* is indicated by *iti* in both these cases.

(C) The *m* of *īm* is sometimes dropped in the Sp. The Pdk restores it and adds *iti* to it indicating thereby that the word which is found in the Sp as simply *ī*, is actually *īm*. Following are the cases where the Pdk has restored *īm* :

Sp	Pp
sámī pṛcyate	*sám / īm ıti /.....1.103.1*
jagdhámī púṇaḥ	*jagdhám / īm ıti / 1.140.2*
sámī vivyāca	*sám / īm ıti / 3.36.8*
sámī sákhāyo	*sám / īm ıti / 9.45.5*

Sp	*Pp*
támī mṛjanti	*tám / īm ıti /* 9.63.17
sámī rátham	*sám / īm ıti /*.....9.71.5
é riṇanti	*ā́ / īm ıti /* 9.71.6
sámī gā́vo	*sám / īm ıti /* 9.72.6
yámī gárbham	*yám / īm ıti /* 9.102.6
sámī vatsám	*sám / īm ıti /* 9.104.2
támī sṛjanti	*tám / īm ıti /* 9.107.17

Out of (A), (B), and (C), (C) is without any exception: (A) has got one exception already noted above; but (B) has got several cases of exception, few of them are discussed below.

The form *dartaḥ* in *RV*1.130.10 is shown in the Pp as *dartarıti dartaḥ*. Here the repeating of *dartaḥ* after *iti* is not in agreement with the general rule that only a verbal form is repeated after *iti*. The form is vocative singular of *dartṛ*.

Similarly, adding *iti* after *ūvuḥ* (1.61.8), *guḥ* (3.7.7), *syuḥ* and *syuḥ* in 2.4.9 and 1.24.7 respectively is not in consonance with the general principle that *iti* should indicate a *ḥ* which results from *r*. Here in all the cases mentioned above the *ḥ* results from *s*. *Uvuḥ* is perfect 3rd pl of root *vā* 'to weave'; *guḥ* is aorist 3rd pl of root *gā*; and *syuḥ* is optative 3rd pl of root *as* 'to be'.

Apart from the purposes of using *iti*-device discussed so far, we come accross few cases where *iti* device is used for individual purposes. For instance, the word *namasyan* (1.72.5) is shown in the Pp as *namasyannıti namasyan*. Here, *namasyan* neither ends in a *pragṛhya*-vowel nor in ḥ resulting from *r*. Still *iti* is added. The reason for such treatment seems to be that immediately preceding *namasyan* there occurs the word *namasyaṃ* which ends in *anusvāra* in the Sp. Naturally, there is a chance of confusion between *namasyam* and *namasyan.* To avoid this he might have added *iti* to *namasyan* and might have stressed this point by repeating it after *iti*

Similarly, when *rathyā* and *rathyebhiḥ* are found juxtaposed together with the lengthening of *a* of *rathyebhiḥ* in the Sp in 1.157. 6, the Pdk adds *iti* to *rathyebhiḥ* and repeats it after *iti* such as *ráthyebhiriti ráthyebhiḥ*. The Sp reads as *rathyā* $\frac{1}{3}$ *ráthyebhiḥ*

Likewise, *praṇapāt* is shown as *pránapāditi prá -napāt* in the Pp under 8.17. 13. The Sp reads...*napāt práṇapāt*...Moreover, *n* of *praṇpāt* is cerebralised. Perhaps, the Pdk wants to show all this. Otherwise, *praṇapāt* does not end either in a *pragṛhya* vowel or in ḥ coming from *r.* Therefore, it cannot be influded either in (A) or in (B). Thus, *iti* explains the individual feature here.

Similarly, in *nấsya té mahimấnam pári ṣṭatḥ* (16.61.8), *staḥ* (present 3rd du of root as) is found as *ṣṭaḥ* and the Pdk wants to indicate it as an special case and therefore, he adds *iti* to it and repeats it after *iti.*

In all these examples which could not be included in any of the catagories (A), (B), and (C), the Pdk can show some reason for adding *iti* to them. But, we do not know what made the Pdk add *iti* after *vaneḥ* (2.6.1) and *vark* (10.8.9). *Vaneḥ* is Optative 2nd sg of root *van* and *vark* is root aorist 3rd sg of the root *vṛj*. Obviously, none of these forms ends in a *pragṛhya*-vowel or in ḥ. They do not suffer any phonetic change either. They do not create any confusion where they occur. Moreover, the form *vark* in 6.26.3 is not shown as *vargiti vark* although it occurs at the end of the *Pāda* There fore, we do not get any reason to support the treatment of the Pdk in these cases.

But it is not the case with *praceta iti pra - cetaḥ* in the Pp under 1.24.14. Here, the Sp is *pracetā rājan* where we get a peculiar *sandhi,* i.e.The loss of of *ḥ* of *pracetaḥ* and the lengthening of its final *a*. The Pdk wants to explain this *sandhi* and therefore, he adds *iti* to this form and stresses the point by repeating it after *iti*.

To sum up : The use of *iti* has the following purposes

i) It indicates a *pragṛhya- vowel,*

ii) It indicates ḥ resulting from *r*.

iii) It restores the original form of a form if such a form suffers any loss of its final phoneme.

iv) It explains a confusing situation when a homophonous words are juxtaposed.

v) It explains a peculiar *snadhi* in the Sp.

And the repetition of the forms after *iti* has the following implications :

i) It distinguishes ḥ coming from *r* of a root from ḥ coming from *r* of a nominal stem.

ii) It stresses a point indicated by *iti* in special cases.

iii) It indicates that the word group preceding *iti* is divisible.

DATA : *itikaraṇa*

Indrābrahmaṇaspatī́ ıti (2.24.12), *iyāte ıti* (7.39.2), *iravatī ıtīrā-vatī* (7.99.3), *iṣàyantī ıti* (4.56.4), *īryethe ıti* (10.106.10), *īsāthe ıti* (7.97.10), *ukṣàmāne ıti* (4.56.2), *ukṣite ıti* (2.3.6), *úpastute ıtúpastute* (2.32.1), *uśatī́ ıti* (3.33.1), *ūtī́ ıti* (1.185.9), *ṛjré ıti* (6.63.9), *ṛtapsu ıtyṛta - psu* (1.180.3), *ṛtavaso ıty ṛta -vāso* (8.101.5), *ṛdhāhe ıti* (1.17.9), *ṛṣve ıti* (7.62.4), *kavikrato ıti kavi - krato* (3.14.7), *kavī́ iti* (8.8.2), *kṛtád-vasū iti kṛtát -vasū* (8.31.9), *kéno iti* (8.66.9), *gòpatī iti gò - patī* (9.19.2), *camù iti* (5.51.4), *tàtro iti* (1.37.14), devī iti (4.55.6), *dyàvi iti* (4.56.5).

akṣāriti (9.81.1), *adarity adaḥ* (1.121.10), *adardarity adardaḥ* (10.67.7), *adhārity abhaḥ* (10.20.10), *avarīvariti* (10.10.129.1), *avarīvuriti* (10.51.6), *ástarity, ástaḥ* (7.18.11), *asparityaspaḥ* (5.15.5), *ávtarity ávaḥ* (10.67.4), *jaritariti,* (3.15.5), *tūtoriti tūtoḥ* (6.26.4), *dardariti dardaḥ* (1.63.7), *dīdhariti dīdhaḥ* (6.17.6), *duhitariti* (6.15.6), netariti (5.50.5), *neṣṭariti* (1.15.3), *pitariti* (6.51.5), *prànetariti prá-netaḥ.* (7.41.3), *bhāriti bháḥ* (1.128.2), *sva i riti svaḥ* (1.52.12), *savitariti* (1.35.11), *vavruriti vavruḥ* (4.1.15), *hotariti* (1.13.1)

II.5. DOUBLE - SANDHI

In the *Saṃhitā*-text of the *RV* we find a few cases of double - *sandhi*. It is interesting to note that the Pdk has detected all such cases and has analysed them restoring the original shape of the words in the Pp. Here, we find another proof that the Pdk analysed the Sp properly understanding the meaning of the text. Here he provides unique help in understanding the meaning of the *RV*

A few example of double-*sandhi* detected by the Pdk are given below;

Sp	Pp
sédu	sáḥ / it / 1.32.15
sédṛbhavah	sàḥ / it/...4.37.6
Sédagne	sàḥ / it /...4.4.7
sédagniḥ	sàḥit / 7.1.14
Sédugraḥ	sàḥ / it.... 7.40.3
sédīse	sàḥ/it/....10.86.16

Sp	Pp
séti	sàḥ/ıti/ 2.12.5
sāsmā́kam	*Sàḥ / asmā́kam /* 1.129.1
sā́si	*sáḥ / asi /* 2.13.2
sā́smākaebhiḥ	*sáḥ / asmākebhiḥ/* 7.12.4
séndra	*sā́ḥ* / indra / 2.13.11
sémàm	*sáḥ / imàm/* 1.14.11
sémā	*sàḥ / imā́ /* 2.24.1
Sémabhi	*sáḥ / īm / 9.94.7*
sā́smin	*sáḥ / asmin /* 10.44.5
sā́bhivegaḥ	*sàḥ / abhi -vegaḥ /* 10.27.1
sā́smai	*Sā́ḥ / asmai /* 2.17.6
Sése	*sàḥ / īse /* 10.68.9
sótá	*sàḥ/ utà /* 2.24.1
sòpamā́	*sáḥ/upa-mā́/* 1.31.15
sòṣām	*sàḥ / uṣām /* 10.86.16
Sáinā́	*Sàḥ / enā́ /* 2.9.6
sàinam	*sàḥ / enam /* 2.22.1
vā́saū́	*vài / asaū́ / 5.17.3*

REFERENCES

1. *RV* 2.34.5

2. *RV* 5.41.19

3. *RV* 8.5.35.

4. *RV* 9.111.2

5. *RV* 9.72.5

6. *RV* 10.94.7

7. *RV* 10.107.3

8. *RV* 10.130.1

9. *RV* 1.116.3.

10. *RV* 10.85.11

11. *RV* 10.94.7

12. But an original voiced consonant has also been shown as devoiced e.g., *hṛdhıḥ/ hṛt - bhıḥ/*. For this there was some difference of opinion which is recorded in the ṚPr 1.5/13 : *varge varge ca prathamāvaghoṣau, yugmau soṣmānā anunāsiko 'nyaḥ/ tasmād anyam avasāne tṛtīyam gārgyaḥ sparśaḥ prathamam śākṭāyanaḥ//*

13. *RV* 1. 100.16.

14. Perhaps on the analogy of *dhūrṣádaḥ /-dhuḥ-sádaḥ/ (RV*2. 34.4) and *dhūrṣádam/ dhūr -sádam/ RV 1.143. 7).*

15. *RV* 2.35.6

16. *RV* 8.92.7

17. *See, JHA, V.N. "On the two Rgvedic compound-forms : ráthaspáti* and *vánaspáti-*; Proceedings of the 25th All India Oriental Conference, Jadavpur, pp 232-33.

18. VPr V. 13

19. VPr v.35 : *janayatyā oṣadhayo vṛṣāyiṣata nahi canāsmabhyamajāvayo valagam.*

20. See *WHITNEY*, APr IV. 31. p.201.

21. VPr. V. 14

22. APr IV. 31. *WHITNEY's* translation is followed here.

23. *APr* IV. 33

24. *APr* IV. 32.

25. *APr* IV. 34

26. I do not agree with S.K. BELVALKAR's statement : 'A further advance was made by the constituion of Pada pāṭha....Which gave each suffix or termination of the noun separately 'System of Sanskrit Grammar, P. 4. We have got only four case-suffixes separated.

27. See P 1.4.14; 1.4.17. The nominative singular ending- *s* is not separated due to its being counted in *sarvanāmasthāna*-suffixes.

28. See P. 1.4.18

29. See Introductory Remarks of this chapter.

30. *RV* 8.43.3.

31. *RV* 4.2.12.

32. *RV* 7.1.7

33. Cf. *ṅyāpprātipadikāt* (P 4.1.1) and *prātipadikārtha-liṅga* (P 2.3.46). Here P also does not consider *ṅībanta* and *ā*banta bases as *prātipadika*. Also see, K.C. *Chatterjee, Technical terms and technique of Sanskrit Grammer*, p.69.

34. *supi ca (P 7.3.102), bahuvacane jhalyet* (P7. 3.103) etc. are stated in the section *aṅgasya* (P 6.4.1.).

35. *RV* 1.22.14.

36. *RV* 10. 179.2

37. *RV* 10. 130. 1

38. *RV* 8.4.6

39. *RV* 10.89. 11

40. *RV* 1.64.1

41. *RV* 1.139.7

42. *RV* 5.64.7

43. *RV* 6.45.21

44. *RV* 10.137.7

45. *RV* 1.1.5

46. *RV* 5.41.19

47. *RV* 1.7.3

48. *RV* 1.116.3

49. *RV* 3.4.2

50. *RV* 3.50.2

51. *RV* 4.19.3

52. *RV* 10.15.4

53. *RV* 1.155.6

54. *RV* 1.108. 2

55. *RV* 8. 101. 5

56. *RV* 8. 38.1

57. The tick-mark indicates that the Pdk has separated the suffix.

58. *Vedic Grammar,* p. 134, 190a.

59. *Sanskrit Grammer,* p. 457, 1207a.

60. *loc. cit*

61. *loc. cit*

62. According to WACKERNAGEL (AIG, II.2, 128) also *suprajas* is a compound stem. See also AIG, III. 285

63. In the *RV* the only form available is *vikaṭe* (10.155.1) The Pdk separates it as *vi-kaṭe*. But we cannot be sure whether it is a compound- separation or suffix- separation.

64. It is a wrong analysis. Because according to the principle

of ICA of the Pdk, *-tama* is to be separated from *ratnadhā* Moreover, *ratnadhā-* is used as an independent form several times in the *RV*. In these cases - *dhā* is separated from *ratna-*, e.g., *ratna-dhāḥ* (1.15.3).

65. It is derived from *devī -tama*. But even the Sp reads *devitame.* It is peculiar case of shortening of the long primary vowel ī. The Pdk also does not restore the original one and keeps as it is. No commentator gives any explanation for this.

66. For the same reason the word *puruṣatvatā* (4.54.3) also is not analysed by the Pdk.

67. This stem can be found in forms like *sanutar etc.*

68. Since the Pdk's treatment of such forms goes against Pāṇinian treatment Patanjali is very unhappy with the Pdk and remarks : *na lakṣaṇena pada-kārā anuvartyāh padakārair nāma lakṣaṇam anuvartyam / yathālakṣaṇam padaṁ kartavyam/.*

69. Cf. P. 8.2.12, 13, 14 and 16. Katyāyana further records *vṛṣaṇvasū*, and *vṛṣaṇasva* where *n* is retained and wants the extention of the definition of *bha* to *vṛṣan*. The Pdk analyses them as *vṛsaṇ - vasū* and *vṛṣaṇasvena* respectively. *vṛṣaṇasva* is left unanalysed.

70. This principle of the Pdk is not in consonance with his general principle that a grammatical lengthening should not be removed. Otherwise we except analysis of *hastābhyām* etc. as *hasta - bhyām*, which is not done.

71. *VASU's* translation.

72. In some vocative forms instead of *-van* we get *-vaḥ* in the Vedic language.

73. The stem here is not probably an anomalous form for *indhanavan.*

74. See chapters on *-mat, -vat,* etc.

75. *RV* 2.111.9.

76. *RV* 10.24.4.

77. *RV* 8.74.13.

78. *RV* 10.102.8.

79. A similar *sandhi* has taken place in the case of *pṛṣadvat* (7.2.4) and the Pdk has analysed the form as *pṛṣat - vat*. See, under *-vat.*

80. The expected form was *dhṛṣatvinaḥ* in which case the Pdk would not have analysed the form.

81. Normally, the Pdk avoids analysis of the forms showing grammatical lengthening.

82. As he has analysed *namobhiḥ* (1.24.14) etc. as *namoḥ - bhiḥ.*

83. *RV* 7.50.1

84. A similar case is *uttarāttāt* which is also not analysed by the Pdk.
See under II.1.2.b.2.

85. *WACKERNAGEL (AIG II.2, 193)* agrees with P.

86. See *WACKERNAGEL,* II.2, pp.746-747.

87. P 5.2.139.

88. P 5.2.138.

89. See *WACKERNAGEL, II.2,* para 630.

90. See *WACKERNAGEL, II.2* 906.

91. Whether it forms substantives is questionable, because we have only one instance i.e., *aṅkuśa*. See WACKERNAGEL II. 2. 738a.

92. We have both *átha* and *áthā in the RV*. The Pdk invariably makes *áthā* as *átha* in the Pp. This indicates that by the time of the Pdk the form *athā* became out of use and to him only *átha* was correct.

93. *Katháṁ* (5.61.2) is also not analysed by the Pdk.

94. In origin it is the accusative neuter (with adverbial shift of accent) of the suffix *-vant;* cf. *tvāvant* 'like thee'.

95. Here *-tas* is added to a fully inflected form i.e. *patsu.*

96. Originally, it is the ablative of *ta-*.

97. Only as the final member of a compound, e.g., *iryā-iva* (10.106.4).

98. See P. 1.4.15.

99. P 8.2.7.

99a. *Vṛṣāyate* can be derived from the stem *vṛṣa-* also.

99b. *prajāvān* is an integrated form (*vṛtti*). It is derived as follows:

prajā asya asti iti

= *prajā - sU - matUP*

= *prajā - mat*

= *prajā - vat*

= *prajā - vat - sU*

= *prajāvān.*

100. "On the Rgvedic denominetive *adhvarīya-*" Journal of the University of Poona, Humanities Section, No. 27, pp. 27-35.

100a. RPr VII. 1, 2.

100b. *Loc. cit.*

101. From the historical point of view it seems that the stems other than short *i*-stems were connected with the suffix *-iya* which developed to some extent independently, with a desiderative sense. For instance, *putrī-yáti* 'desires a son' *māṁsiyáti* 'craves flesh'. *Maṁsiyáti* does not occur in the *RV*, *adhvarīyase* and *rathīyantiva* can be taken in the desiderative sense.

101a. According to modern scholars the denominative suffix *-iya* is obtained after *taviṣīyá*. Thus, from here *ya* with prefixed long *ī* is like *kavīyá* or *sakhīyá-* etc. which again is extended to stems ending in *a* or *ā*. In classical Sanskrit, forms with long *ī* prevails over short *i*.

102. *Vanarṣad* is the only example where *r* is totally dropped in analysis. It is separated as *vana - sad*.

103. Both these forms are denominatives from *Śama*. Pdk's analysis of these forms makes no sense. It seems that the Pdk failed to recognize these forms as denominative forms. Otherwise, with his normal rule these forms should have been analysed as *śama - ye* and *śama - yate*. If can be noted in this connection that J. AVERY "Verb-forms of the *Ṛgveda*" does not record these two forms, under the denominative forms.

104. P VI.4.77.

105. P 3.2.107.

106. *Vasau hrasvāt.*

107. *Vāṁśau ca bhūtakāle svareṇa hrasvāt anuṣi.*

108. "Treatment of the suffix *-vāṁs* in the Padapāṭha", *IL* : 30, pp.119-133.

109. MACDONELL. *Vedic Grammar*, Para 241.

110. P also calls them *padas* by Pl.4.14.

111. *ṚPr II.43 :: sunascicchepaṁ niditaṁ, narā vā saṁsam pūṣaṇam / narā ca saṁsam daivyam tā anānupūrvya-saṁhitaḥ//.*

112. Other places where *dyāvā* and *pṛthivī* are separated by other words in the Sp and treated as compounds in the Pp are : 1.63.1; 1.143.2; 1.159.1; 2.41.20; 5. 43.2; 6.11.1; 7.43.1; 8.97.14; 10.35.3.

113. The VSM-edition reads *mitrarājānā* instead of *mitra rājānā*. This seems to be a wrong reading since the time of the Pdk. Since we have once in 3.56.7 *rājānā mitrāvaruṇā*, it is better to take *mitra* separately from *rājānā* which will mean 'the kings Mitra and *Varuṇa* 'and will fit in the context.

114. P 6.1.135 and 6.1.137 describes the derivation of these forms and the forms of *pari* plus root *kṛ* discussed above. The *sūtras* are : *sUṬ kātpūrvaḥ* and *sampary upebhyaḥ karotau bhūṣaṇe*, 'The augment *sUṬ* is placed before *k* when *sam, pari* and *upa* are followed by the verb *kṛ* and the sense is that of ornamenting' *tr. VASU.*

115. *VASU's tr.*

116. *The dvandva*-compounds of the type *satyānṛte* (7.49.3), *mātarāpitarā* (4.6.7), and so on are also not analysed by the Pdk.

117. See, JHA, V.N. "On the two Ṛgvedic compound-forms *rathaspati-* and *vanaspati-*" Proceedings of the All-India Oriental Conference, 1969, pp.231-38.

118. Uṇādisūtra 5.1 :: *adibhuvo DutaC.*

119. See, MAYRHOFER, EWA i.547.

120. See, Grassmann, WB.38.

121. Under *RV* 8.20.26 says : *niso nalopas chāndasaḥ/ ...... ata evopasargasamudāyo nāvagṛhyate/.*

122. See the *vārttika* under P6.1.9 :: *sanyaṅanta-syeti ced aseḥ sanyanjaiṭaḥ*. Therefore, the form *iyakṣamāna* is derived from the root *aś*. This is the opinion of the *Vārttikakāra*. Patañjali does not agree with this and derives the form from root *yaj*, the *y* of which is dropped due to *varṇalopa*.

123. To quote his words : *...eṣa cchāndaso varṇa- lopaḥ/tad yathā ..... iṣkartāram adhvarasya, niṣkartāram adhvarasyeti prāpte/.*

124. See BR 1059 AND GRASSMANN 880.

125. *On RV* 2.27.9 :: *asvapnajaḥ asañjātasvpnāḥ/ "supāṅ suluk ....." iti jasaḥ suḥ/.*

126. P 3.2.172.

127. On *RV* 2.27.9.

128. *VASU's translation.*

129. *See WACKERNAGEL, AIG III.* para 55, 204, and 407.

MACDONELL, on the other hand, derives these forms with the suffix - *aj; cf. Vedic Grammar, para 303.*

130. *HOCKETT. C.F. A Course in Modern Linguistics,* Indian Edition, 1970, p. 55.

131. Cf. *Nir* 6.19 : *ilābilasayasya.*

132. But, *śraddadhānaḥ* (1.103.3), is analysed as *śrat - dadhānaḥ.*

133. NAVATHE, P.D. has noted this form in his article "Two anomalous cases in the Padapāṭha of the Ṛgveda" PAOC, 1969, p. 249.

134. See PW s.v. *garta; Nir* 3.5; MW gives the wrong division like *gartā -ruk.*

135. NAVATHE does not notice this fact and feels that the violation of rules regarding *gartārugiva* cannot be explained. In his words "This is clearly an error for which no plausible explanation can be offered". Ibid.

136. See *Apr* IV.41 and VPr V.18: *ive ca* and *iva-kārāmreḍitāyaneṣu* respectively.

137. This criterion is used in many other cases also by the Pdk. The particles *na* and *hi* are accented when they are used independently. But, in *nahi* only one accent is shown and therefore, the Pdk takes it as one word. Similarly, the Pdk treats *iva* - forms as compound- forms. For opinions of patañjali and kaiyata, see patañjali's Vyākaraṇa-Mahābhāṣya (Avyayībhāva- tatpuruṣāhnika) by S.D. JOSHI, University of Poona, 1969, pp. 84-85.

138. Thus, we can observe that the separation of *iva* is not conditioned by any phoneme preceding it or by the length of any vowel. It is separated after all case-endings.

139. See P 6.3.1.223.

140. Thus, it can be said that the Pdk had the perfect knowledge about *sa* which is a substitute morpheme for *saha*.

141. Cf. P 6.3.74.

142. See the Chapter : *Prefixes* for examples.

143. By 'separable' I mean: if there is no other separable immediate constitutent in that particular compound.

144. For example : *niṣaṅginaḥ* (3.30.15), *abhīśavaḥ* (1.38.12), *āyudham* (2.15.4), and *āśavaḥ*.

145. See, BRUGMANN, *Comp. Gr. of I-E languages* pp. 457- 480; WHITNEY, *Sanskrit Grammar*, p. 395,; *MACDONELL, Vedic Grammar*, pp. 414 - 415; *BURROW, The Sanskrit Language* p. 278; WILSON, *And Introduction to the grammer of Sanskrit language* pp. 98-99; RAMGOPAL, *Vaidik Vyākaraṇa*(Hindi), pp. 818 - 19.

146. MACDONELL, *op.cit.*, p. 414.

147. Cf. P. 1.4.80 - 82.

148. Cf. P. 1.4.83.

149. *Na nirbadhdhā upasargā arthān nirāhur iti śākaṭāyanaḥ.* 'Prefixes do not convey and meaning when they are not connected with any word.'

150. *Uccāvacāḥ padārthā bhavantīti Gārgyaḥ* ' these prefixes have various meanings, says *Gārgya*'

151. ..... *upasargā viṁśatir arthavāvakāḥ, sahetarābhyām itare nipātāḥ*......these twenty prefixes are meaningful only when they are connected with nouns and verbs; other than these prefixes, nouns, and verbs are the particles.'

152. See, K.C.CHATTERJI, *Technical Terms and Technique of Sanskrit Grammer* pp.398 - 434.

153. *Prabhyā-parā-nir-dur-anu-vyupāpasaṁ-pari- prati-nyatvadhi sūdavāpi upasargā viṁsatir arthavācakāḥ* /'*pra, abhi, ā, parā, nir, dur, an, u, vi, upa, apa, sam, pari, prati, ni, ati, adhi, su, ud, ava, api* are the twenty prefixes.'

154. *Paropāpāva prati paryanvapyatyadhyaṅ pra sam nirdurunni vi svabhi*/

155. *Ā ity arvāgarthe, pra paretyetasya prātilomyam abhityabhimukhyaṁ pratityetasya prātilomyam, ati su ityabhipujarthe, nir dur ityetayoḥ prātilomyam nyaveti vinigrahārthīyā udityctayoḥ prātilomyam sam ityakībhāvam, vyapetyatasya prātilomyam, anv iti sādṛśyāparabhāvam apīti saṁsargam, upetyupajanam, parīti sarvatobhāvam aiśvaryaṁ vaivam uccāvacān arthān prāhus ta upekṣitavyāḥ*//

156. *Prādayaḥ*. Under this rule *Kāśikā* records *nis* and *dus* as variants of *nir* and *dur* in addition to usual twenty, making in all twenty two.

157. K.C. CHATTERJI, *op. cit.* p. 401

158. See, WHITNY's note *JAOS* IX, p. 18.

159. *Upasarganiṣpūrvo' nudāttee pade.*

160. See last para of WHITNEY'S comment on the *TPr* 6.4.

161. For example, *TPr*10.9, according which *ṛ* becomes *ār* if a prefix which ends in *a* or *ā* precedes. According to this, *apa* and *parā* which are excluded in the list at *TPr* 1.15, cannot receive this treatment of *ṛ to ār*. But, they have received like this at *apārtavyā* (5.3.1.1). WHITNEY's wounder runs as under: "Nor have I observed any cases of the different treatment of *parā* and *apa* before *ṛ*; so that here also I do not

discover any reason for the strange restriction of the class of prepositions made at 1.15."

62. For example, *prati* is a *prātipadika* by P.1.2.45. Since it is a *parātipadika*, it will take sU by P 4.1.2. Again, this sU will be elided by P 2.4.82 because *prati* is an avyaya by P 1.1.37 since it is a *nipāta* by P. 1.4.58.

163. No form consisting of more than two nominal stems with any prefix or separable case suffix is met with in the *RV*.

164. Similarly, nor form consisting of more than two prefixes plus nominal stem or verbal form is available in the *RV*.

165. This does not fit in this pattern according to P, because *tasthi* is not nominal stem, But, the Pdk seems to take *tasthi* as a noun. See the section on *-vàms*.

166. *According Pāṇinan system, the n of prapathin* belongs to the suffix-part and not to the stem-part as seems to have been taken by the Pdk.

167. This example is put here as representing the pattern (AB) - C rather the pattern (ABC) -D, because the Pdk does not consider *vidyun* before mat as a *pada*. His fear is that if we consider *vidyun* as a *pada* the final n, will be dropped.

168. Here also according to P the nominative suffix is added and it is dropped by *halṅyābbhyo dirghāt supi*.... Whether this very rule is before the Pdk cannot be said certainly.

169. Nominative.

170. Accusative.

171. Here, according to P, the nominative suffix is added and it is dropped by P 6.1.68.

172. Neuter singular.

173. According to the normal rule of ICA, the separation in this case should be *suprajā - vatīm* (1.111.2). But, here the Pdk seems to assume that *prajavatīm* is qualified by *su-*, rather than assuming that -vati is added to suprajā-.

174. Nominative dual of *supratikā* (f.).

175. The Pdk never put *dur* in his *pada-text. All the rānta*-forms are shown as ending in *ḥ* The reason for such a treatment is twofold : either he considers *duḥ as original or dur has become duḥ* before a pause. I think the Pdk takes *duḥ* as original, because in the case of *duṣpravyah* (4.25.6) he has shown the Pp as *duḥpra - avyaḥ* even though *ḥ* is not followed by a pause.

176. *Nir* as such cannot occur in the Pp because it is always found followed by a pause. In this case it cannot be said definitely that the Pdk assumes *niḥ* as original like *duḥ,* since we do not have any example of that type.

177. By 'free' I mean both the *karmapravacanīya* and the accented preverbs.

178. P_2 = Internal *Pada.*

179. P_1 = External *Pada.*

180. Of course, they can be derived from root *vyac* and there would be no problem.

181. Cf. *Vārttika* under P 2.1.4.

182. Sāy : *upary ācchādanam*. GELDNER : 'Das Ober- gewand'. Thus, *adhi - vāsám* becomes the possible analysis but the Pdk refrains himself from offering this analysis because *i* of *adhi* is not lengthened due to any *sandhi*. However, it should be

noted in this connection that *TS* 4.6.9.2 analyses it as *adhi - vāsam* in its Pp. This suggests an improvement on the Pp of the *RV*.

183. *Anu -sthú* will be the possible division. Say. Under 1.95.3 derives it in the same way on the basis of *Uṇ*. 1.25 : *apaduḥsusu sthaḥ*

184. This and the like are derived from root *añc* with prefix *anu*. But, as the radical portion has suffered considerable change (i.e., *lopa* or *a* of the root) and the the *u* of *anu* is lengthened, the Pdk does not offer any analysis.

185. *anūpa-* from *anvāpa-* from *anu- āp*. Here also since the radical vowel *ā* has been dropped and *u* of *anu* has been lengthened, the Pdk does not divide it.

186. Here, though the radical stem (from root *rudh)* stands separable, the *u* of *anū* is lengthened which is not due to *sandhi* and so no division is attemped by the Pdk.

187. From *apādravan* from *apa- adravan* from *apa*-root *dru* 'to melt'. It is a case of haplology and, therefore,Pdk does neither restore the full form nor separates the prefix. One more difficulty for the Pdk in recognising this form is this that the augment *a* of the Imperfect is also lost here i.e., it is not found as *apādran*.

188. It is found only in the *RV*. It can be derived as *apa - má - sya*.

189. This and the like upto *aparebhiḥ*, may be derived from *apa* with possessive suffix *ra*. The possessive secondary suffix *ra* is never separated from the preceding stem in the Pp. This means that the Pdk did not know that *-ra* was a secondary suffix.

190. This and the like are derived from *apa* + root *añc*. The derivation shows loss of radical *a*, a phonetic change of the final phoneme i.e., *c* to *k* and lengthening of the final *a* of *apa*.

191. This is to be analysed as *apa-* root *añc* - tāt.

192. All these forms are derived from *api-* root *añc* and every where we see some loss of sounds and non-*sandhi* lengthening of sounds. This prevented the Pdk from giving an analysis.

193. Sāy. takes it from *abhi - iṣṭi*. MW analysed this form as *abhi-ṣṭi*. Cf. MW, p. 71, cl.3, : *abhi - ṣṭi-* (s+tifrom root *as*) 'an assistant' protector'. The Pdk does not know this derivation, probably.

194. This is from *abhi+* root *añc* (?). But, root *añc* loses its initial *a* and *i* of *abhi* becomes lengthened. This happens in almost all the forms derived with root *añc* as their second member.

195. No *pada-pāṭha* of the hymn is available. Sāy. explains it as *abhitaḥ prakāsamānāt*. This form occurs in the *AV* and in the *TS* with different case - endings. In the Pp of the *AV* it is analysed as *abhi -iddhaḥ* (7.77.7), and in that of the *TS* it is analysed as *abhi - iddhā* (5.1.7.3).

196. PW. I.355, (von *ā*p mit *abhi*) adv. wie es sich traifft rechtzeitig. *abhīpa* cannot be separated according to the Pdk, because, *āp* has lost its initial *ā* lengthening preceding *i* of *abhi*. Why not then-*taḥ*, the adverbial suffix? It is seen that this suffix is never separated in the Pp of the *RV* throughout. MW, p.74, cl. 3, takes it from 2.*ap* and compares the formation with *anūpa, and translates it as 'from the waters or clouds' Sāy. gives both the meanings :* *ānukulyena* and *abhi- gamanavataḥ*. Probably, the Pdk does not know any example where the portion before-*taḥ* shows a *pada-change*. Therefore, he does not consider the suffix *-taḥ* as a *pada* -forming suffix.

197. This can be derived as *abhī- īś aś* GRASSMANN derives-*īś* from root *aś.* The Pdk is, naturally, in doubt about its derivation and therefore, does not analyse it. The PP of the *Ts* has, ofcourse, analysed it as *abhi-iśu-*.

198. *Abhi-iśūnām* is the expected division as is, latter on, done by the Pp of the *TS* (4.6.62).

199. *Abhi - sát* is the expected division. But, *i* of *abhi* is lengthened without any phonological reason and *s* of *sāt* is changed to s. Therefore, the Pdk avoids any cut.

200. Perhaps, to be derived as *ava-ma* (superlative suffix), a short form of-*tama.* Cf. WHITNEY *Gr.* para 474, P. 176; MAYRHOFER, KWA,I.58. But, *upamān (10.8.1), is slipt up as upa - mān.* Thus, inconsistency is due to the fact that the Pdk thinks *upamān is* from *upa- mān,* but he cannot give such a derivation for *avama-*.

201. This form is derived as *ava-ra* (comparative suffix) This *-ra* is never separated any where in the *pada* -text. The Pdk does not know that *-ra* is a secondary suffix.

202. This form is to be explained as *á - kim* from *kim* 'some one' ind. Cf. SURYAKANTA, *A Grammatical Dictionary of Sanskrit* (Vedic), Delhi, 1953, p.36.

203. This form is to be explained as ā -ké from root *añc*-sāy antike; Ngh. 2.16 ; Naigh. 3.26 'far' Occurs in a compaund once in the RV 4.45.6 as *āke - nipa -saḥ 'wise'.*

204. It can be derived as *á -khaṇḍala.* But since this is the only occurence of the word *khaṇḍala* in the *RV* the Pdk might not be sure how to analyse it.

205. This is derived from *ā - khúm from root khā to dig' from which 'to harm.' Cf. anu -ṣṭhú* from root *sthā* Cf. KUIPER, *Noun-*

Inflexion, p.77, *Khu* is never found used independentlly. Cf. MAYRHOFER, *op. cit.* p.70. The Pp of the *TS* analyses it as *ā -khuḥ* (1.8.6.1). This is an improvement on *śāk.*

206. Sāy. *āgatadiptiyukta* 'possessed of aquired light' from root *ghṛ 'kṣaraṇadiptyoḥ* plus *ni; ghṛṇe* either independently or in a compound does not occur anywhere else in the *RV*. The analysis of the word is not clear to the Pdk.

207. Sāy. *āttavānasmi*. It is an aorist 1st.sg.- form. The loss of length of root *dā* might have caused doubt in the mind of Pdk. Therefore, he does not analyse it. Another; possibility is that the Pdk might have considered *ā* as an augment. We have this long augent in *ānaṭ*.

208. *Sāy. daridraḥ from ā + root dhrai (?)*, cf GK, *nothros; ā* of *ādhraḥ* goes back to a syllable with *nasal* sound; cf. SURYAKANTA, *OP.CIT.*, P.38.

209. All these forms may be derived as *a-api-PW I. 660, takes it from root āp*. In apapitva,- abhipitva-, etc. *pitva* is separated; whereas, in *āpitvam, tvam* is separated. If *āpi* - is derived from root *āp.*' the question of separation of *ā* does not arise.

210. Opinions are divided among scholars on the division this from. ROTH and GRASSMANN take it as *ā-prasya* from root pṛ for which KLUGE (KZ,25,312) raises objection and supports the not dividing of the Pdk. According to KLUGE *āp-ra-sya* should be the etymology. He equates *āpra*-with Gothic *abrs 'stark heftig'*. Sāy. had already explained it as *annādika ra. Sāy has given an alternative etymology for the word with his usual process yad va* which runs as under:

āprasya āpanasītasya ā samantāt Indrasya prīṇayitur. On this etymology ROTH and GRASSMANN have based their derivation. The Pdk, however, cannot know this.

211. Sāy. *ā samantāt bhavatīti* 'pervading'. PW, 'leer:. The Pp of the *TS* does not separate the form *ābhuḥ* (4.5.1.4) although it separates *ā* from *ābhuvaḥ* Also *ā-bhuvam* in Pp of the *Av* 20.67.I. In any case the Pdk of the *RV* should have analyse this form.

212. This is derived from *ā* + root *bhū*. It means present', 'being near at hand.' The Pp of the *TS*, ofcours, 'analyses abhuvah as *ā-bhuvaḥ* (3.1.11.7), which is a clear sign of improvement over the Ppof the *RV*.

213. I do not see any reason why the Pdk has not separated this form. It means 'weapon' and its derivation is not all ambiguous. It is from *ā* + root *yudh*. The Pp of the *TS*, ofcourse, divides *ā́yudham* (4.5.20.4) as *ā́- yudham*.

214. All such forms are supposed to be derived from root *ṛ* with the prefix *ā*. The form *āritáḥ* is not recorded by MW. WACKERNAGEL, ALG, c.575, also takes it from *ā* -root *ṛ* and translates as 'geehrt'. The Pdk does not know this derivation.

215. Sāy gacchantyaḥ. MW, Pp. 149-50, derives it from ā + *root rī* 'to flow upon'.

216. Sāy *āhantrī*. GELDNER,HOS Vol.35, p.385, also follows Sāy and interprets it as beschadigt hat:. PWI.688 derives it from *āruṣa*, 'the name of a duaghter of Manu and mother of Aurva. The context, ofcourse, demands the parapharase given by *Sāy* and GELDNER. The Pdk might be taking it as a proper name. In that case, the question of the separation of *ā* does not arise.

217. It is an *upasarga* in addition to the usual list of twenty prefixes. PwI.711 further derives it from *ā* + *vid*. MW doubtfully compares it with *vahis ava; Gk.ex, Lat.ex MAYRHOFER, op. cit., p.82, equates it with Av.avis 'openly,*

evidently'. But, even when it occurs in compounds like āviḥ-ṛjīkaḥ (4.38.4), *āviḥ* only is separated. Thus, it seems that Pdk takes *āviḥ* as singleunalysale word.

218. There can be two possible derivation of this form : either it can be taken as *ā - śuśukṣáṇiḥ* from root *suc* (desiderative), 'creating brilliance all around' or as *āśu-śukṣáṇiḥ* 'which becomes brilliant soon'. GELDNER, HOS, 33, p.275, fn. la, takes it as *ā - susukṣaṇiḥ* allowing the second derivation also. All other modern scholars have also taken it in the same way as Sāy. But, the Pdk does not want to commit himself to any definite analysis since two ways of derivation are possible. Or, he simpley does not know how to divide it. The Pp of the *TS* analyses it as *ā -śuśukṣáṇiḥ*. (4.1.2.5).

219. This is also a case of ambiguous derivation. It is doubtful like in *āśuśukṣàṇiḥ* above, whether the first component is *ā* or *āśu*. *Sāy.* gives all possible etymologies for it e.g., *ā* + root *śus*, root *aś* + *kānac* and *āśu* + root *san*. PW adds one more possibility i.e.. *ā* + *svas 'to strive after'. Naturally, the Pdk leaves it unanalysed since he is unable to fix a particular etymology of this word.*

220. Sāy says *satrūṇām āskandayitāraḥ 'attacker* of the enemies.' Evidently he derives it from root *skand*. WACKERNAGEL, AIG ii. 196 derives it from *ā* + *sac* + *ra* meaning 'joined'. Due to doubt about the derivation, the Pdk does not analyse the form.

221. Sāy. says *āhantar maryādayā himsitaḥ* GELDNER, also takes more or less the same meaning 'gegenleitig den Mannern'. Whereas, MAYHROFER, op.cit. p.84, takes it as swelling, distended' Cf. PW I.679, P.280. But in any case the first component is *ā* (*prefix*) which should have been separated. I find no reason why the Pdk does not separate it.

222. *Sāy* paraphrases it as *uttamīkṛtam, utedam uttamāyyam* 'done well which was not done well.'

223. But, *ut-tarāt* at 4.26.6. This separation is based on semantic consideration : when *uttara*-means *udgatatara* (See Sāy. on 4.26.6) and also when it is accented on the prefix, Ut-is separated from-*tara* But, when accent is on the suffix and means 'the north direction'. *ut*- is not separated. Perhaps, to show this semantic distinction, this type of method is adopted by Pdk. the Pp of the *TS* also does the same thing.

224. It is a case of double suffixation : *ut-tarāt-tāt. Sāy. uttarāt kāyapradesāt*. Here also since it indicates direction, no analysis is shown by the Pdk.

225. This word is derived from *ud* + root *tan*. Sāy. *ūrdhvatāna. MAYHROFER, also takes it from ud+tan.* I do not find any reason why the Pdk thinks that these are unanlysable forms. It is to be noted that the Pp of the *TS* analyses it as *ut-tāna*- (5.5.3.2)

226. To be derived from *ud* + root *sthā*. The root *sthā* gives sthi in the weak grade and *s* is lost. According to ASCOLI it is a prakrit tendency (Cd. SURYAKANTA, *ibid.* p.51,l , cl.I.) The Pp of the *TS* analyses it as *ut-sthitaḥ* (7.2.9.3). the difficulty for the Pdk of the *RV* is that he does not know the analysis of the word.

227. All such forms are derived from *ud*+root *añc*. The Pdk does not know this derivation of the word. Although he could recognize *ud* as a preverb still it was difficult for him to explain *-īcaḥ*. Therefore, he thought it better not to give analysis at all.

228. Sāy. says *ūrdhvagamaḥ*. At *AV* 4.7.3 Sāy. explains *udarathim as udriktārtijanakam*. PW I.9.19 following Sāy. and translates as 'rising' or 'arising'. GRASSMANN gives another etymology, namely, *udā* from *udan* plaus *rathi* which is quoted by AIG. b. 106. But this explanation does not suit the context. GELDNER does not translate this word because

he is not certain about the derivation and meaning. It appears that the Pdk is in doubt and therefore, he prefers to be silent.

229. The constituents of this word are not certainly known to the Pdk. Sāy. paraphrases it as *urubalau or vistirṇabalau.* PW I.92 translates it as 'copper-coloured'. GELDNER omits this word in his translation. The derivation of this word is not yet clear to the sholars.

230. Sāy. says *ūrdhvaṁ gamayam. TS* has got the forms, like *úddharati* (6.5.5.3), *úddharati* (3.4.8.7), *úddhriyati* (2.2.4.7), *uddhanyā́t* (2.2.10.5) etc. In the first three cases *ud* is kept within two *daṇḍas* with *iti* attached to it, but in the last form *ud* is taken as a component of the compound-verb *uddhanyāt* and thus Pp is given as *uddhanyadityut - hanyāt.* This is based on the fact that in the first three cases *ud* is accented whereas in the last the verb is accented. We do not find the word *uddharan* in the *TS.* Perhaps, the Pdk of the *RV* is not sure whether this word whould be derived from *ud* -root *ḥṛ* or *ud* - root *dhṛ*. Therefore, he did not show any division.

231. It is derived from *ud* + root *añc*. But the words formed from root añc are not analysed in the Pp, since he does not know the derivation of these words.

232. To be derived from *ud* - hitam. Sec, fn. 49 above.

233. In the *TS* the word *uttabdhyai* (6.6.4.6) occurs and in its Pp it is analysed as *uttabdhyai iti ut - stabdhyai.* The Pdk does not understand loss of *s* in root *sthā* or root *stabh / stambh* which is known to the Pdk of the *TS* and P. See, *udaḥ stahāstambhoḥ purvasya* P8.4.61.

234. To be derived as *upa - bd - i. -bd-* represent *p (a), d* from *ped. According to SURYAKANT, *op. cit.*, p.52, the word means 'noise, sound' produced at the sprinkling of *soma*'.

According to MYRHOFER I. 105, the word means trampling or noise. The Pdk could not analyse it since he did not know its derivation.

235. This is from *upabda*. See fn. 90 above.

236. This and like are derived from the prefix *upa* with the suffix *ra*. According to *MAYRHOFER I. 105, the word means 'lower' or 'posterior'. Nowhere this ra* is separated by the Pdk, because he did not know it.

237. Sāy. says *adhaḥ-sāyina*. MAYHROFER, *op.cit.*, I.106, gives the meaning 'inferior, subordinate' and derives as *upa* + *asti*. The Pdk does not analyse it because he does not know its derivation. The word *upastayaḥ* (*AV* 6.15.1) is analysed as *upa -stayaḥ*. Also see *abhiṣṭiḥ*.

238. This is derived from root *añc* which is not separated in the Pp, because he does not recognise the *añc*-derivation. This is consistently followed. See other derivaties of root *añc*.

239. Sāy. explains the meaning as *ārūḍharathaḥ*. OLDENBERG and PISCHEL (Ved. St. I.197) derive it from *upa - ā -nas*. GELDNER and others follows Sāy. but add a question- mark. The Pdk is not sure of the derivation. Even though he may guess *upa* as a separate constituent still the rest of the form was not clear to him. The separation of *upa* will lead to the deffinite commitment about the second constituent.

240. Sāy. explains as *durbuddhiḥ, MAYRHOFER, II.48, 'misfortune' evil deed' and gives the probable derivation as dus* + *śunā*. Cf. SURYAKANTA, *op. cit.*, p.136. Who explains it as a derivation from IE *dhukh* 'with the loss of initail aspiration'. Two denominative forms from this base are also available in the *RV*, e.g., *ducchunāyati* (10.37.12) and *ducchunāyase* (7.53.3). The Pdk very wisely refrains from analysing the form.

241. The Pp of the *TS* splits *duḥ-one* (1.2.14.3), where-as in all other Pps *duroṇe* is treated as one word. According to MAYRHOFER II.51 *dur* is not a preverb but a contraction of *dvār* which means 'door'. the Pdk of the *RV* is justified in not committing himself to a speciffic *derivation.*

242. MAYRHOFER II.51-52, mentions a number or derivations. Especially, the secong member -oṣa is difficult to identify. The Pdk is justified in keeping silence.

243. The form is to be explained as *dur + ya-*. Here, *dur represents dvāra,* See, , MAYRHOFER, *op.cit.* p.53; GRASSMAN, *op.cit.,* p.616. The Pdk probably does not know the derivation.

244. To be explained as *dur + yoṇa-*. This is the only locative sg. from available in the *RV*. Elsewhere, we have *duryoṇam* (Paip.20.8.5), *duryoṇaḥ (MS 1.6.9) and duryoṇe* (Paip.9.16.4). It means 'bad abode.' Sāy. paraphrases it as *duṣṭayonau sthāne, etannāmakasya rājnaḥ prityarthaṁ vā,* 'in a bad place or in order to please the king of this name'. Why the Pdk hesitates to separate *dur* here is not clear.

245. The Sp is *duṣṭara. In the Pp, ofcourse, the phonological change has been accounted for. But no separation is shown which is made by the later Pp ; the Pp of the TS* analyses *duṣṭaram* (4.4.12.2) as *duḥ-taram*. According to SURYAKANTA, *op.cit.*, p.138, the word means 'inconvincible'. But *niṣṭuraḥ* (8.77.2) and *niṣṭure* (8.32.27) are divided by Śāk. as *niḥ-turaḥ* and *niḥ- ture.* Thus, this a clear case of inconsitency on the part of the Pdk of the *RV*.

246. The Sp is *duṣṭáritave.* Thus in the Pp, sometimes, cerebral sound are restored to their original form. But why an *avagraha* is not put after *dus* is not clear. Here agian, the Pdk is inconsistent.

247. See f.65.

248. The etymology of this word is still doubtful. It may be *ni-ṇik* (ni,-a prefix), *ni- ṇik* (by reduplication of the root *nij)* *or* ṇ*ir- nik* (as BENFEY suggest See. SURYAKANTA, *op.cit,* p.156), or *nir-naya* (See, SURYAKANTA, ibid.) According to MAYRHOFER II.161, the word is probably derived from *niny-anc.* The Pdk does not know this and therefore, he avoids may separation.

249. MAYRHOFER, *op.cit.*, p. 161, interprets 'interior, hidden'; cf. WACKERNAGEL, *op.cit* I.992, P.195. SURYAKANTA, *op.cit,* doubtfully derives it from **nirṇaya* The cause of *n* to ṇ is unknown. The Pdk does not know how to divide this word and therefore, he avoids any commitment.

250. For etymology, see GRASSMANN, *op.cit* p.729,; SURYAKANTA, *op.cit., p.156. Nobody gives detailed etymology of it. It is a doubtful case and thus division is not shown. According to MAYRHOFER, the division is ni- tya,* where *ni* is a stem. Kātyāyana gives *ni + tyap.*

251. Its etymology also is doubtful, GRASSMANN, *op.cit.* p.732, takes it from *ni-MAYRHOFER,* op.cit., p.166, takes if from *ni* Thus the word is not divided by the Pdk because the division is not clear to him.

252. The form is to be analysed as *ni-yut-vataḥ*. According to the Pdk's general principles of ICA, he should have divided it as *niyut-vataḥ*. But this cannot be done because *ni- yut-* is not a grammatical *pada* as it end in *t*. If it is a *pada,* the form will be *niyudataḥ*. All right ; then way is not *ni* separated from*-yutvataḥ*. The reason appears to be that *niyut* - is considered to be one semantic unit. If *ni* would have been added after the formation of *-yutvataḥ* the prefix *ni* would have been separated, as has been done in the case of *nitodinaḥ (10.34.7). here also nitod-* is not a *pada,* so the next constituent has been analysed as *ni-todinaḥ*. The Pdk of the *TS,* ofcourse, analyses *niyutvate* (2.1.1.1) as *ni-yutvate.*

253. Sāy. paraphrases as *nitarām remaṇasīlaḥ*. GRASSMANN *op.cit.*, p. 733 takes it from *ni-root ram*. See also MW p.533, cl.1. The Pdk is perhaps, doubtful whether it is to be derived as *ni + ram* or *nir + root am*.

254. Whether it is *ni + root ric* or *nir + ekam* is doubtful and thus the Pdk avoids analysis. Modern scholars derive it from root *ric* with *ni*. See. PW, IV.188; GRASSMANN, *op.cit.*, P.733.

255. Here the expected division, *ni-saṅginaḥ*, is not made. This is because *niṣaṅga*-gives an integrated semantic unit which cannot be preserved if it is analysed as *ni-saṅginaḥ*, is not made. On the other hand, the form *saṅga or saṅgin* is not used independently throughout the *RV* which sometimes becomes one of the deciding factors for analysing any form. But *nitodinaḥ* is analysed as *ni-todinaḥ* in which case the Pdk has todaḥ as an independently occurring form. Moreover, he considers *todinaḥ* as a single semantic word and thus he separates *ni* from it. The Pp of the *TS* analyses *niṣaṅginaḥ* (4.5.11.2) as *ni- saṅginaḥ*.

256. The etymology is abscure. The Pdk is wise in not giving any analysis.

257. Here also the etymology is obscure and therefore, no division is offered by the Pdk. GRASSMANN takes it as the name of the mother of Indra.

257. GRASSMANN op cit., p.736 takes it from *nis-tya*. Cf. P 4.2.104; 8.3.101. But no form ending in *tya* has been analysed in the Pp of the *RV*.

258. CRASSMANN, *op.cit.*, p.736, derives it from root *sap* with *nis*. According to him it means 'Verschwender'. The Pdk, ofcourse, does not know the division.

259. GRASSMANN, *op.cit. p.; 736, derives it from root sah* with *nis*. The Pdk is not sure of the derivation.

260. GRASSMANN, *op.cit.*, p.741, derives it from *ni-root añc*. No from of *añc*-derivation is divided in its components. According to MAYRHOFER II. 171, it is a case formation ; *nīc* + *ā* from *nyaṅ*.

261. Sāy. explains it as *sthānam*. GRASSMANN, records it with ḍ. Historically, the form is derived from *ni* + root *sad*. But the Pdk does not know how to derive it and there fore, leaves it unanalysed.

262. *GRASSMANN, op.cit.*, p.742, derives it from *ni*-root *vyā*. According to MAYRHOFER II. 174-5, *ī* of *nī* is difficult to explain. The Pdk does not know how to derive it, and therefore, keeps silence.

263. To be derived from *ni*-+root *āñc*. The Pdk does not know that it is derived from root *añc*.

264. PW IV.175 derives it from *nis* + root *av* ; GRASSMANN, *op.cit;,* p.733 takes it from *nis* - root *ava* I. Sāy. derives it from *ni* + *rava*. The Pdk is not sure of the derivation.

265. To be derived frop *parā* - root *añc*. Words formed with root *añc* are never separated in the Pp. According to MAYRHOFER II.216, *parākāttāt* contains two ablative suffix. The Pdk is not sure of the derivation.

266. Sāy. explains as *parileśam paritaḥ sukhakaram annam*. MAYRHOFER, *op.cit*, p.217 ; *pari* + *aṁsa* ; GRASSMANN, *op.cit* p.785 : *pari* + root *aiṁs* ; But the Pdk cannot restore the lost *a of aṁsa*. So, he does not analyse.

267. Here the Pdk does not separate *pari* from *vatsarīṇa* because he may not be sure of the word *vatsara*. He does not divide *saṁvatsara* either. According to MAYRHOFER II-132-33, *vatsara* is derived from *vatsa* + a suffix *ra*. The Pdk of the *TS*, ofcourse, divides *parivatsareṇa* as *pari-vatsareṇa* (5.5.7.3). The form *vatsara* does not occur in the *RV*, indepedently.

268. To be derived possibly from *pari* + root as or *pari* + root *sthā*. See MAYRHOFER, II.218-19. The Pdk is sure of the derivation.

269. SURYAKANTA op.cit., p.180 : 'ancient' derive it from *pra*, GRASSMANN, op.cit., p.870 : from *pra. Tna represents zero-grade of the suffix tana.* See MAYRHOFER, II.362. The Pdk may not knew it.

270. To be derived from pra + tama (superletive saffix). But the aspirantion of t is obscare. See RASSMANN, op cit p.873 ; MAYRHOFER, op.cit p.363. The Pdk does not know this and thus makes no attempt at division.

271. The Pp of the *TS* shows *pra - vanam* (2.4.12.1). The Pp of *VS* also offers *pra - vanebhiḥ* (12.50). Sāy. gives two types of interpretation : (1) from root *pru* and (2) from *pra* + root *van.*GRASSMANN, *op.cit., p.880, follows (1). According to MAYRHOFER, II.367, it is derived from pra + vana.* The Pdk is not sure of the derivation and thus does not offer any explanation.

272. *Pravat* is divided as *pra-vat* (9.74.7), when occurred independently but in the case of *pravatvati,* no separation is made. The question of separating - *vati* does not arise because pravat - is not a *pada*. In that case we would have got the form ***pravadvati*. He cannot divide as *pra -vatvati* either because *vatvati* is not a free form.

273. See fn. 12. According to MAYRHOFER, II.370-1, the original meaning of the word is not clear. Therefore, the derivation of the word is not clear either. The Pdk is right in keeping silence.

274. GRASSMANN, *op.cit.,* p.884, takes *skaṇva* as an alternate form of *kaṇva-, Kaṇva* - is known to the Pdk several times. Probably, he does not know that *skanva* is same as *kaṇva* i.e.,

he fails to account for the s between *pra* and *kaṇva*. Therefore, he avoids analysis. According to P 6.1.153, the division is *pra* - *kaṇva* and *a suṭ* is inserted. This is also supported by MAYRHOFER II.372.

275. The Pdk cannot divide *Prāk-tāt* because it is not a *pada*. If it is a *pada* we will have the form **prāgtāt*. He does not separate *pra* because he does not know root *añc*-derivation. Moreover, -*tāt* cannot be a meaningful unit.

276. GRASSMANN, *op. cit.*, p.887 derives it from root *an* with *pra*. The Pp of the *TS* divides it as *pra-anāḥ* (7.2.9.3). The Pdk of the *RV* does not know it and so he does not divide. According to MAYRHOFER, II.282-83, it belongs to *piparti*.

278. GRASSMANN, *op.cit.*, p.887 derives it from *pra*. According to MAYRHOFER, II.376, it is a derivation from *pra*. The Pdk is right in keeping silence.

279. Sāy. explains it as *pūrṇā*. GELDNER HOS. 34 p. 193, fn. 8b derives it from root *prā* and indicates its meaning as *prāti* i.e., *pūrti* 'Fulle' Since *prāta* looks like that the past participle, the question of division does not arise. See MAYRHOFER II.282-3.

280. It means 'distinguished, eminent', *Pra* some times changes to *prā* in a compound denoting non-human being if the following component is formed by a *kṛt*-suffix *ghan* See P 6.3.122 : GRASSMANN, op.cit, p.888 ; The Pdk in very many cases, does not separate when the first member shows lengthening of its final syllable.

281. See fn. 99

282. To be derived from *pra* + *root vṛṣ 'to rain'. Cf. SURYAKNTA, op.cit., p.183 ; GRASSMANN, op. cit., p.888 ; also see fn. 99.*

283. To be derived from *pra* + root *vep*. See GRASSMANN *op.cit.*, p. 889; also see fn. 136 above.

284. I cannot explain why the Pdk has not analysed the compound. There is controversy about the meaning of this form. Sāy. takes it to mean 'consumable, eatable'. But, GELDNER, HOS, 34, p.342, fn 6a, takes it as very quick;. The Pdk is not sure of its derivation and therefore, he does not analyse it.

285. It means 'swiftly finishing'. Here *-ṣaṭ* cannot be separated because-ṣ-is not phonologically conditioned but it is conditioned morphologically. The Pdk cannot divide as *pra-āśuṣāt* is not a separate meaningful unit.

286. See fn. 140.

287. To be derived from root *iṣ* with *pra*. Cf.GRASSMANN, *op.cit.*, p.894 ; MAYRHOFER, *op.cit.*, p.382. No reasonalble explanation for non-separation by the Pdk can be offered.

288. To be derived from *Prati* + root *añc*. The Pdk does not know the *āñc*-derivation. See MAYRHOFER II.360-1

289. To be derived from *prati* + root *i* 'to go'. Cf.GRASSMANN, op.cit., p.870. The Pdk perhaps does not know this derivation.

290. To be derived from *prati* + root *vı*. Cf.GRASSMANN, *op.cit.*, p.870. In case of lengthening of preverbs, the Pdk does not indicate separation.

291. To be derived from *prati* + root *añc*. As usual, the Pdk does not attempt this *añc*-derivation also.

292. To be derived from *vi* + root pan 'to boast'. See GRASSMANN, *op.cit*p.1283. MAYRHOFER III.217 mentions another derivation, namely, from the same stem from which

vipraḥ is also derived. The stem is *vep*. The division of the word is not clear to the Pdk.

293. MAYRHOFER III.217 states that *vipayāmahe* might have been influenced by *vipaniḥ* which occurs in the same context. The Pdk cannot divide as *vi-panyāmahe,* because *panyāmahe* is not a separate semantic unit.

294. See fn.148.

295. To be dorived from vi-pṛk- vat. For the reason why the Pdk has not analysed the form see the fn. on niyu-vat.

296. To be derived from *vi* + root *ruc* + mat. The Pdk has fear that if he analyses viruk - m*ataḥ* it would be *virugmataḥ*. He could not divide as vi - *rukmataḥ* either because *rukmataḥ* is not a separate semantic unit.

297. To be derived from *vi-vas-vat*. The separation as *vivas-vat* would give *vivovat*. *Vi-vasvat* is also not desirable because *vasvat* is not a semantic unit.

298. To be derived from *vi + root vic* 'to divide asunder' *-ta*. It cannot be explained why the Pdk did not separate *vi* from *vikta*.

299. To be derived from *vi+vic*. It is an epithet of *Agni*. Sāy. explains it as *vivecakam*. *Vici* does not occur in the *RV* as an independent form. Perhaps, the Pdk considers that this is the name of Agni. So no question of division of a proper name.

300. To be derived from root *stabh* from *sta*(m)bh with *vi* See GRASSMANN, *op.cit.,* p.1309. The Pdk does not know this analysis. He takes it as an indivisible single word.

301. Here even though the radical noun *stambha* is found without any change the Pdk does not show any division.

This indicates that he does not know this stem. *Stambha* - does not also occur as a free stem in the *RV*. The Pp of the *TS* separates *vi*- from *stambhaḥ* (3.5.2.2.)

302. To be derived from root *spaś* 'to spy' with *ivi*. See GRASSMANN, op.cit., p.1310. The Pdk does not find *spaṭ* occuring freely in the *RV*. He does not divide it due to doubt regarding its derivation.

303. Sāy. explains it as *vyāptitasya karmaṇaḥ* GRASSMANN, expressing doubt takes it from root *sphāy with the prefex vi*. It means 'difficulty'. The etymology is not clear. The Pdk does not know the derivation. He is not sure whether *vi* is a preverb or not.

304. Probably, it is derived from *sphuliṅga* with the prefix *vi* and the pleonastic suffix- *ka* affixed to it. Nowhere the pleonastic suffix-ka has been separated by the Pdk. Therefore, it appears that since he is not sure of the etymology he does not separate *vi* from *sphuliṅgaka*. For etymology see GRASSMANN, *op.cit.*, p.1310.

305. Sāy. explains it as *narakeṇa*. *GRASSMANN derives if from root añc* with prefix *vi* and puts a questionmark. See, GRASSMANN, *op.cit.*, p.1314. SURYAKANTA, *op.cit.*, p.238; root *añc* + vi. This is a derivative of root *añc* and as such the Pdk does not divide it.

306. Sāy. givies two-fold explanation of this word. (1) *viśeṣeṇa vistāryaḥ (from root stṛ* 'to expand') (2) *śatrūṇaṁ hiṁsakaḥ*. GRASSMANN, *op.cit., p.*1269 derives it as an form from root *taṅs* with vi'zu beeilen'. Being doubtful about the eyymology the Pdk does not offer any division.

307. According to GRASSMANN, *op.cit.*, p.1481, the from can be derived either from *sam* or from *sama* This is not known to the Pdk and therefore he does not analyse it.

308. To berived from *sam-ud* ('water')-ra ('water')-ra (suffix). The suffix - *ra* is attested elsewhere also e.g. *apa-ra, ava-ra* etc. It is never separated by the Pdk which indicates that the Pdk does not know this secondary suffix. He does not separate *sam* from *udra* because *udra* cannot be semantically single unit. See, GRASSMANN, *op.cit.*, p.1483 ; SURYAKANTA, *op.cit., p.261 under samudriya.* The Pp of the *SV* analyses it as *sam-udra* and following this *Nir 2.10 gives the etymology as sam udravanti asmāt āpaḥ iti samudraḥ*

309. To be derived from *sami* + root *añc*. Sami is a varient of *sam*. The Pdk does not analyse the *añc*-derivations.

310. To be derived from *sam*-vatsara-. See fn.87.

311. To be derived from *sam-kṛtaḥ* from root *kṛ* or *skṛ* There is a difference of opinion about the origin of the -s-. It may be organic or inorganic. P takes it as inorganic and explains it *as āgama (See P 6.1.137). The Pdk probably could not account for this s and prefered not to divide it. For etymology see, GRASSMAN op.cit., p.1439; SURYAKANTA, opcit,.* p.257. But I am at loss to understand why these forms are not divided when *pariṣkṛṇvan* (9.39.2), *suścandram* (2.34.13) etc. are analysed as *pari-kṛṇvan, su-candram,* etc. One more peculiarity is to be noticed here. Nowhere the phonemes which are in the Sp, whether original or modified by phonological change, are dropped in the Pp. But in the case mentioned above- ṣ-or-ś- is elided in the Pp. This might have two reasons. Either the Pdk wants to indicate that he cannot account for-s- or he wants to show that-s-does not belong to the root. The Pp of the *TS* does not analyse any of these forms which shows the consistency of the Pp of the *TS*.

312. To be derived form *su* + root *gam*. See GRASSMANN op. cit., p.1530 (from *sugmā where gmā* represents *gman*). This etymology is not known to the Pdk. Therefore, he makes no attempt at division.

313. Both GRASSMANN, op.cit.p.1547 and MW p.1231 suggest *su-mnā* as the division on the basis of stems ending in-*da* from root *dā*. The stem *mna* - does not occur freely in the *RV* and so the Pdk fails to find out its derivation and does not, therfore, show division.

314. GRASSMANN, op.cit p.1549 derives it from *su*+root *rabh*. SURYAKANTA, opcit.p.269 expalins it as 'fragrant'. The word *rabhih* (8.5.29) occurs as an independent word but it has different meaning i.e., arm, support' (GELDNER). Moreover, accent of *surabhi* and *rabhi*-differ and *rabhi* with accent on the final syllable does not occur in dependently in the RV. Thus it is quite probable that the Pdk does not know the derivation of the word and so avoids separation.

315. To be derived from *su* + root *sthā* Perhaps, morphemic change in the root *sthā* may have caused confusion in the mind of the Pdk regarding the derivation of the form. Therefore, he does not divide it. For etymology, see GRASSMANN, op,cit., p.15558.

316. Sāy. explains the derivation as *su-ūn-ṛta*. GRASSMANN, : 1) beautiful, 2) happy, 3) blissful. He compares it with *sūnara-*. But opinions differ. WACKERNAGEL derives it as *su-nṛ-ta* (from tva). Cf. AIG.II 2pp. 617- 18. Since the Pdk is not sure of the derivation, he does not divide. The lengthening of *su* is another difficulty to the Pdk.

317. WACKERNAGEL, AIG II. 2, p.617 compares it with *sūnṛta-*. See fn. 172. The etymology is doubtful. Therefore, the Pdk does not indicate any division.

318. Yaska : *Nir* : 9.23 *bharvatirattikarmā*. Sāy, under *RV* 1.143.5 : *bharva hiṁsāyām, yadyapi attibharvatyoḥ adanamevārthaḥ tuthāpi tadavāntarabhedo vagantavyaḥ* the Pdk knows the second component of *sūbharvam*. But, since U of su is lengthened he does not indicate any division.

319. GRASSMANN, *op.cit.*, p.1569 derives it from root *sṛ* He derives *suryā* from *sur, svar* SURYAKANTA, op.cit. p.272 explains *sūrmi as 'radiance'. cf. sūr-ta,* not from root *sṛ* and *sūr-mī 'reed, cane'*. The pdk does not know the division.

320. Cf.P 1.1.16 : 'The final *o* of the vocative singular before the word *iti* according to Śākalya, in non- vedic literature, is *pragṛhya.'*

321. Cf. P. 1.1.14 : *nipātaekājanāṅ.*

322. Cf. RPr 1.70 : *apūrvapadāntagasca* 'Also *o* not occurring at the end of the first part off a compound is *pragrhya.'*

323. See P 1.1.11 : *īdūdeddvivacanam pragṛhyam* 'A dual case affix ending in *ī*, or *ū*, or e is called *pragṛhya,* or excepted vowels which do not admit of *sandhi* or conjunction.'

324. See P 1.1.19 : *īdūtau ca saptamyarthe* 'The final *ī* and *ū* or words giving the sense of the locative case are *pragṛhya.'*

325. See P 1.1.13 : *Se* 'The affix *se* (the vedic substitute of the case affixes) is a *pragṛhya.'* and P 1.1,12 *ī, ū e* after the *m* of the pronoun *adas* are *pragṛhya.'*

326. See p.1.1.17-18

WORKS OF REFERENCE

Sanskrit Texts

(Arranged in the order of Sanskrit Alphabet)

Atharvaveda, ed. by VISHVA BANDHU, Vishveshvarananda Indological Series, No. 13, Parts I-V, Hosiarpur, 1960-62.

Atharvavedaprātiśākhya,, ed. and tr. by WHITNEY W.D.,

JAOS, Vol. VII, 1862.

Aṣṭādhyāyi of Pāṇini, ed. by BOHTLINGK O., Hildescheim, 1964.

Ṛkprātiśākhya of Saunaka, ed. and tr. by SHASTRI M-D., Vols I-III, I, 1959; II, 1931; III, 1937; Lahore.

Ṛgveda-saṁhitā, ed. by SONATAKKE N.S. and KASHIKAR C. G. Vaidaka Samshodana Maṇḍala, Vols. I-V, Poona, 1933 - 1951 ; tr.by GELDNER K.F., *HOS* Vols. 33 - 36, 1951 - 1957.

Aitareya Āraṇyaka, ed. and tr. by KEITH A.B. Oxford 1909.

Kātantravyākaraṇa, ed. by EGGELING J., Calcutta, 1874.

Kāśikāvṛtti of Jayaditya, and Vāmana with commentaries *Nyāsa,* and *Padamañjarī* I - VI, Benares, 1965 -67.

Cāndravyākaraṇa of Candragomin, ed. CHATTERJI K., Deccan College, Poona, Part I, 1953 and Part II, 1961.

Jainendravyākaraṇa, ed. by TRIPATHI Pdt. S. and CHATURVEDI Pdt. M., *Jñānaphit Murtidevi Jaina Grantha Mālā,* Sanskrit Grantha No. 17, Benares, 1956.

Taittirīya Prātiśākhya, ed. and tr. by WHITNEY W.D. JAOS, Vol. IX, 1871.

Taittirīya Saṁhitā, ed. by MAHADEVA SHASTRI A. and RANGACHARYA K., Government Oriental Library Series, Bibliotheca Sanskrit No.4, Vols I-XII, Madras, 1894 - 1898, tr. by KEITH A.B., Parts, I - II, reprint, Delhi, 1967.

Nirukta of *Yāska*, ed. and tr. by SARUP L., Parts I-II, Patna, 1967.

Mahābhāṣya of Patanjali, ed. by KIELHORN F.,BSS Nos. 18,

21, 28; revised by ABHYANKAR K. V., vol. I, 1962, Vol. II, 1965, BORI, Poona; Vol.III, 1885, Bombay.

Mādhyandina-saṁhitāyāḥ Padapāṭhaḥ, ed. by MIMĀṀSAKA Y., Bahalgarh (Haryana), 1971.

Mugdhavodhavyākaraṇa of Vopadeva, ed. by *BOHTLINGK O.* Leipzig, 1847.

Vājasaneyī Prātiśākhya of Kātyāyana, with the commentary of *Uvaṭa*, Benares Sanskrit Series No. 8, Benares, 1883, tr. RASTLGI I., Chowkhamba Sanskrit Series Office, Varanasi 1967.

Vārttika of Kātyāyana, See MBhā.

Śatapatha Brāhmaṇa, Chowkhamba Sanskrit Series, Benares,1950.

Śāṅkhāyana Āraṇyaka, ed. by Apte V.G., Ass No. 90, Poona,1922.

Sāmavedasaṁhitā, ed. by VIDYASAGAR J., Calcutta, 1892.

Sārasvatavyākaraṇa of *Anubhūtisvarupachārya*, ed. by KARA SARMA Pdt, N.K., Kashi Sanskrit Series (Haridas Sanskrit Granthamala) No. 111, Benares, 1935.

Siddhāntakaumudī of *Bhaṭṭoji*, Motilal Banarasidass, Varanasi, 1967.

Modern Works

(Arranged in the order of English Alphabet)

ABHYANKAR K.V.:
"discrepancy between the Saṁhitā and the Pada-texts of the *Ṛgveda*", ABORI, Vol. 52, 1972, pp. 211-214.

ABHYANKAR K.V.:
-"Prolegomena to the *Veda- padapāṭha", ABORI, Vol. 54, 1973, pp. 9-44.*
-Dictionary of Sanskrit Grammar, Baroda, 1961.

AGRAWALA V.S.:
-"Pre-Pāṇinian technical terms". Siddheshwar Varma Comm Vol. II, Hoshiarpur, 1950, pp. 135-37.

ALLEN W.S.:
-Sandhi's-Gravenhage, 1962.

ARNOLD E.V.:
-Vedic Metre in its historical development, Cambridge, 1905.

AVERY J.:
-"Verb-Inflexion in Sanskrit', JAOS, Vol X, pp. 219-324.

BHATE S:
-"Pre-Pāṇinian Grammatical elements in Pāṇini's Aṣṭadhyāyi (Unpublished thesis, University of Poona), Poona, 1970.

BHATTACHARYA B.:
-Yāska's Nirukta, Calcutta, 1958.
-Yāska and Śākalya", Indian Culture, Vol XII, Nos. 1-4, 1945-46, pp. 123-27.

BHATTACHARYA R.S.:

-"Some Chief characteristics of Pāṇini in comparison to his predecessors," JOIB, Vol. II, No. 2, Baroda, 1952, pp. 167-173.

BELVALKAR S.K.:

-*Systems of Sanskrit Grammars*, Poona, 1915.

BOHTLINGK and ROTH:

-*Sanskrit- Worterbuch Vols. I - VII, 1855-1875.*

BURROW T.:

The Sanskrit Language, London 1955.

CARDONA G.:

-*Studies in Indian Grammarians Vol. I, The American Philological Society, Philadelphia, 1969.*

CHATTERJI K.C.:

-*Technical terms and Technique of Sanskrit Grammar*, Calcutta University, 1964.

CHATURVEDI S.P.:

-*"Pāṇini and the Ṛkprātiśākhya" NIA, Vol. I, Poona, 1938-39.*

GHATAGE A.M.:

-*Historical Linguistics and Indo-Aryan Languages*, University of Bombay, 1962.

GHOSH B.K.:

-*"Pāṇini and the Ṛkprātiśākhya" IHQ, X, No. 4, Calcutta, 1934.*

-"Chaturvedi on Pāṇinin and the Ṛkprātiśākhya". *NIA II, No. 1, Poona, 1939, pp. 56-61.*

-"Aspects of the Pre-Pāṇinian Grammar", B.C. Law Comm. Vol. I, Calcutta, 1945, pp. 334-345.

GOLDSTUCKER T.:

-*Pāṇini : His place in Sanskrit Literature, Indian Education, Chowkhamba Sanskrit Series, Varanasi, 1965.*

GRASSMANN H.:

-*Wörterbuch zum Ṛgveda,* otto harrassowitz, Wiesbaden, 1955.

HOCKETT C.F.:

-*A Course in Modern Linguistics,* Indian Edition, Delhi, 1970.

JHA V.N.

-"On the two Ṛgvedic compound- form *ráthaspàti* and *Vànaspàti* "PAIOC, 25th session, Jadavpur University, 1969, pp. 231-238.

-"*Ṛgvedīyapadapāṭhe upasargāḥ', Pdt. Rajeshwar Shastri Dravid Felicitation Volume, Bharati Parishat, Allahabad, 1971, pp. 37-39 (Vedic Section).*

-"*Śākalya's theory of avāsana-sandhi*", *JOIB,* Vol. XXI, No. 3, 1972, pp. 174-183.

-"The *mat*-derivatives and their treatment in the *Padapāṭha of the ṚGVEDA', BDCRI, Vol. XXXI-XXXII, Iravati Karve Comm. Vol., 1971-72, pp. 116-19.*

-Śākalya and "Pāṇini" *BDCRI, Vol. XXXIII, 1973, pp. 223-26.*

-"The Negative Particle *a/an* in the *Ṛgvedapadapāṭha*" *Archiv Orientalni,* vol. No. 1, 1974, pp. 37-38.

JOG K.P.

-"On the Rgvedic denominative *adhvarīya-*", JUPHS, No. 27, pp. 27-35.

JOSHI S.D.:

Patanjali's Vyākaraṇa- Mahābhāṣya (Avyayībhāva-tatpuruṣāhnika), University of Poona, 1969.

KASHIKAR C.G.

-"The Problem of the *gaḷantas* in the Ṛgveda-padapāṭha", PAIOC, 13th session, Nagpur University, 1946, pp. 39-46.

KATRE S.M.:

-*Dictionary of Pāṇini,* Parts I-III, Deccan College, Poona, 1964.

KLUGE F.:

-"KLEINE BEMERKUNGEN" KZ, Vol. 25, pp. 309-14.

KUIPER F.B.J.

-Notes on Vedic noun-inflexion, 1942.

LANMANN:

-"Noun-Inflexion in the Veda" *JAOS*, X.

LIEBICH B.:

-Zur einfuhrung in die indische einheimische Praschwisenschaft, II, Heidelber, 1919.

MACDONELL A.A.:

-Vedic Grammar Indological Book House, Varanasi, 1968.

-A Vedic Grammar for Students, Oxford, 1916.

MAYRHOFER M.:

-KurzgefaBtes etymologisches Wörterbuch des Altindischen, Band I, 1956, Band II, 1963, Heidelberg.

MONIER-WILLIAMS

A Sanskrit -English Dictionary, Oxford, 1899.

NAVATHEN P.D

"Treatment of the suffix-*vāṁs* in the *Padapāṭha" II*, Vol. 30, Katre Felicitation Vol., Part II, 1969, pp. 119-133.

"Two anamalous cases in the *padapaṭha* of the Ṛgveda "*PAIOC*,, 25th session, Jadavpur University, 1969, pp.247-50.

OLDENBERG H.:

Rgveda. Textkritische und exegetische Noten, Berlin, 1909-12.

POKORNY J.

-Indogermanisches etymologisches Wörterbuch, Band I, 1959.

RAMGOPAL

-Vaidika Vyākaraṇa (Hindi), National Publishing House, Delhi, Part I, 1965.

Sehgal S.R :

"Dr. Roth's studies on the *Pada-pāṭha*", *ABORI,Vol. XXXI*, 1950, pp. 279-84.

SEN S.

-*A Comparative Grammar of Middle Indo-Aryan*, Poona, 1960.

SHARMA K.L.

"Prātiśākhyas and the Padapāṭha", Charudeva Shastri Felicitation Vol., Delhi, 1974, pp. 133-148.

SHASTRI M.D

"The relation of Pāṇini's technical devices to his predecessors"
PAIOC, IV, Allahabad, 1926, pp. 465-474.

STAAL J.F.:

Word Order in Sanskrit Universal Grammar, Foundation of Language, Vol. V, Dordrech, 1967.

SURYAKANTA

-*A Grammatical Dictionary of Sanskrit (Vedic),* Delhi, 1953.

THIEME P.:

Pāṇini and the Veda, Allahabad, 1935.
-"Pāṇini and the Ṛkprātiśākhya", IHQ. XIII, No.1, Calcutta, 1937.

TARGER L. **and** SMITH H.L

-*An outline of English Structure,* 1951.

TURNER R.L

-*Some Problems of Sound change in Indo-Aryan,* P.d. Gune Memorial Lectures : 1, University of Poona, 1960

VARMA S.:

-*Etymologies of Yāska, Hosiarpur, 1953.*
-*Critical Studies in Phonetic Observations of Indian Grammarians,* Delhi, 1961.

WACKERNAGEL

-*Atlindische Grammatic,* Gottingen, Band I-III, 1964.

WEBER

"Taittirīya-padapāṭha", Indische Studien, Vol. 13, 1873, pp.1-128.

WHITNEY W.D

-*Sanskrit Grammar*, Delhi, 1962.

-*The Roots, Verb-forms and Primary Derivatives of the Sanskrit Language*, Motilal Banarsidass, Varanasi, 1963.

WINTERNITZ

-*A History of Indian Literature, Vol. 1, Calcutta, 1927*

INDEX OF WORDS

Numbers refer to the pages